Technician Class

FCC License Preparation for Element 2 Technician Class Theory

by
Gordon West
WB6NOA

Fifth Edition

Master Publishing, Inc.

Also by Gordon West, WB6NOA

General Class
FCC License Preparation for
Element 3 General Class Theory

Extra Class
FCC License Preparation for
Element 4 Extra Class Theory

GROL-Plus
General Radiotelephone Operator License
Plus Ship Radar Endorsement

(*with* Fred Maia, W5YI)

FCC Commercial Radio License Preparations for
Element 1, Element 3, and Element 8 Question Pools

This book was developed and published by:
Master Publishing, Inc.
Lincolnwood, Illinois

Editing by:
Pete Trotter, KB9SMG

Thanks to the following for their assistance with this book: Alan Martin, Ph.D., J.D., KB3HIP; Jack Hudson, W9MU; and Fred Maia, W5YI, for his technical review of the RF safety and FCC material contained in this book. Thanks, also, to our "www" proofers: Bill, WA6CAX; Art, W7AEG; Ben, N6FM; Don, N9ZGE; Ken, KF6AYX; Diana, KG4VFZ; and Suzy, N6GLF.

Printing by:
Arby Graphic Service
Lincolnwood, Illinois

Photograph Credit:
All photographs that do not have a source identification are either courtesy of Radio Shack, the author, or Master Publishing, Inc. originals.
Cover photo by Julian Frost, N3JF.

Fifth Edition
9   8   7   6   5   4   3   2   1

Table of Contents

QUESTION POOL NOMENCLATURE
The latest nomenclature changes and question pool numbering system recommended by the Volunteer Examiner Coordinator's question pool committee (QPC) for question pools have been incorporated in this book. The Technician Class (Element 2) question pool has been rewritten at junior-high-school and high-school reading levels, respectively. This question pool is valid from July 1, 2003 until June 30, 2007.

FCC RULES, REGULATIONS AND POLICIES
The NCVEC QPC releases revised question pools on a regular cycle, and deletions as necessary. The FCC releases changes to FCC rules, regulations and policies as they are implemented. This book includes the most recent information released by the FCC at the time this copy was printed.

Welcome to the fabulous, fun hobby of Amateur Radio! It has never been easier to enter the amateur radio service than now!

Changes to Amateur Radio regulations announced by the Federal Communications Commission on December 30, 1999, that became effective April 15, 2000, have made it easier than every to obtain your entry-level Technician class ham radio license — and to move up through all the license classes to earn the top Extra class license.

And when I say "made it easier than ever" I really mean it! The Technician class examination question pool has been reduced from 943 Q&A's down to 510. The new Element 2 written examination that you will take now has just 35 total questions on it, down from 65. *Absolutely no knowledge of Morse code is required for your entry-level ham license.* And there aren't many math skills required, either.

In just one exam session, you can satisfy all of the requirements to earn your Technician class amateur radio license. Within days of passing your written exam (you need to answer 26 of the 35 questions correctly — that's just 74%) you can be on the air talking through repeaters, transmitting via satellites to work other stations thousands of miles away, and even getting a taste of some ionospheric skywave worldwide contacts.

And once you get started, you won't want to stop at Technician! Everyone will want the General class license that gives you worldwide privileges on every single ham band. To study for your Element 3 exam, use my *General Class* book. And it's very easy to learn Morse code using my tapes or computer software. The FCC has reduced the required code speed to just 5-words-per-minute. It's the only code test required for the General, and that qualifies you for the top ham radio ticket — the Extra class license. Hey, *even you* can learn the code at 5-wpm in just one weekend!

Extra class is the top Amateur Radio license. When you're ready to move up to that level, I have a book to help you study for that written exam as well — *Extra Class.*

Three license classes. One Morse code speed. It couldn't be easier to get involved in one of the most fascinating and fun hobbies in the world!

Ready to get started? Hurry up — I am regularly on the airwaves and I hope to make contact with you very soon with your new Technician class call sign.

73

Gordon West, WB6NOA

About This Book

This book provides you with all of the study materials you need to prepare yourself to take and pass the Element 2 written examination to obtain your Technician class amateur radio license. Technician class is the entry-level amateur operator/primary station license issued by the Federal Communications Commission — the FCC. *Absolutely no Morse code test is required* for the Technician class license, which will give you unlimited VHF and UHF ham band privileges.

Our book also provides you with valuable information you need to be an active participant in the amateur ranks. To help you get the most out of *Technician Class,* here's a look at how our book is organized:

- *Chapter 1* provides an overview of the amateur service and a quick look at all of the exciting things you can do with just your entry-level Technician class license.

- *Chapter 2* tells you about all of the ham radio operating privileges you will have with your new Technician class license — including additional privileges you can earn if you pass the *optional* 5-wpm Morse code test.

- *Chapter 3* gives an overview of the amateur service, and a brief history of ham radio regulations. It contains details on the December, 1999 FCC Report & Order that greatly simplified the Amateur Radio service licensing structure, which streamlined the number of examination elements and reduced the emphasis on Morse code for all classes of ham radio licenses. It's your orientation to ham radio.

- *Chapter 4* describes the Element 2, Technician class written examination, and contains all 510 questions that comprise the Element 2 question pool. 35 of these questions will be on your written examination. If you answer 26 of them correctly (74%) you'll pass the exam and receive your FCC license. Along the way, as you study these questions, you'll be learning important things you need to know to get started on the air as a licensed ham.

- *Chapter 5* focuses on Morse code. Even though you don't need the code to become a Technician class operator, it has never been easier to move up through the ranks of amateur radio knowing the code at just 5-words-per-minute. We urge you to learn the code!

- *Chapter 6* will tell you what to expect when you take your Element 2 written exam, where to find an exam session, how you will apply for and receive your new FCC license, and more — all the details you need to know to get your license and get on the air.

- The *Appendix* has valuable lists and reference information. And reading the *Glossary* will get you up to speed on some of the amateur radio "lingo" that you might not understand as you begin studying our book.

Getting Into Ham Radio

WELCOME TO AMATEUR RADIO!

There are many great stories about the origin of our "ham" nickname, and soon you will decide on your favorite. Many people call us "hams" because we always seem to be ready to "show off" the magic of our little wireless gadgets. It won't be long before you'll be doing this, too!

Amateur radio operators INVENTED wireless communications. Did you know that Guglielmo Marconi – who often is credited with inventing radio – considered himself an amateur? Amateur operators were 100 years ahead of your little cell phone. Our century-old Morse code dots and dashes were a forerunner to that little PDA that's tucked away in your pocket or purse. Just ask any ham operator who knows his history, and you'll be told that this new hobby and service you are preparing to join truly did shape everything that is going on with wireless communications today and in the future.

Nearly every country in the world has an amateur radio service, and we all share certain ham radio frequency bands globally. There are more than 2,000,000 licensed amateur radio operators throughout the world, and we number nearly 700,000 here in the U.S.

There's a lot of fun to be had in the ham radio hobby you're about to join!

WHY DO I NEED A LICENSE?

Unlike a lot of electronic communications devices that you already use – like cordless phones in your home, cell phones on the road, or short-range FRS or CB radios – the ham radio equipment you will learn to use has capabilities to communicate across town, around the world, and even into outer space. So, in order to keep things orderly, all hams are required to demonstrate that they understand the rules, regulations, and international frequency assignments placed on amateur radio.

All countries require their ham radio operators to be licensed; to know their country's local radio rules and regulations, and to know a little about how radios work in order to pass that "entrance exam." Here in the U.S., the exam for the entry-level Technician class amateur operator license is a snap. Chapter 4 gives you all the details!

Once you pass our 35-question multiple choice "entrance exam," you'll be issued your first amateur radio license by the FCC (Federal Communications Commission). Absolutely no knowledge of Morse code is required for your Technician class ham radio license.

Your brand new Technician class license will authorize you to operate with unrestricted access on all ham bands above 50 MHz. Ham "bands" are internationally-designated groups of frequencies reserved for amateur radio operation. In the next Chapter, and throughout this book, you'll learn about frequencies in cycles per second (hertz), ham bands in wavelengths, and exactly where our ham bands are located on the radio dial.

YOUR FIRST RADIO

The first radio that most Technician class operators start out with is a dual-band handheld transmitter/receiver. You'll tune into frequencies that are automatically relayed to other ham radio operators throughout your city via repeaters. The keypad on the front of your little handheld may also be used to dial up internet radio links. Imagine walking down the street with your handheld talking to a fellow ham radio operator in Australia – or maybe in Antarctica! Or how about calling home on a free ham radio "autopatch" network – or listening to freeway traffic reports that are more frequent and accurate than those on your car radio!

Many dual-band handheld ham radios also have the capability to tune in worldwide shortwave broadcasts, AM and FM radio stations, television audio, scan the police, paramedics, and fire frequencies, and even do a little eavesdropping backstage on wireless microphone frequencies. These are very sophisticated pieces of radio equipment with many fun and interesting capabilities designed in.

You'll probably want to get a dual-band handheld transceiver for your first ham radio.

Later, after you've learned how to operate properly and are ready to expand into other ham radio capabilities, you can consider buying a mobile radio that can be mounted in your car or pickup, and even used as a "base station" in your home. But my strong recommendation for your first radio is the dual-band handheld.

After you've developed your operating skills, you may want a mobile set for your car or pickup. They can be used as base stations in your house, too.

What about a radio tower? Well, while the Eiffel Tower in Paris was one of the world's first antenna towers, today's antennas for ham radio can be very discreet. They can be safely placed in attics, or be stealth hookups to a nearby window screen. So, no, you won't need a huge tower to get started in your new hobby and service.

WHAT ELSE CAN YOU DO? PLENTY!

Your new handheld can plug into a global positioning system (GPS) and relay your location to ham satellites or mountaintop digital repeaters tied into the internet. Your fellow hams – even mom – could track your every movement. Or maybe you'd like plug your handheld into a tiny color video sender and show all the hams around you what it looks like from the top of that mountain you just hiked!

Your new Technician class license allows you every ham radio privilege on all of the VHF and UHF bands. Imagine talking thousands of miles away by bouncing 6-meter band signals off of the ionosphere. Six-meter sky wave excitement occurs summer and fall, and many Technician no-code operators have worked hundreds of other ham stations throughout the world on 6-meter single sideband. Yes, we'll explain all about "single sideband" in upcoming pages.

Are you into radio control (R/C) of model airplanes and boats? There are channels reserved only for use by licensed ham radio operators for this type of activity on 6-meters, too!

What else can you do with all of your new Technician class no code privileges? You could set up your 2-meter ham station to bounce signals off the face of the Moon! Or send a digital stream of information off a meteor trail. Or yak with a pal on the other side of the country through one of the many ham radio satellites orbiting up there for exclusive use by hams. And for out-of-the-world communications with your new 2-meter ham band Technician class privileges, you can speak regularly with the ham radio operator astronauts passing 240 miles overhead in the International Space Station. Yes, the ISS has a complete ham station installed and, when it's overhead, its within line-of-sight range of your handheld!

There's still more you can do just with that entry-level Technician class license.

If you're also into computers, hams have access to hundreds of wireless frequencies to send high speed information "packets" over the airwaves, absolutely-error-free wireless e-mails, digital slow scan color photos, and a relatively new binary phase-shift-keying computer-to-computer mode that occupies only a sliver of radio bandwidth called PSK-31.

Live television? As a Technician class ham radio operator, we can put you on some frequencies where you will join fellow amateur radio television operators to beam crystal clear, live-action television all over the state! We call this "ATV."

If you're the technical type getting into ham radio, we will help you explore your workshop for magnetrons, waveguides, microwave horns, satellite telecommand big dish arrays, and show you how to work the tropospheric cloud layer for some extraordinary long-range contacts on usually short-range frequencies.

If you're non-technical, we can use a computer to download all the frequencies to your handheld radio memory circuits to turn you into a walkin' talkin' computin' radio operator with equipment not much larger than your favorite cell phone. You don't have to be an engineer to become a ham operator!

Not just a hobby, but a service

There's a serious side to our hobby, when ham radio becomes a public service. When emergencies strike, ham operators are at their shining best. At any major or local disaster, ham operators are often the first to handle outgoing and incoming emergency calls.

Our ham radio nets stay on the air through hurricanes, during tornadoes, and even in the event of major city disasters. Following the 9/11 attack on New York's World Trade Center, ham operators worked for more than a month providing additional emergency communications capabilities to the rescue workers. Our ham radio network of mobile radios, relay stations and remote base equipment continuously keeps emergency responders in contact with many necessary resources.

Many of our ham radio emergency traffic handlers are always at home and always on the air. You wouldn't know that they are visually impaired or perhaps confined to a wheelchair because there is no disability that would keep ham radio operators from working on the amateur radio service airwaves. Visit **www.handiham.org.**

Join a club – get yourself an "Elmer"

When you pass your upcoming Technician class ham exam, your local ham radio clubs may send you a letter with a warm welcome inviting you to join them at an upcoming club meeting. You should go!

Club members – who are now your fellow amateur operators – can help you select radio equipment, program your new radio, and even come to your house and to help set-up that home or vehicle radio installation. These willing helpers who are eager to "show you the ropes" are known as "Elmers," and your Elmer can teach you the practical, on-the-air aspects of amateur radio. Ham radio is one big fraternity!

What are some other ways to learn about your new hobby? One of the best is to read some of the ham radio magazines. One that focuses exclusively on Technician class frequencies if *CQ VHF – Ham Radio Above 50 MHz* (visit **www.cq-vhf.com**). Their parent magazine, *CQ – Amateur Radio* contains excellent articles that will help you learn, as well.

The largest ham radio magazine is *QST – Amateur Radio*. It is published by the American Radio Relay League (ARRL), which is the national association for amateur radio in the United States (visit **www.arrl.org**). *73 – Amateur Radio Today* and *Worldradio* are also fun to read.

And before I let you go on to the next Chapter of my book – which details all of the Technician class frequency privileges you'll earn when you pass your exam – keep in mind that there are more frequencies and bands that you will earn as you upgrade your ham license. As a General and Extra class operator with some Morse code dots and dashes under your belt, you'll gain many more long-range bands to keep you in touch around the world. You could even become a volunteer examiner with the General and Extra class licenses, and then you could give the same tests you are about to pass.

So let's get started now with Technician class study. In the next Chapter, we'll take an in-depth look at the frequency privileges you'll earn with your Technician class license. I can't wait to hear you on the air with your new call sign. Welcome to our Amateur Radio service!

Technician Class Privileges

There is plenty of excitement out there on the amateur VHF and UHF bands with just the Technician class license. You don't need to learn Morse code to get all of the "radio real estate" described in *Table 2-1*. But if you do learn the code and pass the CW test at the same time you take the Element 2 written examination for your Technician license, you'll earn privileges on some "bonus" CW and voice frequencies that you'll be allowed to use as a Technician class operator.

SPECTRUM, WAVELENGTH, AND FREQUENCY

Before we look at the actual Technician class privileges you'll earn with your new FCC Amateur Radio license, let's take a minute to understand the fundamentals of what is meant by the radio terms *spectrum, wavelength,* and *frequency.*

Figure 2-1 on the next page shows the entire electromagnetic energy spectrum, and highlights where the radio frequencies fall within the total spectrum. The low end of the spectrum starts with audio and VLF (Very Low Frequency) frequencies. At the top end of the overall spectrum – above the radio frequencies – are light, X-Rays, and Gamma Rays.

The region from 20,000 hertz to 30 gigahertz is where radio waves are found. Within that region, the radio spectrum is divided up for various uses. The commercial radio AM band is found from 550 kHz (kilohertz) to 1650 kHz. FM radio stations operate between 88 MHz (megahertz) to 108 MHz. One hertz is equal to one cycle per second. That means that an AM signal at 720 kHz on you radio dial is oscillating at 720,000 cycles per second, and an FM signal at 91.5 MHz on your dial is oscillating at 91,500,000 cycles per second.

Figure 2-2 adds some detail to this explanation. The table at the top shows where some of the frequencies lie, and where Amateur Radio operators have privileges. The illustrations show how wavelength and frequency are related. The easiest thing to remember is LOWER LONGER, HIGHER SHORTER. Lower frequency radio waves travel longer distances in one cycle (wavelength), and higher frequency radio waves travel shorter distances in one cycle.

When we say that we are going to operate on the 6-meter band, that means the wavelength of the frequency we will be using is about 6-meters long – or that one cycle of the frequency travels about 236 inches (or 19 feet) in one cycle. On the 70 centimeter band, one wavelength is about 27.5 inches long (or about 2.3 feet) in one cycle.

In general, antennas need to be equal to wavelength (or ½ or ¼ wavelength) in order to efficiently send and receive radio signals. And, finally, radiowaves travel at approximately the speed of light, or 300,000,000 meters per second. So, there's a lot of stuff happening in a big hurry out there on the radio waves!

Now, let's take a look at the Technician class frequency privileges, and how they are used for various purposes.

Figure 2-1. The electromagnetic spectrum detailing the radio frequency spectrum
Soruce: FCC

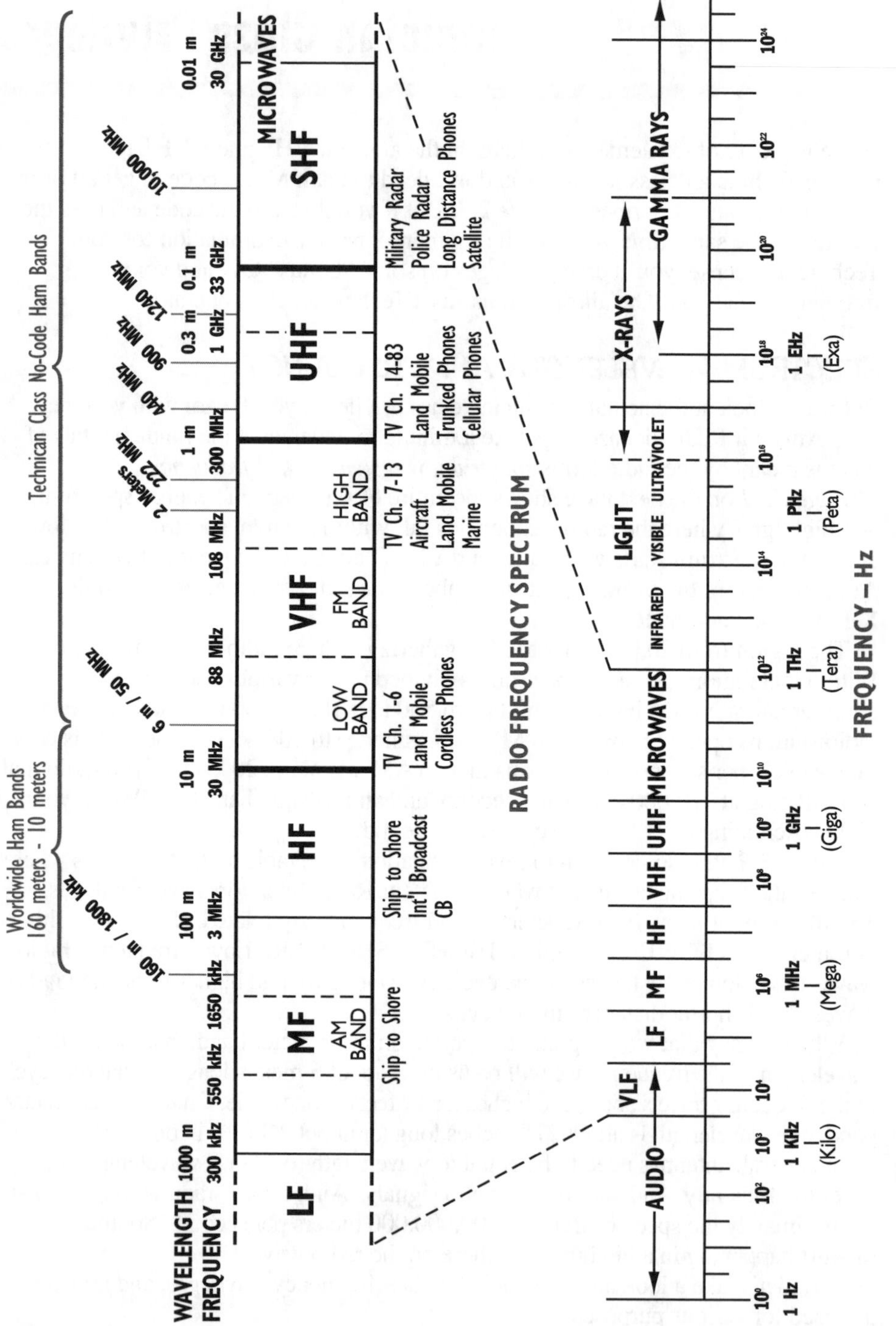

Figure 2-2. Radio Bands, Frequency and Wavelength

Category	Abbrev.	Frequency	Amateur Band Wavelength
Audio	AF	20 Hz to 20 kHz	None
Very Low Frequency	VLF	3 to 30 kHz	None
Low Frequency	LF	30 to 300 kHz	None
Medium Frequency	MF	300 to 3000 kHz	160 meters
High Frequency	HF	3 to 30 MHz	80, 40, 30, 20, 17, 15, 12, 10 meters
Very High Frequency	VHF	30 to 300 MHz	6, 2, 1.25 meters
Ultrahigh Frequency	UHF	300 to 3000 MHz	70, 33, 23, 13 centimeters
Superhigh Frequency	SHF	3 to 30 GHz	9, 5, 3, 1.2 centimeters
Extremely High Frequency	EHF	Above 30 GHz	6, 4, 2.5, 2, 1 millimeter

Frequency Spectrum

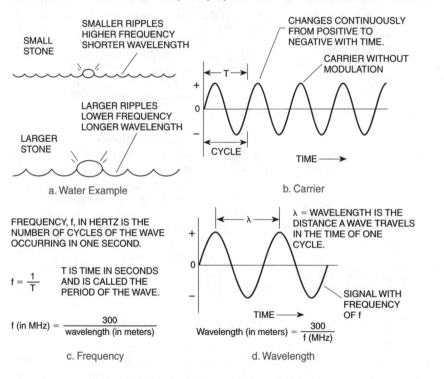

a. Water Example

b. Carrier

$$f = \frac{1}{T}$$

$$f \text{ (in MHz)} = \frac{300}{\text{wavelength (in meters)}}$$

c. Frequency

$$\text{Wavelength (in meters)} = \frac{300}{f \text{ (MHz)}}$$

d. Wavelength

Carrier, Frequency, Cycle and Wavelength

TECHNICIAN CLASS PRIVILEGES

The Technician class is the entry-level license where you get started in the amateur service. It's now easier than ever to enter the amateur radio service as a Technician class operator — with or without the code.

If you're not going to take the code test as a Technician class operator, you will have plenty of excitement on radio frequencies above 30 MHz. You will have full operating privileges on all of the exciting VHF, UHF, SHF, and microwave bands shown in *Table 2-1*. You can work skywaves on 6 meters to communicate all over the country; on the 2-meter band, you'll operate through repeaters and orbiting satellites. On the 222 MHz band, you may operate through linked repeaters; on the 440 MHz band, you might try amateur television, satellite, and remote base operation; and on 1270 MHz there are more frequencies for amateur television, satellites, repeater linking, and data point-to-point systems. And then there are the microwave bands where dish and loop Yagi antennas will beam out signals a lot farther than you might think.

Even without the worldwide CW and voice privileges earned by passing the 5-wpm code test, the Technician class without code has plenty of worldwide excitement on 6 meters, and our new satellites may carry your signals thousands of miles away. Let's explore the different bands for the Technician class operator *without* the Morse code Element 1 certificate.

Table 2-1. Technician Class No-Code Operating Privileges

Wavelength Band	Frequency	Emissions	Comments
6 Meters	50.0–54.0 MHz	All modes	Sideband voice, radio control, FM repeater, digital computer, remote bases, and autopatches. Even CW. (1500 watts PEP output)
2 Meters	144–148 MHz	All modes	All types of operation including satellite and owning repeater and remote bases. (1500 watt PEP output)
1¼ Meters	222–225 MHz	All modes	All band privileges. (1500 watt PEP output)
70 cm	420–450 MHz	All modes	All band privileges, including amateur television, packet, Internet linking, FAX, and FM voice repeaters. (1500 watt PEP output.)
33 cm	902–928 MHz	All modes	All band privileges. Plenty of room! (1500 watt PEP output.)
23 cm	1240–1300 MHz	All modes	All band privileges. (1500 watt PEP output)
13 cm	2300-2310 MHz 2390-2450 MHz	All modes	Amateur television

6-METER WAVELENGTH BAND, 50.0-54.0 MHZ

The Technician class operator will enjoy all amateur service privileges and maximum output power of 1500 watts on this worldwide band. Are you into radio control (R/C) and want to escape the interference between 72 and 76 MHz? On 6 meters, your Technician class license allows you to operate on exclusive radio control channels at 50 MHz and 53 MHz, just for licensed hams. *Table 2-2* shows the ARRL 6-meter wavelength band plan.

On 6 meters, the Technician class operator can get a real taste of long-range skywave skip communications. During the summer months, and during selected days and weeks out of the year, 50-54 MHz, 6-meter signals are refracted by the ionosphere, giving you incredible long-range communication excitement. It's almost a daily phenomenon during the summer months for 6 meters to skip all over the country. This is the big band for the Technician class no-code operator because of this type of ionospheric, long-range, skip excitement. There are even repeaters on 6 meters. So make 6 meters "a must" at your future operating station.

Table 2-2. 6-Meter Wavelength Band Plan, 50.0-54.0 MHz

MHz	Use
50.000–50.100	CW weak signal
50.060–50.080	CW Beacon FM
50.100–50.300	SSB, CW
50.100–50.200	DX window & SSB DX calling
50.225	Domestic SSB calling frequency and QSO each side
50.300–50.600	Non-voice communications
50.620	Digital/Packet calling frequency
50.800–50.980	Radio control
	20 kHz channels
51.000–51.100	Pacific DX window
51.120–51.480	Repeater inputs (19)
51.120–51.180	Digital repeater inputs
51.620–51.980	Repeater outputs (19)
51.620–51.680	Digital repeater outputs
52.000–52.480	Repeater inputs (23)
52.020, 52.040	FM simplex
52.500–52.980	Repeater outputs (23)
52.525, 52.540	FM simplex
53.000–54.480	Repeater inputs (19)
53.000, 53.020	FM simplex
53.1/53.2/53.3/53.4	Radio control
53.500–53.980	Repeater outputs (19)
53.5/53.6/53.7/53.8	Radio control
53.520	Simplex
53.900	Simplex

2-METER WAVELENGTH BAND, 144-148 MHZ

The 2-meter band is the world's most popular spot for staying in touch through repeaters. Here is where most all of those hand-held transceivers operate, and the Technician class operator receives unlimited 2-meter privileges! *Table 2-3* gives the 2-meter wavelength band plan adopted by the ARRL VHF/UHF advisory committee.

The United States, and many parts of the world, are blanketed with clear, 2-meter repeater coverage. They say there is nowhere in the United States you can't reach at least one or two repeaters with a little hand-held transceiver. 2-meters has you covered! Here are examples:

Handie-talkie channels	Tropo-DX-ducting	Remote base
Transmitter hunts	Internet radio links	Simplex operation
Autopatch	Contests	Rag-chewing
Moon bounce (EME)	Traffic handling	Emergency nets
Meteor bursts	Satellite downlink	Sporadic-E DX
Packet radio	Satellite uplink	Aurora

The Technician class license allows 1500 watts maximum power output for specialized 2-meter communications, and also permits you to own and control a 2-meter repeater.

Table 2-3. ARRL 2-Meter Wavelength Band Plan, 144-148 MHz

MHz	Use
144.00–144.05	EME (Earth-Moon-Earth) (CW)
144.05–144.06	Propagation beacons (old band plan)
144.06–144.10	General CW and weak signals
144.10–144.20	EME and weak-signal SSB
144.20	National SSB calling frequency
144.20–144.275	General SSB operation, upper sideband
144.275–144.30	New beacon band
144.30–144.50	New OSCAR subband plus simplex
144.50–144.60	Linear translator inputs
144.60–144.90	FM repeater inputs
144.90–145.10	Weak signal and FM simplex
145.10–145.20	Linear translator outputs plus packet
145.20–145.50	FM repeater outputs
145.50–145.80	Miscellaneous and experimental modes
145.80–146.00	OSCAR subband—satellite use only
146.01–146.37	Repeater inputs
146.40–146.58	Simplex
146.61–146.97	Repeater outputs
147.00–147.39	Repeater outputs
147.42–147.57	Simplex
147.60–147.99	Repeater inputs

1¼-METER WAVELENGTH BAND, 219-220 MHz

On the 222 MHz band, the frequencies 219 MHz to 220 MHz may be used by point-to-point digital message forwarding stations operated by Technician class licensees or higher. These stations must register with the American Radio Relay League 30 days prior to activation, and these stations must not interfere with primary marine users near the Mississippi River, or any other primary user of this band. Remember, before you turn on a point-to-point digital message forwarding station, you must first register your operation with the American Radio Relay League 30 days before going on the air on 219 to 220 MHz.

The 100 kHz channels for point-to-point fixed digital message forwarding stations, 50 watts PEP limit, are shown in *Table 2-4*.

Table 2-4. ARRL 1¼-Meter Wavelength Band Plan, 219-220 MHz

MHz	Use
219–220	Point-to-point fixed digital message forwarding systems. Must be coordinated through ARRL. 100 kHz Channels. 50W PEP limit.

Channel	Freq. (MHz)	Channel	Freq. (MHz)
A	219.050	F	219.550
B	219.150	G	219.650
C	219.250	H	219.750
D	219.350	I	219.850
E	219.450	J	219.950

MHz	Use
220–222	No longer available

1 ¼-METER WAVELENGTH BAND, 222-225 MHZ

Table 2-5 shows the usage allocation for this band. The Technician class license permits you to use the entire band at 1500 watts maximum output power. If you need some relief from the activity on 2 meters, the 222-225 MHz band is similar in propagation and use. 222 MHz to 225 MHz is now exclusively assigned to our Amateur Radio service.

Table 2-5. ARRL 1¼-Meter Wavelength Band Plan, 222-225 MHz

MHz	Use
222.00–222.15	Weak-signal modes (FM only)
222.00–222.05	EME (Earth-Moon-Earth)
222.05–222.06	Propagation beacons
222.10	SSB and CW calling frequency
222.10–222.15	Weak signal CW and SSB
222.15–222.25	Local coordinator's option: Weak signal, ACSB, repeater inputs, control points
222.25–223.38	FM repeater inputs only
223.40–223.52	FM simplex
223.50	Simplex calling frequency
223.52–223.64	Digital, packet
223.64–223.70	Links, control
223.71–223.85	Local coordinator's option: FM simplex, packet, repeater outputs
223.85–224.98	Repeater outputs only

70-CM WAVELENGTH BAND, 420-450 MHZ

As you gain more experience on the VHF and UHF bands, you will soon be invited to the upper echelon of specialty clubs and organizations. The 450-MHz band is where the experts hang out. *Table 2-6* presents the ARRL 70-cm (centimeter) wavelength band plan. Amateur television (ATV) is very popular, so there's no telling who you may see as well as hear. This band also has the frequencies for controlling repeater stations and base stations on other bands, plus satellite activity. With a Technician class license, you may even be able to operate on General class worldwide frequencies if a General class or higher control operator is on duty at the base control point. You would be able to talk on your 450-MHz hand-held transceiver and end up in the DX portion of the 20-meter band. As long as the control operator is on duty at the control point, your operation on General class frequencies is completely legal!

The 450 MHz band is also full of packet communications, RTTY, FAX, and all those fascinating FM voice repeaters. If you are heavy into electronics, you'll hear fascinating topics discussed and digitized on the 450-MHz band. A Technician class operator has full power privileges as well as unrestricted emission privileges. Visit:
➡ **www.wa6twf.com**

Table 2-6. ARRL 70-cm Wavelength Band Plan, 420-450 MHz

MHz	Use
420.00–426.00	ATV repeater or simplex with 421.25-MHz video carrier control links and experimental
426.00–432.00	ATV simplex with 427.250-MHz video carrier frequency
432.00–432.07	EME (Earth-Moon-Earth)
432.07-432.08	Propagation beacons (old band plan)
432.08–432.10	Weak-signal CW
432.10	70-cm calling frequency
432.10–433.00	Mixed-mode and weak-signal work
432.30-432.40	New beacon band
433.00–435.00	Auxiliary/repeater links
435.00–438.00	Satellite only (internationally)
438.00–444.00	ATV repeater input with 439.250-MHz video carrier frequency and repeater links
442.00–445.00	Repeater inputs and outputs (local option)
445.00–447.00	Shared by auxiliary and control links, repeaters and simplex (local option); (446.0-MHz national simplex frequency)
447.00–450.00	Repeater inputs and outputs

33-CM WAVELENGTH BAND, 902-928 MHZ

Radio equipment manufacturers are just beginning to market equipment for this band. Many hams are already on the air using home-brew equipment for a variety of activities. If you are looking for a band with the ultimate in elbow room, this is it! *Table 2-7* shows the 33-cm wavelength band plan adopted by the ARRL.

Table 2-7. ARRL 33-cm Wavelength Band Plan, 902-928 MHz

MHz	Use
902.0–903.0	Weak signal (902.1 calling frequency)
903.0–906.0	Digital Communications (903.1 alternate calling frequency)
906.0–909.0	FM repeater inputs
909.0–915.0	ATV
915.0–918.0	Digital Communications
918.0–921.0	FM repeater outputs
921.0–927.0	ATV
927.0–928.0	FM simplex and links

23-CM WAVELENGTH BAND, 1240-1300 MHZ

There is plenty of over-the-counter radio equipment for this band. Technician class operators may run any legal amount of power—with 20 watts about the usual safe limit. The frequencies are in the microwave region, and this band is excellent to use with local repeaters in major cities.

Like the 450-MHz band and the 2-meter band, this band is sliced into many specialized operating areas. You can work orbiting satellites, operate amateur television, or own your own repeater with your Technician class license. *Table 2-8* presents the 23-cm wavelength band plan adopted by the ARRL.

Table 2-8. ARRL 23-cm Wavelength Band Plan, 1240-1300 MHz

MHz	Use
1240–1246	ATV #1
1246–1248	Narrow-bandwidth FM point-to-point links and digital, duplexed with 1258-1260 MHz
1248–1252	Digital communications
1252–1258	ATV #2
1258–1260	Narrow-bandwidth FM point-to-point links and digital, duplexed with 1246-1252 MHz
1260–1270	Satellite uplinks, reference WARC '79
1260–1270	Wide-bandwidth experimental, simplex ATV
1270–1276	Repeater inputs, FM and linear, paired with 1282-1288 MHz, 239 pairs every 25 kHz, e.g., 1270.025, 1270.050, 1270.075, etc. 1271.0-1283.0 MHz uncoordinated test pair
1276–1282	ATV #3
1282–1288	Repeater outputs, paired with 1270-1276 MHz
1288–1294	Wide-bandwidth experimental, simplex ATV
1294–1295	Narrow-bandwidth FM simplex services, 25-kHz channels
1294.5	National FM simplex calling frequency
1295–1297	Narrow bandwidth weak-signal communications (no FM)
1295.0–1295.8	SSTV, FAX, ACSB, experimental
1295.8–1296.0	Reserved for EME, CW expansion
1296.0–1296.05	EME exclusive
1296.07–1296.08	CW beacons
1296.1	CW, SSB calling frequency
1296.4–1296.6	Crossband linear translator input
1296.6–1296.8	Crossband linear translator output
1296.8–1297.0	Experimental beacons (exclusive)
1297–1300	Digital communications

10-GHZ (10,000 MHZ!) BANDS AND MORE

There are several manufacturers of ham microwave transceivers and converters for this range, so activity is excellent. Gunnplexers are the popular transmitter. Using horn and dish antennas, 10 GHz is frequently used by hams to establish voice communications for controlling repeaters over paths from 20 miles to 100 miles. Output power levels are usually less than one-eighth of a watt! It's really fascinating to see how directional the microwave signals are. If you live on a mountain-top, 10 GHz is for you.

All modes and licensees except Novices are authorized on the bands shown in *Table 2-9.* There is much Amateur Radio experimentation on these bands.

Table 2-9. Gigahertz Bands

2.30–2.31 GHz	10.0–10.50 GHz*	119.98-120.02 GHz
2.39–2.45 GHz	24.0–24.25 GHz	142.0-149.0 GHz
3.30–3.50 GHz	47.0–47.20 GHz	241.0-250.0 GHz
5.65–5.925 GHz	75.50-81.0 GHz	All above 300 GHz

*Pulse not permitted

EARN ADDED TECHNICIAN CLASS PRIVILEGES WITH YOUR MORSE CODE CERTIFICATE

In the previous sections of this Chapter, we describe in detail all of your Technician class privileges above 30 MHz without having to know anything about Morse code dots and dashes. Now we want to tell you about the *additional* band privileges you will have as a Technician if you just make up your mind to learn the code and pass that simple, 5-wpm test.

80-METER WAVELENGTH BAND, 3500-4000 KHZ

Your valid code certificate gives you privileges on the 80-meter band for CW only from 3675 to 3725 kHz.

40-METER WAVELENGTH BAND, 7000-7300 KHZ

Passing a 5-wpm code test gives you Morse-code-only privileges on this band from 7100 to 7150 kHz. This is a popular night-time and early morning band because signals in code can reach up to 5,000 miles away!

15-METER WAVELENGTH BAND, 21,000-21,450 KHZ

Technician class operators holding the code certificate for 5-wpm may operate CW from 21.1 MHz to 21.2 MHz in this portion of the worldwide band. You can expect daytime range in excess of 10,000 miles using CW.

10-METER WAVELENGTH BAND, 28,000-29,700 KHZ

Passing a code test at 5-wpm allows you to operate on sub-bands available to grandfathered Novice class operators and grandfathered Technician-plus operators. You may operate code and digital computer communications from 28.1 MHz to 28.3 MHz, and monitor 28.2 MHz to 28.3 MHz for low-power propagation beacons. Now here's the good news — you may operate single-sideband voice between 28.3 MHz to 28.5 MHz, and literally work the world during band openings during daylight hours.

Table 2-10 summarizes the additional operating privileges you will have as a Technician class operator who holds a Morse code certificate – as well as the VHF/UHF privileges discussed earlier.

See, it really is worth the little bit of extra effort needed to learn the code so you can pass that Element 1, 5-wpm code test. Even if you never upgrade, you will always retain these operating privileges as a Technician class operator. And as soon as you pass the test, you'll have exam credit good for 365 days, making it even easier to upgrade to General class.

So once you pass Technician, don't stop! Go onto General class, and ride the worldwide airwaves of excitement, and still have all of your Technician class privileges on VHF and UHF, too.

After you pass your Technician written Element 2 exam, your next step is our second book, *General Class.* The General class license opens up all of the worldwide bands for long-range communications. Code speed is just 5-wpm. If you pass your code test during the Tech test, you have 365 days to cash in on this CW certificate for General class.

Table 2-10. Technician Class Operating Privileges with Morse Code Certificate

Wavelength Band	Frequency	Emissions	Comments
80 Meters	3675–3725 kHz	Code only	Limited to Morse code (200 watt PEP output limitation)
40 Meters	*7100–7150 kHz	Code only	Limited to Morse code (200 watt PEP output limitation)
15 Meters	21,100–21,200 kHz	Code only	Limited to Morse code (200 watt PEP output limitation)
10 Meters	28,100–28,500 kHz	Code	Morse code (200 watt PEP
	28,100–28,300 kHz	Data and code	output code limitation)
	28,300–28,500 kHz	Phone and code	Sideband voice (200 watt code PEP output limitation)

Plus These Existing VHF/UHF Frequency Privileges (No code test required)

Wavelength Band	Frequency	Emissions	Comments
6 Meters	50.0–54.0 MHz	All modes	Morse code, sideband voice, radio control, FM repeater, digital computer, remote bases, and autopatches (1500 watts PEP output)
2 Meters	144–148 MHz	All modes	All types of operation including satellite and owning repeater and remote bases. (1500 watt PEP output)
1¼ Meters	219–220 MHz	Data	Point-to-Point digital message forwarding
	222–225 MHz	All modes	All band privileges. (1500 watt PEP output)
70 cm	420–450 MHz	All modes	All band privileges, including amateur television, packet, RTTY, FAX, and FM voice repeaters. (1500 watt PEP output)
33 cm	902–928 MHz	All modes	All band privileges. Plenty of room! (1500 watt PEP output)
23 cm	1240–1300 MHz	All modes	All band privileges. (1500 watt PEP output)
13 cm	2300-2310 MHz		
	2390-2450 MHz	All modes	Ham T.V. Links; Satellites

* U.S. licensed operators in other than our hemisphere (ITU Region 2) are authorized 7050-7075 kHz due to shortwave broadcast interference.

AN IMPORTANT WORD ABOUT SHARED FREQUENCIES

In this Chapter, we discussed the Amateur Radio frequency privileges you will receive when you pass your exam and receive your license and call letters from the FCC. It is important, however, that you know that every ham band above 225 MHz is shared on a secondary basis with other services. This means that the primary users get first claim to the frequency!

For example, Government radiolocation (radar) is a primary user of some bands. And a multitude of industrial, scientific and medical services have access to the 902-928 MHz band. Just because the frequency is allocated to the amateur service does not mean that others do not have prior right or an equal right to the spectrum. You must not interfere with other users of the band.

There also are instances where amateurs must not cause interference to other stations, such as foreign stations operating along the Mexican and Canadian borders, military stations near military bases, and FCC monitoring stations. Also, amateur operators must not cause interference in the so-called National Radio Quiet Zones which are near radio astronomy locations. The astronomy locations are protected by law from Amateur Radio interference. Operation aboard ships and aircraft also is restricted. The FCC also can curtail the hours of your operation if you cause general interference to the reception of telephone or radio/TV broadcasting by your neighbors.

Every amateur should have a copy of the Amateur Radio Service Part 97 Rules and Regulations. It would be good for you to especially read Part 97.303 on frequency sharing.

> You can obtain a copy of the current Part 97 Rules from the W5YI Group by calling 1-800-669-9594.

SUMMARY

Enjoy the excitement of being a ham radio operator and communicate worldwide with other amateur operators without a code test. Your Technician class operator license allows you all ham operator privileges on all bands with frequencies greater than 50 MHz. You have operating privileges on the worldwide 6-meter band, on the world's popular 2-meter and 222-MHz repeater bands, on the amateur television, satellite communications, and repeater-linking 440-MHz and 1270-MHz bands, and on the line-of-sight microwave bands at 10 GHz and above.

Remember, you may enter the amateur service as a Technician class operator, passing Element 2, without a code test. You will receive full privileges on all of the VHF/UHF bands we have just described.

If you decide to take the 5-wpm Element 1 code test and pass it, you'll also receive the additional privileges on 10-, 15-, 40-, and 80-meters to join in with grandfathered Novice operators and higher class operators using these portions of the band.

Taking and passing Element 1, the simple 5-wpm code test, will satisfy the requirements for code for General class worldwide communications, and provide you with 365 days of exam credit toward your General class, Element 3 license upgrade.

3

A Little Ham History!

Ham radio has changed a lot in the 100 years since radio's inception. In the past 25 years, we have seen some monumental changes! So, before we get started preparing for the exam, I'm going to give you a little history lesson about our hobby, its history, and an overview of how you'll progress through the amateur ranks from your first, entry-level Technician class license to the top amateur ticket – the Extra class license. We know this background knowledge will make you a better ham! I'll keep it light and fun, so breeze through these pages.

In this chapter you'll learn all of the licensing requirements under the FCC rules that became effective April 15, 2000. And you'll learn about the six classes of license that were in effect *prior* to those rules changes. That way, when you run into a Novice, Technician Plus or Advanced class operator on the air, you'll have some understanding of their skill level, experience, and frequency privileges.

Marconi (shown here in 1896) was an amateur who was very serious about radio. We know you're going to have a lot of fun with your new ham radio hobby!
(Courtesy Marconi Co. Archives)

WHAT IS THE AMATEUR SERVICE?

There are nearly 700,000 Americans who are licensed amateur radio operators in the U.S. today. The Federal Communications Commission, the Federal agency responsible for licensing amateur operators, defines our radio service this way:

"The amateur service is for qualified persons of all ages who are interested in radio technique solely with a personal aim and without pecuniary interest."

Ham radio is first and foremost a fun hobby! In addition, it is a service. And note the word "qualified" in the FCC's definition – that's the reason why you're studying for an exam; so you can pass the exam, prove you are qualified, and get on the air.

Millions of operators around the world exchange ham radio greetings and messages by voice, teleprinting, telegraphy, facsimile, and television worldwide. Japan, alone, has more than a million hams! It is very commonplace for U.S. amateurs to communicate with Russian amateurs, while China is just getting started with its amateur service. Being a ham operator is a great way to promote international good will.

The benefits of ham radio are countless! Ham operators are probably known best for their contributions during times of disaster. In recent years, many recreational sailors in the Caribbean who have been attacked by modern-day pirates have had their lives saved by hams directing rescue efforts. Following the 9/11 terrorist attacks on the World Trade Center and the Pentagon, literally thousands of local hams assisted with emergency communications. In addition, over the years, amateurs have contributed much to electronic technology. They have even designed and built their own orbiting communications satellites.

The ham community knows no geographic, political or social barrier. If you study hard and make the effort, you are going to be part of our fraternity. Follow the suggestions in my book and your chances of passing the written exam are excellent. If you are fascinated by radio communication, learning will be easy and fun!

A BRIEF HISTORY OF AMATEUR RADIO LICENSING

Before government licensing of radio stations and amateur operators was instituted in 1912, hams could operate on any wavelength they chose and could even select their own call letters. The Radio Act of 1912 mandated the first Federal licensing of all radio stations and assigned amateurs to the short wavelengths of less than 200 meters. These "new" requirements didn't deter them, and within a few years there were thousands of licensed ham operators in the United States.

Since electromagnetic signals do not respect national boundaries, radio is international in scope. National governments enact and enforce radio laws within a framework of international agreements which are overseen by the International Telecommunications Union. The ITU is a worldwide United Nations agency headquartered in Geneva, Switzerland. The ITU divides the radio spectrum into a number of frequency bands, with each band reserved for a particular use. Amateur radio is fortunate to have many bands allocated to it all across the radio spectrum.

In the U.S., the Federal Communications Commission is the government agency responsible for the regulation of wire and radio communications. The FCC further allocates frequency bands to the various services in accordance with the ITU plan – including the Amateur Service – and regulates stations and operators.

By international agreement, in 1927 the alphabet was apportioned among various nations for basic call sign use. The prefix letters K, N and W were assigned to the United States, which also shares the letter A with some other countries.

In the early years of amateur radio licensing in the U.S., the classes of licenses were designated by the letters "A," "B," and "C." The highest license class with the most privileges was "A." In 1951, the FCC dropped the letter designations and gave the license classes names. They also added a new Novice class – a one-year, non-renewable license for beginners that required a 5-wpm Morse code speed proficiency test and a 20-question written examination on elementary theory and regulations, with both tests taken before one licensed ham.

In 1967, the Advanced class was added to the Novice, Technician, General and Extra classes. The General exam required 13-wpm code speed, and Extra required 20-wpm. Each of the five written exams were progressively more comprehensive and formed what came to be known as the *Incentive Licensing System.*

In the '70s, the Technician class license became very popular because of the number of repeater stations appearing on the air that extended the range of VHF and UHF mobile and handheld stations. It also was very fashionable to be able to patch your mobile radio into the telephone system, which allowed hams to make telephone calls from their automobiles long before the advent of cell phones.

In 1979, the international Amateur Service regulations were changed to permit all countries to waive the manual Morse code proficiency requirement for "...stations making use exclusively of frequencies above 30 MHz." This set the stage for the creation of the Technician "no-code" license, which occurred in 1991, when the 5-wpm Morse code requirement for the Technician class was the eliminated. New licensees were now permitted to operate on all amateur bands above 30 MHz. Applicants for the no-code Technician license had to pass the 35-question Novice and 30-question Technician class written examinations but, for the first time, not a Morse code test. Technician class amateurs who also passed a 5-wpm code test were awarded a Technician-Plus license. Besides their 30 MHz and higher no-code frequency privileges, Tech-Plus licensees gained the Novice CW privileges and a sliver of the 10 meter voice spectrum.

By this time, there was a total of six Amateur Service license classes – Novice, Technician, Technician-Plus, General, Advanced, and Extra – along with five written exams and three Morse code tests used to qualify hams for their various licenses.

The Amateur Service Is Restructured

In 1998, the FCC began a review of the amateur radio service with the objective of streamlining the licensing process, eliminating unnecessary and duplicated rules, and reducing the emphasis on the Morse code tests. The result of this review was a complete restructuring of the U.S. amateur service that became effective April 15, 2000. Today, applicants can only be examined for three amateur license classes:

- Technician class – the VHF/UHF entry level license;
- General class – the HF entry level license, and
- Amateur Extra class – a technically-oriented senior license.

In addition, there now is only one Morse code test speed at 5 words-per-minute (Element 1), which is required for the General class license.

Individuals with licenses issued before April 15, 2000, have been "grandfathered" under the new rules. This means that Novice, Technician-Plus and Advanced class amateurs are able to modify and renew their licenses indefinitely. Technician-Plus amateur licenses will be renewed as Technician class, but these licensees will retain their HF operating privileges indefinitely. The FCC elected not to change the operating privileges of any class, so you may hear some of these "grandfathered" hams when you get on the air.

Self-Testing In The Amateur Service

Prior to 1984, all amateur radio exams were administered by FCC personnel at FCC Field Offices around the country. In 1984, the FCC adopted a two-tier system beneath it called the VEC System to handle amateur radio license exams. It also increased the length of the term of amateur radio licenses from five to ten years.

The VEC (Volunteer Examiner Coordinator) System was formed after Congress passed laws that allowed the FCC to accept the services of Volunteer Examiners (or VEs) to prepare and administer amateur service license examinations. The testing activity of VEs is managed by Volunteer Examiner Coordinators (or VECs). A VEC acts as the administrative liaison between the VEs who administer the various ham examinations and the FCC, which grants the license.

A team of three VEs, who must be approved by a VEC, is required to conduct amateur radio examinations. General class amateurs may serve as examiners for the Technician class and the 5-wpm code test. Advanced class amateurs may administer exams for Elements 1, 2 and 3. The Extra class written Element 4 may only be administered by a VE who holds an Extra class license.

In 1986, the FCC turned over responsibility for maintenance of the exam questions to the National Conference of VECs, which appointed a Question Pool Committee (QPC) to develop and revise the various question pools according to a schedule. The QPC is required by the FCC to have at least ten times as many questions in each of the pools as may appear on an examination. As a rule, one question pool is changed annually.

The previously-mandated ten written exam topics were eliminated and the VEC's Question Pool Committee (QPC) now decides the content of each of the three written examinations. Both the Technician class Element 2 and General class Element 3 written examinations contain 35 multiple-choice questions. The Extra class Element 4 written examination has 50 questions.

That completes your history lesson. Now let's turn our attention to the privileges you'll earn as a new Technician class operator.

LICENSE PRIVILEGES

An amateur operator license conveys many privileges. As the control operator of an amateur radio station, you will be responsible for the quality of the station's transmissions. Most radio equipment must be authorized by the FCC before it can be widely used by the public but, for the most part, this is not true for amateur equipment!

Unlike the citizen's band service, amateurs may design, construct, modify and repair their own equipment. But you must have a license to do this, and even though it is easier than ever, there are certain things you must know before you can obtain your license from the FCC. Everything you need to know is covered in this book.

OPERATOR LICENSE REQUIREMENTS

To qualify for an amateur operator/primary station license, a person must pass an examination according to FCC guidelines. The degree of skill and knowledge that the candidate demonstrates to the examiners determines the class of operator license for which the person is qualified.

Anyone is eligible to become a U.S. licensed amateur operator (including foreign nationals, if they are not a representative of a foreign government). There is no age limitation – if you can pass the examinations, you can become a ham!

One of the reasons for the existence of the amateur service is to provide communications in times of emergency. Although hardly ever used on the ham bands during an emergency anymore, CW (Morse code) is one way to pierce through interference when other modes cannot get through. Packet radio is another very special type of emergency communications that uses your personal computer over the airwaves. Now that there is an opportunity to become an amateur operator Technician class licensee, you can concentrate on packet communications without ever having to worry about learning the Morse code for emergency communications.

Why Morse Code?

Morse code is *required* under the terms of international radio regulations (Article S25 of the International Telecommunications Union's International Radio Regulations) for hams operating on those worldwide frequencies shared by other amateur radio operators throughout the globe. Passing the simple 5-wpm Morse code test will meet these requirements.

OPERATOR LICENSE CLASSES AND EXAM REQUIREMENTS

Today, there are three amateur operator licenses issued by the FCC – Technician, General, and Extra. Each license requires progressively higher levels of learning and proficiency, and each gives you additional operating privileges. This is known as *incentive licensing* – a method of strengthening the amateur service by offering more radio spectrum privileges in exchange for more operating and electronic knowledge.

There is no waiting time required to upgrade from one amateur license class to another, nor any required waiting time to retake a failed exam. You can even take all three examinations and the Morse code test at one sitting if you're really brave! *Table 3-1* details the amateur service license structure and required examinations.

Table 3-1: Current Amateur License Classes and Exam Requirements
(Effective April 15, 2000)

License Class	Exam Element	Type of Examination
Technician Class	2	35-question, multiple-choice written examination. Minimum passing score is 26 questions answered correctly (74%).
General Class	3	35-question, multiple-choice written examination. Minimum passing score is 26 questions answered correctly (74%). Also requires passing Element 1 Morse code test.
Extra Class	4	50-question, multiple-choice written examination. Minimum passing score is 37 questions answered correctly (74%).
Morse Code	1	Demonstrate ability to receive Morse code at a 5-word-per-minute rate. (See Chapter 5 for more information and an example test.)

ABOUT THE WRITTEN EXAMS

What is the focus of each of the written examinations, and how does it relate to gaining expanding amateur radio privileges as you move up the ladder toward your Extra class license? *Table 3-2* summarizes the subjects covered in each written examination element. Visit: ➡️**www.aa9pw.com**

Table 3-2. Question Element Subjects

Exam Element	License Class	Subjects
Element 2	Technician	Elementary operating procedures, radio regulations, and a smattering of beginning electronics. Emphasis will be on VHF and UHF operating.
Element 3	General	HF (high-frequency) operating privileges, amateur practices, radio regulations, and a little more electronics. Emphasis is on HF bands.
Element 4	Extra	Basically a technical examination. Covers specialized operating procedures, more radio regulations, formulas and heavy math. Also covers the specifics on amateur testing procedures.

No Jumping Allowed

All written examinations for an amateur radio license are additive. You *cannot* skip over a license class or by-pass a required examination as you upgrade from Technician to General to Extra. For example, to obtain a General class license, you must first take and pass the Element 2 written examination for the Technician class license, plus the Element 3 written examination and the required Element 1 5-wpm code test. To obtain the Extra class license, you must first pass the Element 2 (Technician) and Element 3 (General) written examinations, and the 5-wpm Element 1 code test, and then successfully pass the Element 4 (Extra) written examination. Again, you only need to pass the 5-wpm Morse code test once.

TAKING THE ELEMENT 2 EXAM

Here's a summary of what you can expect when you go to the session to take the Element 2 written examination for your Technician class license. Detailed information about how to find an exam session, what to expect at the session, what to bring to the session, and more, is included in Chapter 6.

Examination Administration

All amateur radio examinations are administered by a team of at least three Volunteer Examiners (VEs) who have been accredited by a Volunteer Examiner Coordinator (VEC). The VEs are licensed hams who volunteer their time to help our hobby grow.

How to Find an Exam Session

Examination sessions are organized under the auspices of an approved VEC. A list of VECs is located in the Appendix on page 208. The W5YI-VEC and the ARRL-VEC are the 2 largest examination groups in the country, and they test in all 50 states. Their 3-member, accredited examination teams are just about *everywhere*. So when you call the VEC, you can be assured they probably have an examination team only a few miles from where you are reading this book right now!

Want to find a test site fast?
Visit the W5YI-VEC website at **www.w5yi.org**, or call 800-669-9594.

Taking the Exam

The Element 2 written exam is a multiple-choice format. The VEs will give you a test paper that contains the 35 questions and multiple choice answers, and an answer sheet for you to complete. Take your time! Make sure you read each question carefully and select the correct answer. Once you're finished, double check your work before handing in your test papers.

The VEs will score your test immediately, and you'll know before you leave the exam site whether you've passed. Chances are very good that, if you've studied hard, you'll get that passing grade!

GETTING YOUR FIRST CALL SIGN

Once the VE team scores your test and you've passed, the process of getting your official FCC Amateur Radio License begins – usually that same day.

At the exam site, you will complete NCVEC Form 605, which is your application to the FCC for your license. If you pass the exam, the VE team will send on the required paperwork to their VEC. The VEC reviews the paperwork submitted by your exam team and then files your application with the FCC. This filing is done electronically, and your license will be granted and your call sign posted on the FCC's website within a few days. As soon as you see your new call sign, you are permitted to go on the air as a licensed amateur – even before your paper license arrives in the mail! See Chapter 6 for more details on this process.

Vanity Call Signs

Your first call sign is assigned by the FCC's computer, and you have no choice of letters. However, once you have that call sign, you can apply for a Vanity Call Sign. Again, see Chapter 6 for details.

HOW MANY CLASSES OF LICENSES?

Once you've passed your Element 2 exam and go on the air as a new Technician class operator, you'll be talking to fellow hams throughout the U.S. and around the world. Here's a summary of the new and "grandfathered" licenses that your fellow amateurs may hold, and a recap of the level of expertise they have demonstrated in order to gain their licenses.

New License Classes

Following the FCC's restructuring of Amateur Radio that took effect April 15, 2000, there are just three written exams and three license classes – Technician, General, and Extra. There is only one Morse code test, and that is 5-wpm. But persons who hold licenses issued prior to April 15, 2000, may continue to hold onto their license class and continue to renew it every 10 years for as long as they wish.

"Grandfathered" Licensees

As mentioned previously, individuals licensed prior to April 15, 2000, will continue to enjoy band privileges based on their licenses. So, once you get on the air with your new Technician class privileges, every now and then you might meet a Novice operator while yakking on 10 meters, or sending CW on 15, 40, or 80 meters.

And you'll see some older licenses saying "Technician Plus," which belong to grandfathered Technician class operators licensed prior to April 15, 2000, who passed their 5-wpm code test and who get to keep their code credit indefinitely as long as they renew their license. Technician Plus operators will have their licenses renewed as Technician class with permanent code operating credit.

And then there are the Advanced class operators who may continue to hold onto their license class designation until they finally decide to move up to Extra class – without any further code requirement.

When you look at the Frequency Charts in this book that tell you the various band privileges, you will continue to see designated sub-bands for Extra, Advanced,

General, Tech Plus, Tech, and Novice. These sub-bands privileges haven't changed – any ham licensed prior to April 15, 2000, is automatically "grandfathered" to their original frequency privileges and will not lose a single kilohertz of operating room. But they'll get more privileges if they upgrade to the top – the Extra class!

NOW, ABOUT THAT CODE TEST

In order to upgrade to General class you'll have to take and pass the 5-wpm Element 1 Morse code test. And you need to be a General class licensee to upgrade to Extra class.

As explained in Chapter 2, if you are a new Technician class operator after April 15, 2000, and pass the 5-wpm code test, your license will still say "Technician." You'll be given a Certificate of Successful Completion of Examination (CSCE) by the VE team that gives you the test. The CSCE is only good for 365 days for your General class upgrade, and you'll need to re-take the code test again if you don't upgrade before the CSCE expires. While the CSCE only allows exam credit for 365 days, it does convey *permanent* HF operating privileges on four worldwide band segments at 80, 40, 15, and 10 meters.

If you don't know the Morse code, it's easy to learn! I have developed a fun, educational, and very unique audio course for learning the dots and dashes by sound. Using my audio course along with the code information included in Chapter 5 that will help you memorize the characters, it shouldn't take you more than a couple of weeks to get the feel of the code. If you're musical, you might have it down in just 10 days. Chances are you can pick up my audio course at the same place where you purchased this book. And while you're at it, go ahead and look at the General class Element 3 book and see how easy that test is, too.

IT'S EASY!

Probably the primary pre-requisite for passing any amateur radio operator license exam is the will to do it. If you follow my suggestions in this book, your chances of passing the Technician exam are excellent. And once you pass, then it's on to our *General Class* book.

Yes, indeed, the year 2000 brought some big changes to ham radio, and everyone comes out a winner! There has never been a better time to join the ranks of ham radio hobbyists. So study hard! We hope to hear you on the air very soon.

Getting Ready for the Exam

4

Your Technician class written examination will consist of 35 multiple-choice questions taken from the 510 questions that make up the 2003-07 Element 2 pool. Each question on your examination and the multiple-choice answer will be identical to what is contained in this book.

This chapter contains the official, complete 510-question FCC Element 2 Technician class question pool from which your examination will be taken. Again, your exam will contain 35 of these questions, and you must get 74% of the questions correct – which means you must answer 26 questions correctly in order to pass. This chapter also contains important information about how the exam is constructed using the questions taken from the Element 2 pool.

If you're also going to take the Element 1, 5-wpm Morse Code test, you can do it at the same test session, or schedule it later. Or, you can schedule the Code test before your written examination, and receive a 365-day credit for passing the test.

What? Not into dots and dashes? Then forget about the code, and just go for Technician class, Element 2. If you decide to do the code five years from now, no problem! There is absolutely no time limit on when you must take the Code test when you hold the Technician class license.

Your examination will be administered by a team of 3 or more Volunteer Examiners (VEs) – amateur radio operators who are accredited by a Volunteer Examiner Coordinator (VEC). You will receive a Certificate of Successful Completion of Examination (CSCE) when you pass the examination. This is official proof that you have passed the exam and it will be given to you before you leave the exam center. In just a few days, you'll find your call letters on the worldwide web, and as soon as you know them you are licensed to go on the air!

THE 2003-07 QUESTION POOL

There is no more important examination for the amateur service than the entry-level Technician class test. This exam must always remain "fresh" and reflect those operating areas that a new ham may get involved in. The exam must contain a balance of questions that range from entry-level operating practices to the importance of knowing all about RF safety. Further, the entry-level exam should cover the basics of electricity and how radios work. Knowing this material will make you a better Amateur Radio operator when you get on the air!

This new Technician class question pool was carefully developed by the National Conference of Volunteer Exam Coordinators Question Pool Committee (QPC). The QPC chairman is Scotty Neustadter, W4WW, and the other committee members are Bart Jahnke, W9JJ, John Johnson, W3BE, and Fred Maia, W5YI.

WHAT THE EXAMINATION CONTAINS

The examination questions and the multiple-choice answers (one correct answer and three "distracters") for all license class levels are public information. They are widely published and are identical to those in this book. *There are no "secret" questions.* FCC rules prohibit any examiner or examination team from making any changes to any questions, including any numerical values. No numbers, words, letters, or punctuation marks can be altered from the published question pool. By studying all 510 Element 2 questions in this book, you will be reading the same exact questions that will appear on your 35-question Element 2 written examination. But which 35 out of the 510 total questions?

Table 3-1. FCC Element 2 Technician Class Question Pool

Subelement	Topic	Total Questions	Exam Questions
T1	FCC Rules	64	5
T2	Methods of Communication	35	2
T3	Radio Phenomena	25	2
T4	Station Licensee Duties	37	3
T5	Control Operator Duties	34	3
T6	Good Operating Practices	37	3
T7	Basic Communications Electronics	51	3
T8	Good Engineering Practice	104	6
T9	Special Operations	41	2
T0	Electrical, Antenna Structure, & RF Safety Practices	82	6
TOTALS		510	35

Table 3-1 shows how the Element 2, 35-question examination will be constructed. The question pool is divided into 10 subelements. Each subelement covers a different subject and is divided into topic areas. For example, for the Element 2 examination, 6 questions of the 35 total will be taken from subelement T8 on Good Engineering Practice. On Radio Phenomena (T3), you will find 2 questions; and on FCC Rules (T1) you will have 5 questions.

All Volunteer Examination teams use the same multiple-choice question pool. This uniformity in study material ensures common examinations throughout the country. Most exams are computer-generated, and the computer selects one question from each topic area within each subelement for your upcoming Element 2 exam.

Trust me – trust me, every question on your upcoming Element 2 exam will look very familiar to you by the time you finish studying this book

QUESTION CODING

Each and every question in the 510 Element 2, Technician class question pool is numbered using a **code.** *The coded numbers and letters reveal important facts about each question!*

The numbering code always contains 5 alphanumeric characters to identify each question. Here's how to read the question number so you know exactly how the examination computer will select one question out of each group for your exam.

Once you know this information, you can increase your odds of achieving a "max" score on the exam, especially if there is a specific group of questions which seems impossible for you to memorize or understand. When you get to Element 4, Extra class – a very tough exam – this trick will really come in handy!

Let's pick a typical question out of the pool – T8A03 – and let me show you how this numbering code works:

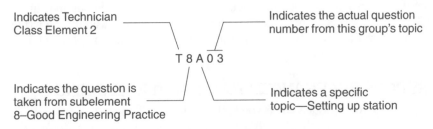

Figure 4-1. Examination Question Coding

- The first character "T" identifies the license class question pool from which the question is taken. "T" is for Technician. "G" would be for General, and "E" would be for Extra.

- The second digit, an "8", identifies the subelement number, 1 through 0. Technician subelement 8 deals with good engineering practice.

- The third character, "A", indicates the topic area within the subelement. Topic "A" deals with your ham radio equipment including "setting up station."

- The fourth and fifth digits indicate the actual question number within the subelement topic's group. The "03" indicates this is the third question about good engineering practice, and within the topic area of setting up the station. There are 14 individual questions in topic area T8A, *but only one out of this topic group will appear on the test.*

Here's the Secret Study Hint

Only one exam question will be taken from any single group! A computer-generated test is set up to take one question from one single topic group. It cannot skip any one group, nor can it take any more than one question from that group.

Your upcoming Element 2, Technician class, written exam is relatively easy with no bone-crusher math formulas. The same thing is true for the Element 3 exam, General, found in my *General Class* book. But when you get to the *Extra Class* book, there may be one or two groups that have formulas so complicated that you may want to wait until the very end to digest them. And if you decide to skip them completely, guess what – how many questions out of any one group? That's right, only one per group. This means you are not going to get hammered on any upcoming test with a whole bunch of questions dealing with a specific group item. Great secret, huh?

Study Time

How long will it take you to prepare for your upcoming exam?

The Technician class question pool in this book is valid from July 1, 2003, through June 30, 2007. It contains a total of 510 questions – but don't panic! Most questions are repeated several different ways, and these "repeats" reinforce what you've already learned. It is probably going to take about 30 days to work through this book and prepare for your Technician class test. Remember, you may not skip over Technician and take the General written test first – you must take the written exams in order: Element 2 Technician, Element 1 Morse code and Element 3 General, and Element 4 Extra.

QUESTIONS REARRANGED FOR SMARTER LEARNING

The first thing you'll notice when you look at how the Element 2 question pool is presented in this book is that I have *completely rearranged the entire Technician class question pool* to precisely follow my weekend ham radio training classes. This rearrangement will take you *logically* through each and every one of the 510 Q & A's. The questions are arranged here by 29 topic areas in a way that eliminates the need for you to jump back and forth between topic groups or subelements to match up questions on similar topics.

For example, I have taken all of the questions in the pool that talk about where you can operate your ham radio and grouped them together into one area that allows you to better understand all of the material that relates to this topic. This arrangement of the Q&A's follows a natural learning process beginning with what ham radio is, what radio waves are, how they get from here to there, a peek under the cover of the modern Technician class ham set, and ends with safety issues to keep you safe and sound in your new amateur radio hobby.

Trust me, the reorganization of all of the test questions in the 510 pool has been tested and finely-tuned in hundreds of my weekend classes. This method of learning WORKS! You will probably cut the amount of study time in half simply by following the question pool from front to back as presented here in my book!

Let me assure that each and every Element 2 Q&A is in this book. A cross-reference of all 510 questions is found on pages 219 to 220 in the back of the book, along with the syllabus used by the Question Pool Committee to develop this new Element 2 pool.

This book – and my Technician class audio course – contain all 510 Technician class questions, 4 possible answers, the noted correct answer, and my upbeat description of how the correct answer works into the real world of amateur radio. We also include **KEY WORDS** that will help you remember the correct answer and provide you with a fast review of the entire question pool just before you sit for the big Tech exam.

We also include many web addresses that can provide you with hours of fascinating study on selected "hot topics" that will help you really understand the real world of ham radio behind the Q & A's. You can visit the site while you study, or visit them after you've earned your Technician class licenses and are on the air.

When you visit some of these websites, it may not be immediately apparent why we are suggesting that you go there. Some addresses take you to the sites of local ham clubs. Most of these are specialty clubs, and they contain lots of information on how to operate on repeaters, or satellites, or provide educational resources on learning about electronics or antennas or how radios work.

And a disclaimer – while we have worked hard to make sure all of these addresses are current at the time of publication, websites move, addresses change, or sites simply go away. So if you find an address that doesn't work, feel free to drop us an e-mail so we can update this for the next printing of our book. And if you know of a website that you think is a gem, then send us that information and we'll consider it for our next printing.

> *Here's our e-mail address:*
> **masterpubl@aol.com**

How to Read the Questions

Using an actual question from page 32, here is a guide to explain what it is you will be studying as you go through all of the Q&As in the book:

Official Q&A

T1D02 What age must you be to hold an amateur license?
A. 14 years or older
B. 18 years or older
C. 70 years or younger
D. There are no age limits

Correct Answer

ANSWER D: *There are no age limits.* There are Amateur Radio operators who are as young as 5 years old! Also, most kids love the Morse code. [97.5b1] ➡ **www.w5yi.org**

FCC Part 97 Rule Citation   Suggested Website   Key Words To Remember

Topic Areas

Here is a list of my topic areas showing the page where it starts in the book. Again, there is a complete cross reference list of the Q&As in numerical order on pages 217 to 220 in the Appendix, along with the official Question Pool Syllabus.

STUDY SUGGESTIONS

Finally, as you get ready to start study the questions, here are some suggestions to make your learning easier:

1. Read over each multiple-choice answer carefully. Some answers start out looking good, but turn bad during the last 2 or 3 words. If you speed read the answers, you could very easily go for a wrong answer because you didn't read them all the way through. Also, don't count on the multiple-choice answers always appearing in the exact same A-B-C-D order on your actual computer-generated test. While they won't change any words in the answers, they will sometimes scramble the A-B-C-D order.

2. Keep in mind that there is only one question on your test that will come from each group, and track how many groups in each sub-element.

3. Give this book to a friend, and ask him or her to read you the correct answer. You now give her the question wording.

4. Mark the heck out of your book! When the pages begin to fall out, you're probably ready for the exam!

5. Take this book along with you everywhere you go. Avoid reading it while driving the car or riding a bicycle. Remember, audio cassette tapes on Technician class theory are available, too, so if you want to listen to me read the questions and answers to you while you're out driving, or laying on the beach, we can do this.

6. Highlight the keywords one week before the test. Then speed read the brightly highlighted key words twice a day before the exam.

Are you ready to work through the 510 Q & A's? Put a check mark by the easy ones that you may already know the answer for, and put a little circle by any question that needs a little bit more study. Save your highlighting work until a few days before your upcoming test. Work the Q & A's for about 30 minutes at a time. I'll drop in a little bit of humor to keep you on track; and if you actually need my live words of encouragement, you can call me on the phone Monday through Thursday, 10:00 a.m. to 4:00 p.m. (California time), 714/549-5000.

THE QUESTION POOL, PLEASE

Okay, this is the big moment – your Technician class, Element 2, question pool. Don't freak out and get overwhelmed with the prospect of learning 510 Q & A's. You will find that the topic content is repeated many times, so you're really going to breeze through this test without any problem!

What exactly is ham radio?
A few questions to get you started!

T1A02 What are two of the five fundamental purposes for the amateur service in the United States?
- A. To protect historical radio data, and help the public understand radio history
- B. To help foreign countries improve communication and technical skills, and encourage visits from foreign hams
- C. To modernize radio schematic drawings, and increase the pool of electrical drafting people
- D. To increase the number of trained radio operators and electronics experts, and improve international goodwill

ANSWER D: The Federal Communications Commission rules, found in Part 97, describe the amateur service as "a radio communications service for the purpose of self-training, intercommunication and technical investigation, carried out by amateurs, that is, duly authorized persons interested in radio technique solely with a personal aim and without pecuniary interest." Hams are well-known for their emergency communications capabilities; and when we are not handling disaster radio traffic, we can be found on the airwaves finding new ways to send signals from here to there as a hobby and service. Other purposes of ham radio include *increasing the number of trained operators and improving international goodwill.* [97.1] ➡ **www.qrz.com**

T1A03 What is the definition of an amateur station?

With a transceiver like one of these, you can hold your ham station in the palm of your hand.

- A. A radio station in a public radio service used for radiocommunications
- B. A radio station using radiocommunications for a commercial purpose
- C. A radio station using equipment for training new broadcast operators and technicians
- D. A radio station in the amateur service used for radiocommunications

ANSWER D: Your *ham station* will consist of a radio device, at a particular location, that will be *used for amateur communications.* This station can go anywhere that you go, and might be mobile, a base, or a handheld set. You also are allowed to choose any authorized frequency in any authorized band. You can change radio equipment type at anytime. [97.3a5] ➡ **www.eHam.net**

T1D03 What government agency grants your amateur radio license?
- A. The Department of Defense
- B. The State Licensing Bureau
- C. The Department of Commerce
- D. The Federal Communications Commission

ANSWER D: Your Technician class *license*, as well as all radio licenses here in the United States, are *granted by the Federal Communications Commission.*
➡ http://wireless.fcc.gov

UNITED STATES OF AMERICA
FEDERAL COMMUNICATIONS COMMISSION

 ## AMATEUR RADIO LICENSE

KB9SMG

DETER E TROTTER

Ham License

T1D01 Who can become an amateur licensee in the US?
A. Anyone except a representative of a foreign government
B. Only a citizen of the United States
C. Anyone except an employee of the US government
D. Anyone

ANSWER A: There is no nationality requirement to become an amateur operator in the United States, but *representatives of foreign governments are ineligible.* [97.5b1] ➡ www.arrl.org

---

T1D02 What age must you be to hold an amateur license?
A. 14 years or older
B. 18 years or older
C. 70 years or younger
D. There are no age limits

ANSWER D: *There are no age limits.*
There are Amateur Radio operators who are as young as 5 years old! Also, most kids love the Morse code. [97.5b1]
➡ www.w5yi.org

Kids love ham radio!

T1C07 What is your responsibility as a station licensee?
A. You must allow another amateur to operate your station upon request
B. You must be present whenever the station is operated
C. You must notify the FCC if another amateur acts as the control operator
D. You are responsible for the proper operation of the station in accordance with the FCC rules

ANSWER D: When a fellow ham is using your equipment and station call sign, remember *it is your responsibility to make sure everything is legal.* [97.103a] ➡ www.hamgallery.com

---

How easy is it to get my first ham license?
A look at licensing requirements.

T1C02 What are the US amateur operator licenses that a new amateur might earn?
A. Novice, Technician, General, Advanced
B. Technician, Technician Plus, General, Advanced
C. Novice, Technician Plus, General, Advanced
D. Technician, Technician with Morse code, General, Amateur Extra

ANSWER D: Beginning April 15, 2000, there are now 3 amateur radio classes – Technician with or without Morse code, General class, and Amateur Extra class. Any answer with "Novice" or "Advanced" in it would be wrong because the question reads, "a new amateur might earn." Even though there are grandfathered Novice, Technician-Plus, and Advanced class operators out there in radio land, the question really wants you to know the answer as *Technician class, Technician class with Morse code, General class, and Amateur Extra class.* [97.9a]

T1D06 What is a Volunteer Examiner (VE)?
A. A certified instructor who volunteers to examine amateur teaching manuals
B. An FCC employee who accredits volunteers to administer amateur license exams
C. An amateur, accredited by one or more VECs, who volunteers to administer amateur license exams
D. An amateur, registered with the Electronic Industries Association, who volunteers to examine amateur station equipment

ANSWER C: General, Advanced, and Extra class *amateur operators* may be *accredited by* one or more *Volunteer Examiner Coordinators* to volunteer their time *to administer amateur license exams.* When you take your upcoming examination for a new license, it will be fellow ham radio operators, accredited by a VEC, who will give you the exam. It takes three or more accredited Volunteer Examiners to conduct a test session. [97.509a] ➡ **www.ac6v.com**

T1D07 What minimum examinations must you pass for a Technician amateur license?
A. A written exam, Element 1 and a 5 WPM code exam, Element 2
B. A 5 WPM code exam, Element 1 and a written exam, Element 3
C. A single 35 question multiple choice written exam, Element 2
D. A written exam, Element 2 and a 5 WPM code exam, Element 4

ANSWER C: No more Morse code test for the entry-level license! To pass the *Technician amateur examination,* you will study the *Element 2* written theory here in my book, or on my audio tapes. Got the tapes? They're fun! [97.503b1]

T1D04 What element credit is earned by passing the Technician class written examination?
A. Element 1   C. Element 3
B. Element 2   D. Element 4

ANSWER B: Right now, you are studying to pass the *Technician class examination, Element 2.* If you plan to learn CW, the Morse code element is Element 1. General class theory is Element 3, and Extra class theory is Element 4. As long as you keep your license current and don't let it expire by more than 2 years, you will not need to retake any of your amateur radio exams. [97.501c]

T1C05 What is the normal term for an amateur station license grant?

A. 5 years
B. 7 years
C. 10 years
D. For the lifetime of the licensee

ANSWER C: Amateur station *licenses* are granted for a *term of ten years.* You will need to renew your license at that time, and renewing will probably be as simple as e-mail to the FCC. There won't be any reminder notices sent out, so every now and then check the expiration date of your license and don't forget to renew! [97.25a]

T1C01 Which of the following is required before you can operate an amateur station in the US?

A. You must hold an FCC operator's training permit for a licensed radio station
B. You must submit an FCC Form 605 together with a license examination fee
C. The FCC must grant you an amateur operator/primary station license
D. The FCC must issue you a Certificate of Successful Completion of Amateur Training

ANSWER C: When you pass your examination, your accredited Volunteer Examination Team will file the test results electronically with the FCC, and many times your *call letters will be granted by the FCC* in less than a week! As soon as you find out your new call letters, you can go on the air. It will take approximately 30 days for your actual paper license to arrive in the mail. Ask your Volunteer Examination Team what phone number to call, or

Make sure the FCC has issued your call sign before you go on the air for the first time.

go the FCC website to find out what your new call letters are. You will not need to wait for that paper license – you can go on the air immediately with your new call sign. [97.5a] ➡ **http://wireless.fcc.gov**

T1C03 How soon after you pass the examination elements required for your first Amateur Radio license may you transmit?

A. Immediately
B. 30 days after the test date
C. As soon as the FCC grants you a license and the data appears in the FCC's ULS data base
D. As soon as you receive your license from the FCC

ANSWER C: Good news! You will not need to wait very long to begin operating with your first Amateur Radio license. *As soon as you see your FCC license grant* on the Internet, or make a phone call to someone who can read you your new call sign from the FCC database, *YOU ARE ON THE AIR!* On the internet, go to http://wireless.fcc.gov, click on "license search" and then search by name entering your last name first, then a comma, and then your first name. The paper copy of your license will come in about three to four weeks. If your Volunteer Examination Team and Coordinator file electronically, you should see a grant within 48 hours of electronic submission. [97.5a] ➡ **www.buck.com**

T4A05 Why must an amateur operator have a current US postal mailing address?
A. So the FCC has a record of the location of each amateur station
B. To follow the FCC rules and so the licensee can receive mail from the FCC
C. Because all US amateurs must be US residents
D. So the FCC can publish a call-sign directory

ANSWER B: When you fill out the FCC Form 605 to apply for your amateur operator/primary station license, it asks for your *mailing address so you can receive mail from the FCC.* Where do you want to get the license? At your home? At your office? At a friend's house? It's a hassle to change your mailing address, so make it some spot that you plan to get your mail for the next few years. [97.23] ➡ **www.ac6v.com/#index**

FCC 605 Main Form	Quick-Form Application for Authorization in the Ship, Aircraft, Amateur, Restricted and Commercial Operator, and General Mobile Radio Services	Approved by OMB 3060 - 0850 See instructions for public burden estimate

required showing as described in the instructions.

8) Are attachments (other than associated schedules) being filed with this application?	( ) Yes No

Applicant/Licensee Information

9) FCC Registration Number (FRN): **0008583833**

10) Applicant /Licensee is a(n): (**I**) Individual / Corporation   Unicorporated Association / Limited Liability Corporation   Trust / Partnership   Government Entity / Consortium   Joint Venture

11) First Name (if individual): **Joe**	MI: **J**	Last Name: **Diode**	Suffix: **Sr.**

11a) Date of Birth (required for Commercial Operators (including Restricted Radiotelephone)): ____(mm)/____(dd)/____(yy)

12) Entity Name (if other than individual):

13) Attention To:

14) P.O. Box:	And/Or	15) Street Address: **1500 MHz Way**

16) City: **Rectifier**	17) State: **WI**	18) Zip Code: **5333X**	19) Country: **USA**

20) Telephone Number: **414-434-0111**	21) FAX Number:

22) E-Mail Address: **JDIODE@WEST.NET**

FCC 605 – Main Form
October 2002 - Page 1

FCC Form 605

T4A03 What penalty may the FCC impose if you fail to provide your correct mailing address?
A. There is no penalty if you do not provide the correct address
B. You are subject to an administrative fine
C. Your amateur license could be revoked
D. You may only operate from your address of record

ANSWER C: It is very important that you keep your amateur radio license up-to-date with respect to your mailing address. If you move and don't report your new address to the FCC, you might end up having your license revoked. From time to time the Federal Communications Commission will send out important Universal Licensing System (ULS) information, including a special password that you will need to know to file amendments to your license in case you move, change your name, or need to correct a spelling error. FCC MAILINGS ARE NOT FORWARDED. If they get their mail back as "moved," *your license could be revoked.* Always keep the FCC up to date on your current address! [97.23] ➡ **www.amateur-radio.org**

T4A06 What is one way to notify the FCC if your mailing address changes?

A. Fill out an FCC Form 605 using your new address, attach a copy of your license, and mail it to your local FCC Field Office

B. Fill out an FCC Form 605 using your new address, attach a copy of your license, and mail it to the FCC office in Gettysburg, PA

C. Call your local FCC Field Office and give them your new address over the phone

D. Call the FCC office in Gettysburg, PA, and give them your new address over the phone

ANSWER B: You will need to *fill out an FCC Form 605* if you ever change your address. Send a copy of your license, not the original, *to the FCC in Gettysburg, PA.* NEVER give up your original license. Copies are fine. [97.21a1]
➡ **www.hamnet.net**

T1C04 How soon before the expiration date of your license may you send the FCC a completed Form 605 or file with the Universal Licensing System on the World Wide Web for a renewal?

A. No more than 90 days
B. No more than 30 days
C. Within 6 to 9 months
D. Within 6 months to a year

ANSWER A: Don't try and renew your license too early! Whether you renew on the computer or use Form 605, don't try to *renew* until your license is *within 90 days of expiration.* Licenses are good for 10 years, so keep it in a safe place where you're going to remember what you did with it 10 years from now! [97.21a3i]
➡ **www.hamgallery.com**

T1C11 If you forget to renew your amateur license and it expires, may you continue to transmit?

A. No, transmitting is not allowed

B. Yes, but only if you identify using the suffix "GP"

C. Yes, but only during authorized nets

D. Yes, any time for up to two years (the "grace period" for renewal)

ANSWER A: Your new Technician class license will usually be granted for 10 years. It is renewable without a test. You usually renew within 90 days of expiration. Although there is a 2-year grace period after your license expires, *you may NOT operate during the grace period.* ➡ **www.w5nc.org**

T1C06 What is the "grace period" during which the FCC will renew an expired 10 year license?

A. 2 years
B. 5 years
C. 10 years
D. There is no grace period

ANSWER A: You are not allowed to operate during a grace period; however, *you keep your privileges for 2 years.* After that, they are lost for good. So is your call sign. Don't forget to renew! [97.21b] ➡ **www.arnewsline.org**

What's so special about a ham radio call sign?
You'll be the only one in the world when you get yours from the FCC!

T1E11 How does the FCC issue new amateur radio call signs?
A. By call sign district in random order
B. The applicant chooses a call sign no one else is using
C. By ITU prefix letter(s), call sign district numeral and a suffix in strict alphabetic order
D. The Volunteer Examiners who gave the exams choose a call sign no one else is using

ANSWER C: The FCC will issue a new *amateur radio call sign* beginning with the letter A, K, N, or W. Entry-level call signs usually begin with the letter K and one additional sequential letter. Next comes your call sign district number. After that the new entry-level license will have *3 additional letters in strict alphabetical order.* The call sign issuing process is electronic; and once your examination team processes your paperwork to the Volunteer Examiner Coordinator, your wait is only a couple of additional days for the computer to issue your unique call sign. As soon as you know your call sign from the computer listing, you can go on the air with your new ham license! [97.17d] ➡ **www.w5yi.org**

T1E02 What letters must be used for the first letter in US amateur call signs?
A. K, N, U and W
B. A, K, N and W
C. A, B, C and D
D. A, N, V and W

ANSWER B: *In the United States, all ham call signs begin with A, K, N, or W.* This is because, as an aid to enforcement, all transmitting stations are required to identify themselves at intervals when they are in operation. Radio does not respect national boundaries. By international agreement, the first characters of the call sign indicate the country in which the station is authorized to operate. The only prefixes allocated to United States amateur stations are: AA-AL, KA-KZ, NA-NZ, and WA-WZ. ➡ **www.qsl.net**

U.S. Call Sign Areas

T1E03 What numbers are normally used in US amateur call signs?
A. Any two-digit number, 10 through 99
B. Any two-digit number, 22 through 45
C. A single digit, 1 though 9
D. A single digit, 0 through 9

ANSWER D: You can get a good idea where someone is by the number in their call sign—unless they moved to another state and didn't change their call sign. You can buy colorful charts that illustrate the geographic area assigned to *Amateur Radio call sign numbers, 0-9.* ➡ **www.wm7d.net/hamradio**

T1E01 Which of the following call signs is a valid US amateur call?
A. UZ4FWD
B. KBL7766
C. KB3TMJ
D. VE3BKJ

ANSWER C: There are *never more than two letters preceding the number in a ham call sign,* followed by another letter, or two, or three. Answer B has too many letters, and ends up with numbers – so it's incorrect. And since Answers A and D don't begin with A, K, N, or W, they also are wrong.

T1E12 Which station call sign format groups are available to Technician Class amateur radio operators?
A. Group A
B. Group B
C. Only Group C
D. Group C and D

ANSWER D: Your brand *new Technician class call sign* will usually consist of 2 letters, a number, and 3 additional letters. This will be *from Group D.* Years ago, Technician class operators might have received a call sign beginning with the letter N, a number, and 3 additional letters. This was from Group C, but all of these call signs are already taken. So unless they go back and re-issue Group C call signs, the correct answer to this question is Group C and D for a Technician class operator. Don't hold your breath for a call sign beginning with the letter N – there are no more available at this time. (See page 204 for a complete explanation of the FCC's call sign system and the Vanity Call Sign application process.) ➡ **www.dxer.com**

T1E06 What must you transmit to identify your amateur station?
A. Your "handle"
B. Your call sign
C. Your first name and your location
D. Your full name

ANSWER B: *Use your own call sign* – not someone else's call sign – when operating from your own station. [97.119a] ➡ **www.aa9pw.org**

T5B01 How often must an amateur station be identified?
A. At the beginning of a contact and at least every ten minutes after that
B. At least once during each transmission
C. At least every ten minutes during and at the end of a contact
D. At the beginning and end of each transmission

ANSWER C: Give your call letters regularly. Remember, even though the law doesn't require that you give them at the beginning of the transmission, it makes good sense to start out with your call letters. The rules require that you *give your call letters every 10 minutes and at the end of your contact.* [97.119a]

Call Signs

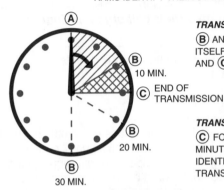

Ⓐ START OF TRANSMISSION—EVEN THOUGH IT IS NOT REQUIRED, MOST HAMS IDENTIFY THEIR STATION AT THE START OF A TRANSMISSION.

TRANSMISSIONS LONGER THAN 10 MINUTES:
Ⓑ AN AMATEUR STATION MUST IDENTIFY ITSELF EVERY 10 MINUTES OF TRANSMISSION, AND Ⓒ AT THE END OF A TRANSMISSION.

TRANSMISSIONS LESS THAN 10 MINUTES:
Ⓒ FOR TRANSMISSIONS LESS THAN 10 MINUTES, THE AMATEUR STATION MUST IDENTIFY ITSELF AT THE END OF THE TRANSMISSION.

Identifying Amateur Transmissions

T5B03 What is the longest period of time an amateur station can operate without transmitting its call sign?

A. 5 minutes
B. 10 minutes
C. 15 minutes
D. 30 minutes

ANSWER B: Some hams *use a 10-minute timer* to remind them to give their call signs. §Part 97 stipulates: "Each amateur shall give its call sign at the end of each communication, and every ten minutes or less during a communication." [97.119a] ➡ www.w5yi.org

T5B02 What identification, if any, is required when two amateur stations end communications?

A. No identification is required
B. One of the stations must transmit both stations' call signs
C. Each station must transmit its own call sign
D. Both stations must transmit both call signs

ANSWER C: No matter how brief or long, you must *always give your own call sign at the end of your contact.* [97.119a] ➡ www.heilsound.com

T5C01 If you answer someone on the air and then complete your communication without giving your call sign, what type of communication have you just conducted?

A. Test transmission
B. Tactical signal
C. Packet communication
D. Unidentified communication

ANSWER D: Jumping into a conversation to give a quick comment *without proper identification* with your FCC call letters is considered an *unidentified communication.* Always give your call sign! [97.119a]

T5B08 If you are using a language besides English to make a contact, what language must you use when identifying your station?

A. The language being used for the contact
B. The language being used for the contact, provided the US has a third-party communications agreement with that country
C. English
D. Any language of a country that is a member of the International Telecommunication Union

ANSWER C: It is okay to talk with another amateur in a foreign language to practice the other language as long as you identify your station in English every 10 minutes. *FCC rules require U.S. amateurs to give their call signs in English.* [97.119b2] ➡ **www.hamgallery.com**

T1E07 How might you obtain a call sign made up of your initials?

A. Under the vanity call sign program
B. In a sequential call sign program
C. In the special event call sign program
D. There is no provision for choosing a call sign

ANSWER A: When you pass your entry-level Technician class examination, you'll be issued a call sign generated by the FCC computer. This call sign will consist of 2 letters, a number, and 3 additional letters. Once you spot your call sign grant on the Federal Communications Commission computer data base, you are allowed to go on the air immediately. A paper FCC license will come to you within about 30 days. Once that arrives, you are eligible to *replace the computer-issued call sign with a vanity call sign* of your choosing. You also may request a call sign that was previously assigned to you that may have expired many years ago, or a call sign of a close relative or former license holder who is now deceased. The easiest way to get a vanity call sign is to contact The W5YI Group at

Many hams order license plates with their call sign.

800-669-9594 and ask for their vanity call sign application package. You could try do it yourself on-line at the FCC website, but The W5YI Group will make it a hassle-free, uncomplicated process. Trust me on this! [97.19] ➡ **www.w5yi.org.**

T1E08 How may an amateur radio licensee change his call sign without applying for a vanity call?

A. By requesting a systematic call sign change on an NCVEC Form 605
B. Paying a Volunteer Examiner team to process a call sign change request
C. By requesting a specific new call sign on an NCVEC Form 605 and sending it to the FCC in Gettysburg, PA
D. Contacting the FCC ULS database using the Internet to request a call sign change

ANSWER A: You look on the computer and you see your brand new call sign – and you absolutely hate the last 3 letters! You may *apply for a new systematic call sign* by completing NCVEC Form 605 and sending it into the VEC that originally handled your initial license process. You will find their name and address on your test-passing Certificate of Successful Completion of Examination (CSCE). Also, if you notice your brand new license has a misspelling or a problem with your street address, contact the VEC at the address listed on the CSCE. It is the VEC's responsibility to electronically file for your call sign, and they can help you correct any errors. [97.21(A) (3)(ii)] ➡ **www.powerstream.com/tech.html**

T1E09 How may an amateur radio club obtain a station call sign?
A. You must apply directly to the FCC in Gettysburg, PA
B. You must apply through a Club Station Call Sign Administrator
C. You must submit FCC Form 605 to FCC in Washington, DC
D. You must notify VE team on NCVEC Form 605

ANSWER B: I strongly encourage you to join a local ham radio club when you earn your Technician class license. Club members will give you a warm, hearty welcome into our hobby, and they might assist you in programming your first ham radio handheld. This same club may be interested in *obtaining* its own *club station call sign.* They will accomplish this relatively easily *through a club station call sign administrator.* The administrator will carefully examine the application to insure only one call sign is assigned to the club's radio officer. It would be in violation of the rules for any ham to brainstorm 10 or 20 "different" ham radio clubs on paper, and then apply for 10 to 20 club call signs. The FCC has taken quick action on this in the past, and the relatively new club station call sign administrator keeps a sharp eye that only one call sign is granted to the club's radio officer. [97.17b2] ➡ **www.w5yi.org**

T1E10 Amateurs of which license classes are eligible to apply for temporary use of a 1-by-1 format Special Event call sign?
A. Only Amateur Extra class amateurs
B. 1-by-1 format call signs are not authorized in the US Amateur Service
C. Any FCC-licensed amateur
D. Only trustees of amateur radio clubs

ANSWER C: Halloween is coming up, and you want to set up a very special ham station down at the local haunted house. You might be eligible for a letter-number-letter format call sign of your choice for this special event station, and *any FCC licensed amateur is eligible* to apply *for* such a temporary *special event call sign.* ➡ **www.hamquick.com**

Where can I operate my ham radio?

Take your gear everywhere – there's only a few restrictions.

T1C08 Where does a US amateur license allow you to operate?

A. Anywhere in the world
B. Wherever the amateur service is regulated by the FCC
C. Within 50 km of your primary station location
D. Only at the mailing address printed on your license

ANSWER B: Once you have a license, *you may operate anywhere the FCC has jurisdiction.* About the only exception is in a commercial aircraft. No operation is allowed on an airliner without special permission. [97.5d]

➡ **www.radioamateuronline.com**

T4A02 When may you operate your amateur station somewhere in the US besides the address listed on your license?

A. Only during times of emergency
B. Only after giving proper notice to the FCC
C. During an emergency or an FCC-approved emergency practice
D. Whenever you want to

ANSWER D: Just because your license has a permanent station location on it, don't think for a second that this is the only place you may operate your ham set. *You can operate it anywhere in the U.S.* and its territories and possessions without notifying the FCC. However, using your portable ham set on a commercial airplane is taboo. Using your ham set on cruise ships requires the permission of the captain.

Once you are a licensed amateur operator, your amateur station can operate from anywhere within the U.S., its territories and possessions — even remote mountain lakes and wilderness areas — without notifying the FCC.

T4A04 Under what conditions may you transmit from a location different from the address printed on your amateur license?

A. If the location is under the control of the FCC, whenever the FCC Rules allow
B. If the location is outside the United States, only for a time period of less than 90 days
C. Only when you have written permission from the FCC Engineer in Charge
D. Never; you may only operate at the location printed on your license

ANSWER A: You can drive around *all over the USA* and continue to operate your ham equipment *without further notifying the FCC.* You are NOT restricted to just the location printed on your license. But keep in mind that operating in a foreign country may require some additional paperwork before you leave the USA.
➡ **www.hfpack.com**

T1B12 When are you allowed to communicate with an amateur in a foreign country?
    A. Only when the foreign amateur uses English
    B. Only when you have permission from the FCC
    C. Only when a third party agreement exists between the US and the foreign country
    D. At any time, unless it is not allowed by either government

ANSWER D: *We may speak with every amateur operator in the world.* Most foreign hams speak English as the common ham radio language. We are not prohibited from talking with any foreign ham radio operator at this time. [97.111a1]

T4A01 When may you operate your amateur station aboard a cruise ship?
    A. At any time
    B. Only while the ship is not under power
    C. Only with the approval of the master of the ship and not using the ship's radio equipment
    D. Only when you have written permission from the cruise line and only using the ship's radio equipment

ANSWER C: Thinking of taking a cruise with your new Technician class privileges? Many times you may *obtain permission to operate* a handheld radio aboard a cruise ship, as long as it does not interfere *with* and is separate from the ship's radio equipment. You must first seek *approval of the master of the ship*, usually the ship's captain, along with the blessing of *the ship's radio officer.* [97.11a] ➡ **www.alphadelta.com**

T4A10 When may you operate your amateur station aboard an aircraft?
    A. At any time
    B. Only while the aircraft is on the ground
    C. Only with the approval of the pilot in command and not using the aircraft's radio equipment
    D. Only when you have written permission from the airline and only using the aircraft's radio equipment

ANSWER C: In rare circumstances, *a commercial aircraft pilot may give you specific permission to operate* your handheld transceiver. You will never be able to operate your equipment when the aircraft is operating under instrument flight rules (IFR). With everyone very concerned about air safety, the likelihood of a pilot giving you permission is next to zip. But if you get stuck down on the ground, away from the gate, and you are going to be holding for a long period of time on the deck (as I once was in a snow storm), you may ask the pilot if you can make a handheld call while you are waiting out the storm. [97.11a] ➡ **www.qrparci.org**

T1B14 What does it mean for an amateur station to operate under reciprocal operating authority?
    A. The amateur is operating in a country other than his home country
    B. The amateur is allowing a third party to talk to an amateur in another country

C. The amateur has permission to communicate in a foreign language
D. The amateur has permission to communicate with amateurs in another country

ANSWER A: Over 75 countries hold *reciprocal operating agreements* with the USA. The *permit to operate in different countries* is usually obtained ahead of time, and some European countries don't require any special paperwork other than having copies of your USA license and reciprocal agreement paperwork. This allows us to operate in another country when we travel around the world. See the list of countries with which we have reciprocal operating agreements in the Appendix. [97.107]

T1E05 In which ITU region is Guam?
A. ITU Region 1   C. ITU Region 3
B. ITU Region 2   D. ITU Region 4

ANSWER C: You can't see it on the map, but located between Japan and Australia *Guam is well within Region 3.*

T1E04 In which ITU region is Alaska?
A. ITU Region 1   C. ITU Region 3
B. ITU Region 2   D. ITU Region 4

ANSWER B: Look at the ITU regions map and notice that *Alaska is indeed in Region 2.* It's a little hard to see, but Hawaii also is in Region 2.

➡ **www.ah0a.org**

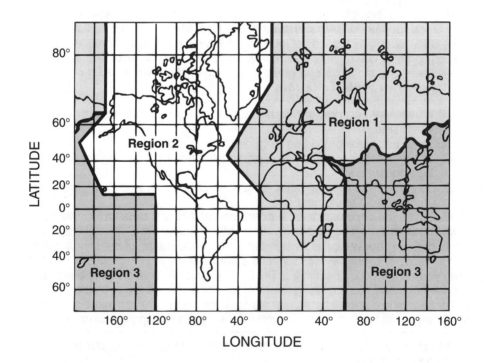

ITU Regions

Control Operator

Who's in control here?
Your control operator privileges and responsibilities.

T4B01 What is the definition of a control operator of an amateur station?
A. Anyone who operates the controls of the station
B. Anyone who is responsible for the station's equipment
C. Any licensed amateur operator who is responsible for the station's transmissions
D. The amateur operator with the highest class of license who is near the controls of the station

ANSWER C: This is a fancy name for you, *the person who holds an amateur operator/primary station license.* You, or any other ham you designate, are in control of all transmissions, and are *responsible for the proper operation of the station.* [97.3a12] **www.kenwood.net/amateur**

T4B02 What is the FCC's name for the person responsible for the transmissions from an amateur station?
A. Auxiliary operator
B. Operations coordinator
C. Third-party operator
D. Control operator

ANSWER D: The official name for the *person responsible* for the radio transmissions from an amateur station *is the control operator.* This is an important position if you, as a licensed amateur operator, have been appointed to be the control operator for a club station or for the equipment from which you are presently transmitting. [97.3a12] **www.hamradio.com**

T4B03 When must an amateur station have a control operator?
A. Only when training another amateur
B. Whenever the station receiver is operated
C. Whenever the station is transmitting
D. A control operator is not needed

ANSWER C: Every ham station must have a responsible *control operator present whenever it is transmitting,* unless it's an automated repeater station under "automatic control." The FCC defines a control operator as: "An amateur operator designated by the licensee of an amateur station to also be responsible for the emissions from that station." Automatic control means the use of devices or procedures for control without the control operator being present at the control point when the station is transmitting. [97.7] **www.icomamerica.com**

T4B04 What is the term for the location at which the control operator function is performed?
A. The operating desk
B. The control point
C. The station location
D. The manual control location

ANSWER B: Some repeaters that may be used for phone patches are controlled by radio links. This means that the actual *control point* is with the *control operator* and his tiny handheld transceiver. As a Technician, you could be a control operator with the control point worn on your belt! [97.3a13]

T4B05 What is the control point of an amateur station?
A. The on/off switch of the transmitter
B. The input/output port of a packet controller
C. The variable frequency oscillator of a transmitter
D. The location at which the control operator function is performed

ANSWER D: This is where you have complete *capabilities to turn the equipment on, or shut it off* in case of a malfunction. Every ham radio station is required to have a *control point*. [97.3a13]➡ **www.hamstation.com**

T4B08 What is the name for the operating position where the control operator has full control over the transmitter?

A. Field point
B. Auxiliary point
C. Control point
D. Access point

ANSWER C: Where you operate the equipment and have *full capabilities* to turn it on and off is called *the control point*. [97.3a13]

T5A01 If you are the control operator at the station of another amateur who has a higher-class license than yours, what operating privileges are you allowed?

A. Any privileges allowed by the higher license
B. Only the privileges allowed by your license
C. All the emission privileges of the higher license, but only the frequency privileges of your license
D. All the frequency privileges of the higher license, but only the emission privileges of your license

ANSWER B: If you operate another amateur's equipment, *you may operate only with the privileges allowed by your license,* even though the equipment is owned by another ham with more privileges. [97.105b] ➡ **www.chq-inc.com**

T4B06 When you operate your transmitting equipment alone, what is your official designation?

A. Engineer in Charge
B. Commercial radio operator
C. Third party
D. Control operator

ANSWER D: Your new call letters are soon to arrive, and you have already purchased your radio ahead of time. This is perfectly okay. Just don't transmit until you know your new call sign. When you do transmit, whether you are alone or with others, *your official designation is CONTROL OPERATOR.* [97.3a12]
➡ **www.yaesu.com/amateur**

When you operate your station you are the "control operator," and you are at the station's "control point."

T5A03 When an amateur station is transmitting, where must its control operator be, assuming the station is not under automatic control?

A. At the station's control point
B. Anywhere in the same building as the transmitter
C. At the station's entrance, to control entry to the room
D. Anywhere within 50 km of the station location

ANSWER A: If you let another ham use your station, your *control operator responsibilities* require you to *stay in the room, right at the radio equipment* control point, supervising the communications. [97.109b]
➡ **www.dxer.com**

T4B07 When does the FCC assume that you authorize transmissions with your call sign as the control operator?
    A. At all times
    B. Only in the evening hours
    C. Only when operating third party traffic
    D. Only when operating as a reciprocal operating station
ANSWER A: Your call sign is unique, and there is no one else in the world with your exact call letters. The call sign is assigned to YOU, not to the ham equipment. This means that your local ham radio set-up at the county fair is open to any ham with their own call letters to use, and be very careful that you don't leave your call letters stuck on the face of the radio because *the FCC will assume that this call sign heard on the air was authorized by you as the responsible control operator.* Remember, the call sign is issued to YOU, not the equipment. [97.103b]

T5A05 If you transmit from another amateur's station, who is responsible for its proper operation?
    A. Both of you
    B. The other amateur (the station licensee)
    C. You, the control operator
    D. The station licensee, unless the station records show that you were the control operator at the time
ANSWER A: As a control operator, *both you and the station licensee are responsible* for the transmissions from that station. [97.103a] ➡ **www.qcwa.org**

T5A06 If you let another amateur with a higher class license than yours control your station, what operating privileges are allowed?
    A. Any privileges allowed by the higher license, as long as proper identification procedures are followed
    B. Only the privileges allowed by your license
    C. All the emission privileges of the higher license, but only the frequency privileges of your license
    D. All the frequency privileges of the higher license, but only the emission privileges of your license
ANSWER A: If a friend with a higher-class license comes over and operates your equipment, he or she may *transmit with the privileges allowed by his or her higher-class license.* Just because he or she is using your equipment doesn't change his or her privileges. [97.105b] ➡ **www.qth.com**

T5A07 If a Technician class licensee uses the station of a General class licensee, how may the Technician licensee operate?
    A. Within the frequency limits of a General class license
    B. Within the limits of a Technician class license
    C. Only as a third party with the General class licensee as the control operator
    D. A Technician class licensee may not operate a General class station
ANSWER B: Your ham neighbor down the street is a General class operator. He has gone fishing and he wants you to come in and feed his pet bird. He said have fun

with his ham station. Would you be allowed to operate on HIS privileges? The answer is ABSOLUTELY NOT. As a Technician class licensee, *you must stay within the limits of your privileges* even though you are at someone else's equipment who has a higher grade of license. Now, if the General class operator is standing right there, that's another story. But in the absence of any other higher class operator, regardless of the station you are operating, you are limited to ONLY your privileges. [97.105(B)] ➡ **www.michiganradio.com**

T5A02 Assuming you operate within your amateur license privileges, what restrictions apply to operating amateur equipment?
    A. You may operate any amateur equipment
    B. You may only operate equipment located at the address printed on your amateur license
    C. You may only operate someone else's equipment if you first notify the FCC
    D. You may only operate store-purchased equipment until you earn your Amateur Extra class license

ANSWER A: Have fun with all types of radio equipment on the privileges of your new Technician class license. The Technician class license has *no restrictions on what type of amateur radio equipment you operate within your license privileges.* ➡ **www.hamradio.com**

T4B10 How many transmitters may an amateur licensee control at the same time?
    A. Only one
    B. No more than two
    C. Any number
    D. Any number, as long as they are transmitting in different bands

ANSWER C: *You may have any number of radios* at your station. I have over 25 radios in my shack! [97.5d] ➡ **www.irony.com/ham-howto.html**

You can own as many different ham radios as you wish as long as you operate them within the privileges of your license class. This ham has 3 mobile sets in his pick-up!

Want to communicate with my ham radio?

It's perfectly legal to let a 3rd party talk on your set.

T5A09 Why can't unlicensed persons in your family transmit using your amateur station if they are alone with your equipment?

A. They must not use your equipment without your permission

B. They must be licensed before they are allowed to be control operators

C. They must first know how to use the right abbreviations and Q signals

D. They must first know the right frequencies and emissions for transmitting

ANSWER B: In order to be the control operator of an Amateur Radio station, *your family member must be properly licensed.* [97.109b]

T5C06 If you let an unlicensed third party use your amateur station, what must you do at your station's control point?

A. You must continuously monitor and supervise the third-party's participation

B. You must monitor and supervise the communication only if contacts are made in countries that have no third-party communications agreement with the US

C. You must monitor and supervise the communication only if contacts are made on frequencies below 30 MHz

D. You must key the transmitter and make the station identification

ANSWER A: Don't even leave the room when a third party is using your ham set. Your license is at stake, so *stay right there with the third party* to insure compliance with all FCC rules. [97.115b1] ➡ **www.natcommgroup.com**

T5C04 What is the definition of third-party communications?

A. A message sent between two amateur stations for someone else

B. Public service communications for a political party

C. Any messages sent by amateur stations

D. A three-minute transmission to another amateur

ANSWER A: Did you know you can *let other people talk over your ham set who might not be ham radio operators*? That's right, but you must stay right at the microphone to act as the "control operator" to make sure that they abide by the rules. When you link your ham radio into the telephone service, the people you call are considered "third-party." [97.3a44] ➡ **www.rainreport.com**

It's perfectly okay to let others talk over your radio as long as you stay at the control point

T5C03 What kind of payment is allowed for third-party messages sent by an amateur station?

A. Any amount agreed upon in advance

B. Donation of repairs to amateur equipment

C. Donation of amateur equipment

D. No payment of any kind is allowed

ANSWER D: *You may not receive payment* for handling any type of third-party traffic. This includes payment for long-distance phone charges incurred during the third-party traffic. [97.11a2]

T5C05 When are third-party messages allowed to be sent to a foreign country?
A. When sent by agreement of both control operators
B. When the third party speaks to a relative
C. They are not allowed under any circumstances
D. When the US has a third-party agreement with the foreign country or the third party is qualified to be a control operator

ANSWER D: Your ham radio station is not a substitute for the regular international telephone service. If a *third party* wishes to use your ham station *to talk with another ham in a foreign country (with which there is a third-party agreement),* the third party's communications must be of a personal nature and relatively unimportant. [97.115a2] ➡ **www.radioamateur.com/english**

T5C07 Besides normal identification, what else must a US station do when sending third-party communications internationally?
A. The US station must transmit its own call sign at the beginning of each communication, and at least every ten minutes after that
B. The US station must transmit both call signs at the end of each communication
C. The US station must transmit its own call sign at the beginning of each communication, and at least every five minutes after that
D. Each station must transmit its own call sign at the end of each transmission, and at least every five minutes after that

ANSWER B: It's common for U.S. amateur operators to handle third-party communications with those countries with whom we have a third-party agreement. *The U.S. station must transmit both its own call sign and the call sign of the foreign operator* at the end of each communication. [97.115c]
➡ **www.dxer.com**

List of Countries Permitting Third-Party Traffic					
Country	**Call Sign Prefix**	**Country**	**Call Sign Prefix**	**Country**	**Call Sign Prefix**
Antigua and Barbuda	V2	El Salvador	YS	Paraguay	ZP
Argentina	LU	The Gambia	C5	Peru	OA
Australia	VK	Ghana	9G	Philippines	DU
Austria, Vienna	4U1VIC	Grenada	J3	Pitcairn Island	VR6
Belize	V3	Guatemala	TG	St. Christopher & Nevis	V4
Bolivia	CP	Guyana	8R	St. Lucia	J6
Bosnia-Herzegovina	T9	Haiti	HH	St. Vincent & Grenadines	J8
Brazil	PY	Honduras	HR	Sierra Leone	9L
Canada	VE, VO, VY	Israel	4X	South Africa	ZS
Chile	CE	Jamaica	6Y	Swaziland	3D6
Colombia	HK	Jordan	JY	Trinidad and Tobago	9Y
Comoros	D6	Liberia	EL	Turkey	TA
Costa Rica	TI	Marshall Is	V6	United Kingdom	GB
Cuba	CO	Mexico	XE	Uruguay	CX
Dominica	J7	Micronesia	V6	Venezuela	YV
Dominican Republic	HI	Nicaragua	YN	ITU-Geneva	4U1ITU
Ecuador	HC	Panama	HP	VIC-Vienna	4U1VIC

What are my operating privileges?
A look at frequencies for Technician class operators.

T5A04 Where will you find a detailed list of your operating privileges?
A. In the OET Bulletin 65 Index
B. In FCC Part 97
C. In your equipment's operating instructions
D. In Part 15 of the Code of Federal Regulations

ANSWER B: In the front of this book, I describe the specific Technician class privileges by frequency, bands, and also band plans. Many ham radio equipment manufacturers also offer colorful band plan charts that you can hang on the wall or put under the glass of your radio station desk. In the back of this book I encourage you to write me and ask for the free certificate and colorful band plan charts that are available to you with a large, self-addressed envelope and stamps. Take advantage of this offer when you get your new call sign. You will also find a very detailed, but quite dry, presentation of *operating frequencies and privileges in FCC Rule Part 97* on the internet. ➡ **www.w5yi.org**

T1B01 What are the frequency limits of the 6 meter band in ITU Region 2?
A. 52.0 - 54.5 MHz
B. 50.0 - 54.0 MHz
C. 50.1 - 52.1 MHz
D. 50.0 - 56.0 MHz

ANSWER B: First of all, "ITU Region 2" is here in the United States, up to Alaska and Greenland, and all the way down to South America. Region 1 is Europe and Africa, and Region 3 is the South Seas and the Far East. Here in *Region 2*, our *6-meter band* extends from *50 MHz to 54 MHz.* [97.301a] ➡ **www.hamoperator.org**

50 MHz   54 MHz
6-Meter Wavelength Band Privileges

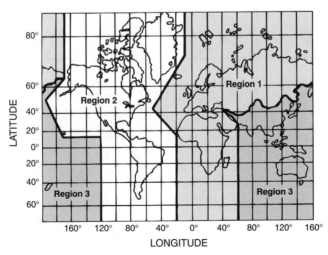

ITU Regions

T1B02 What are the frequency limits of the 2 meter band in ITU Region 2?
A. 144.0 - 148.0 MHz   C. 144.1 - 146.5 MHz
B. 145.0 - 149.5 MHz   D. 144.0 - 146.0 MHz
ANSWER A: Here in the USA, our *2-meter band* extends from *144 MHz to 148 MHz*. [97.301a] ➡ **www.hamstation.com**

144 MHz	148 MHz

2 Meter Wavelength Band Privileges

T2A08 In what radio-frequency range do amateur 2-meter communications take place?
A. UHF, Ultra High Frequency range   C. HF, High Frequency range
B. MF, Medium Frequency range   D. VHF, Very High Frequency range
ANSWER D: The radio spectrum is divided up into specific ranges, as shown below. Let's first convert wavelength in meters to megahertz (millions of cycle). It's easy – whether you have megahertz or meters, simply divide it into 300. Two meters into 300 comes out 150 MHz. Now we need to recall the radio spectrum:

UHF	300 MHz-3,000 MHz	HF	3 MHz-30 MHz
VHF	30 MHz-300 MHz	MF	0.3 MHz-3 MHz

Convert Frequency to Wavelength

$$\lambda(\text{meters}) = \frac{300}{f(\text{MHz})}$$

Convert Wavelength to Frequency

$$f(\text{MHz}) = \frac{300}{\lambda(\text{meters})}$$

The 2-meter ham band, with actual frequencies of 144-148 MHz, is right in the middle of the *30-300 MHz range, very high frequency, abbreviated VHF.* Don't worry that the 2-meter band works out to around 150 MHz, not actually 144-148 MHz as authorized by the FCC. When we speak of a ham radio band in METERS, we are only giving an approximate location of where that band is in relationship to the radio spectrum. Got it? ➡ **www.eham.net**

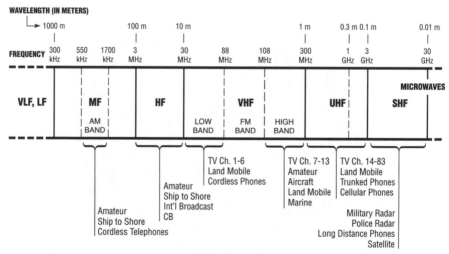

As Frequency increases, wavelength becomes shorter, as you can see from this radio frequency spectrum chart. Transmissions that require greater bandwidth, such as TV, use higher frequencies.

T2B14 What emission privilege is permitted a Technician class operator in the 219 MHz - 220 MHz frequency range?
A. Slow-scan television
B. Point-to-point digital message forwarding
C. FM voice
D. Fast-scan television
ANSWER B: Are you into computers? The Technician class operator has plenty of frequencies for computer communications, and even dedicated frequencies for digital message forwarding on 219-220 MHz. If you're reading my book on the Mississippi, sorry, but along the Mississippi these frequencies are part of a marine radio band for waterway comms, and are not to be used by Amateur Radio operators. But everywhere else, *219-220 MHz is a swell spot for digital message forwarding.* [97.305c]

T1B03 What are the frequency limits of the 1.25 meter band in ITU Region 2?
A. 225.0 - 230.5 MHz   C. 224.1 - 225.1 MHz
B. 222.0 - 225.0 MHz   D. 220.0 - 226.0 MHz
ANSWER B: The *1.25 meter band* is the popular "222" band, extending from *222 MHz to 225 MHz.* We originally had a couple more MHz of this band, but the Federal Communications Commission took it away because it was underutilized by ham operators. We should use all of our frequencies, or stand the chance of losing them. [97.301f] ➡ **www.ac6v.com**

25 WATTS
222 MHz   225 MHz

1.25 Meter Wavelength Band Privileges

T2B07 What emission types are Technician control operators allowed to use on the amateur 1.25-meter band in ITU Region 2?
A. Only CW and phone
B. Only CW and data
C. Only data and phone
D. All amateur emission privileges authorized for use on the band
ANSWER D: When you pass your upcoming 35-question Element 2 Tech exam, you will have all amateur emission privileges from 6 meters and shorter wavelength bands including *all amateur emission privileges on the 1.25-meter band.* How many MHz is 1.25 meters? That's right – 222 to 225 MHz. [97.305]

T1B11 If you are operating on 223.50 MHz, in what amateur band are you operating?
A. 15 meters   C. 2 meters
B. 10 meters   D. 1.25 meters
ANSWER D: The *223 MHz band* is more commonly called *1.25 meters* and sometimes 1-1/4 meters. Check this out by using the equation in question T2A08 on page 52. The calculator keystrokes are: "Clear 300 ÷ 223.50 = ." The closest choice will be 1.25 meters. [97.301f] ➡ **www.gpo.gov**

T1B04 What are the frequency limits of the 70 centimeter band in ITU Region 2?
A. 430.0 - 440.0 MHz   C. 420.0 - 450.0 MHz
B. 430.0 - 450.0 MHz   D. 432.0 - 435.0 MHz

ANSWER C: The *70 cm band* is also known as the *"440" band.* Our privileges extend all the way down to *420 MHz, and all the way up to 450 MHz.* When you buy a new dual-band radio, one band is usually 2 meters, and the other band is this band, the 440 MHz band. [97.301a] ➡ **www.wa6twf.com**

420 MHz   450 MHz

70-CM Wavelength Band Privileges

T1B15 What are the frequency limits for the amateur radio service for stations located north of Line A in the 70-cm band?

A. 430 - 450 MHz   C. 432 - 450 MHz
B. 420 - 450 MHz   D. 440 - 450 MHz

ANSWER A: The United States and Canada have adopted the "Line A" as a buffer zone for certain types of radio stations. This keeps normal "line-of-sight" radio energy from interfering with the other country's communications. *Amateurs are restricted from transmitting on the 70-cm band between 420 – 430 MHz* if they are located *north of "Line A."* This is because Canada has a different type of radio allocation in the bottom part of the 70-cm band. [97.303(f)(1)]
➡ **www.rac.com**

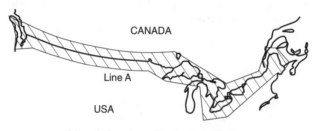

CANADA

Line A

USA

Line A Amateur Radio Restrictions

T1B05 What are the frequency limits of the 33 centimeter band in ITU Region 2?

A. 903 - 927 MHz   C. 900 - 930 MHz
B. 905 - 925 MHz   D. 902 - 928 MHz

ANSWER D: The *33 cm band* extends *from 902 MHz to 928 MHz,* and we compete with a lot of low-power, unlicensed equipment that share these same frequencies. There is very little ham radio equipment for this band, so we must continue to develop our own equipment for these frequencies and use all portions of the band, or stand the chance of losing this band to the low-power, unlicensed, cordless phones and garage door openers that use these frequencies. [97.301a]

902 MHz   928 MHz

33-CM Wavelength Band Privileges

T1B06 What are the frequency limits of the 23 centimeter band in ITU Region 2?

A. 1260 - 1270 MHz   C. 1270 - 1295 MHz
B. 1240 - 1300 MHz   D. 1240 - 1246 MHz

ANSWER B: The *23 cm band* extends from *1240 MHz to 1300 MHz,* and is a good one for amateur television, repeater operation, and point-to-point simplex where there is plenty of ready-made equipment for this band. If you buy a "tri-band" transceiver, chances are it will have 2 meters, 440 MHz, and full capabilities for the 23 cm band from 1240 MHz to 1300 MHz. [97.301a]

0.23 m

1240 MHz   1300 MHz

0.23-Meter (23 Centimeters) Wavelength Band Privileges

T1B07 What are the frequency limits of the 13 centimeter band in ITU Region 2?
 A. 2300 - 2310 MHz and 2390 - 2450 MHz
 B. 2300 - 2350 MHz and 2400 - 2450 MHz
 C. 2350 - 2380 MHz and 2390 - 2450 MHz
 D. 2300 - 2350 MHz and 2380 - 2450 MHz

ANSWER A: We are just beginning to explore the *13 cm band* with "home brew" equipment. Another way to operate on these frequencies is with a transverter that adds microwave capabilities to your existing VHF/UHF base or mobile unit. Now the big question is, "How are you going to remember which of these frequencies is correct on the test?" A simple way is to *look at the* correct answer for the *lower portion of the band, 2300 to 2310 MHz,* and recall that you have been sitting for the exam for about 10 minutes – and this is the only correct answer that has 10 MHz for the lower portion of the correct band. Keep in mind that some computer-generated exams will scramble the A, B, C, D answer order. 10 MHz, 10 minutes. Got it? [97.301a] ➡ **www.aa9pw.com**

2310 MHz   2390 MHz

2300 MHz   2450 MHz

13-CM Wavelength Band Privileges

T8A04 Which of the following devices would be useful to create an effective Amateur Radio station for weak-signal VHF communication?
 A. A hand-held VHF FM transceiver
 B. A multi-mode VHF transceiver
 C. An omni-directional antenna
 D. A mobile VHF FM transceiver

ANSWER B: Your no-code Technician class license puts you in the mainstream of exciting, 2-meter and 432-MHz operation. You can bounce signals off of the moon with your no-code license, and talk with stations hundreds of miles away off of meteor trails. Perhaps work the amateur satellites, or try sending signals thousands of miles within atmospheric temperature inversions. This excitement is available to you as a no-code operator, but you need more than just a simple FM transceiver. Look for a *multi-mode VHF transceiver* to get started on the 2-meter band, using CW and upper sideband *for weak signal work.* There also is a satellite weak signal "window" between 145.800 MHz to 146.000 MHz where no FM is recommended. It takes a multi-mode radio on CW and SSB to work weak signal VHF activities. Weak signal SSB calling frequencies are 144.200 on 2 meters, and 432.100 on 70 cm. ➡ **www.aesham.com**

T2B15 Which sideband is normally used for VHF/UHF SSB communications?

A. Upper sideband

B. Lower sideband

C. Double sideband

D. Double sideband, suppressed carrier

ANSWER A: When you get your new Technician class license, you might be fascinated with all of the weak signal activity down at the bottom of the 2-meter band at 144.200 MHz, and also 432 MHz. No FM down here! All *VHF/UHF voice weak signal communications are UPPER SIDEBAND.* ➡ www.wswss.org

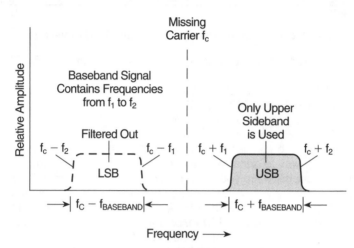

SSB signals are Amplitude Modulated (AM)
with the carrier and one sideband suppressed.

T1B08 If the FCC rules say that the amateur service is a secondary user of a frequency band, and another service is a primary user, what does this mean?

A. Nothing special; all users of a frequency band have equal rights to operate

B. Amateurs are only allowed to use the frequency band during emergencies

C. Amateurs are allowed to use the frequency band only if they do not cause harmful interference to primary users

D. Amateurs must increase transmitter power to overcome any interference caused by primary users

ANSWER C: We share the 900-MHz band with the vehicle locator service, which is *the primary user* of the frequencies. Same thing with 70 cm—we share it with military radiolocation services. They *have first rights to these frequencies.* [97.303] ➡ www.gatewayelex.com

---

T5B12 If you are using a frequency within a band assigned to the amateur service on a secondary basis, and a station assigned to the primary service on that band causes interference, what action should you take?

A. Notify the FCC's regional Engineer in Charge of the interference

B. Increase your transmitter's power to overcome the interference

C. Attempt to contact the station and request that it stop the interference

D. Change frequencies; you may be causing harmful interference to the other station, in violation of FCC rules

ANSWER D: Since our *operation is on a secondary basis*, we must *change frequencies* to not cause interference to the primary service station. [97.303]

T1B13 If you are operating FM phone on the 23-cm band and learn that you are interfering with a radiolocation station outside the US, what must you do?

A. Stop operating or take steps to eliminate this harmful interference
B. Nothing, because this band is allocated exclusively to the amateur service
C. Establish contact with the radiolocation station and ask them to change frequency
D. Change to CW mode, because this would not likely cause interference

ANSWER A: While this may be a rare occurrence, FM phone communications in the 23-cm band could cause interference to a radiolocation station outside of the United States, and *if you are* informed you are *causing interference,* you should *stop operating immediately.* [97.303h]

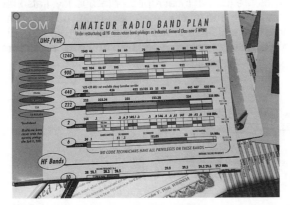

Band plans subdivide ham radio bands for specific uses, such as data, repeaters, and weak signal CW.

For a free band plan chart visit ➡ **www.icomamerica.com**

How can my handheld act like a big base station?
Powerful repeaters let you talk and listen at long distance – and send and receive wireless color pictures, too!

T5C12 What device is commonly used to retransmit amateur radio signals?

A. A beacon

B. A repeater

C. A radio controller

D. A duplexer

ANSWER B: The *device that retransmits amateur radio signals* within a specific ham band *is called a repeater.* When you get your new Technician class license, first do about one week of monitoring without transmitting, listening to repeater communications. This will give you a good idea on what the proper operating procedures are for that local repeater frequency. I also recommend you join the local repeater club and let club members help you program your new radio equipment for some of the local repeater frequencies. You also will want to buy a repeater frequency directory. ➡ **www.artscipub.com/repeaters**

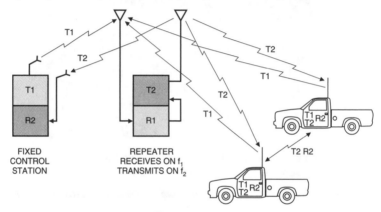

Repeater

Source: *Mobile 2-Way Radio Communications*, G. West, Copyright ©1992 Master Publishing, Inc., Lincolnwood, IL

T9A01 What is the purpose of repeater operation?

A. To cut your power bill by using someone else's higher power system

B. To help mobile and low-power stations extend their usable range

C. To transmit signals for observing propagation and reception

D. To communicate with stations in services other than amateur

ANSWER B: Repeaters are sponsored by ham radio clubs and individual hams for everyone to use. They are usually placed high atop a mountain or a very tall building. Mobile and portable sets operate through *repeaters* with *dramatically extended range.* Even base stations are permitted to use repeaters for added communications distance. There is usually no charge for joining a repeater group. Some repeaters have autopatch, and those repeaters may require special access codes and financial support. ➡ **www.vxstdusa.com**

T2B13 What name does the FCC use for voice emissions?

A. RTTY

B. Data

C. CW

D. Phone

ANSWER D: *Phone (or radiotelephone)* is another name for *voice communications.* [97.3c5] ➡ **www.hambook.com**

T2B09 What is the name of the voice emission most used on VHF/UHF repeaters?
A. Single-sideband phone
B. Pulse-modulated phone
C. Slow-scan phone
D. Frequency-modulated phone
ANSWER D: We use *frequency modulation (FM)* on most *VHF and UHF repeaters.* ➡ **www.cara-ampr.org**

T8C09 Why is FM voice so effective for local VHF/UHF radio communications?
A. The carrier is not detectable
B. It is more resistant to distortion caused by reflected signals than the AM modes
C. It has audio that is less affected by interference from static-type electrical noise than the AM modes
D. Its RF carrier stays on frequency better than the AM modes
ANSWER C: *FM is good* even *when there is amplitude-modulated noise* or when signals are weak. ➡ **www.texastowers.com**

T8C15 Where should the squelch be set for the proper operation of an FM receiver?
A. Low enough to hear constant background noise
B. Low enough to hear chattering background noise
C. At the point that just silences background noise
D. As far beyond the point of silence as the knob will turn
ANSWER C: With any of your new FM radios, *turn the squelch control just to the point that it silences the background noise,* but don't turn it any further. If you set the squelch control too far into silence, it will block weak incoming signals.

T9A05 When using a repeater to communicate, which of the following do you need to know about the repeater?
A. Its input frequency and offset
B. Its call sign
C. Its power level
D. Whether or not it has an autopatch
ANSWER A: When you first get started on the VHF and UHF airwaves with your new Technician class license, operating through repeaters will be a great way to extend your local communications range. All *repeaters transmit on one frequency, and listen on another simultaneously.* This means *you need to know* ahead of time what the *repeater input is and the offset* to hear the repeater output. Some amateur mobile and handheld VHF/UHF transceivers have an automatic repeater offset feature. This is good. But what is BETTER is to ask the sales personnel at the location where you buy your equipment to please clone your new radio to local frequencies in your area so you can begin tuning in all of the radio excitement without having to search for local repeaters and local simplex traffic in

A Repeater

your area. Preprogrammed equipment is a terrific way to start out operating on repeater channels with everything preset and cloned for your local area repeater operation. You should also buy local repeater directories at the same time that you purchase your new equipment so you know what repeaters are where in your area, and in locations where you plan to travel. ➡ **www.amcominc.com**

T9A11 What does it mean to say that a repeater has an input and an output frequency?
A. The repeater receives on one frequency and transmits on another
B. The repeater offers a choice of operating frequency, in case one is busy
C. One frequency is used to control the repeater and another is used to retransmit received signals
D. The repeater must receive an access code on one frequency before retransmitting received signals

ANSWER A: All *repeaters transmit (output) on one frequency, and listen (input) on another* simultaneously. Repeater directories publish the repeater frequencies by output. The plus (+) or minus (-) indicates the input "split" that you dial in on your VHF or UHF ham set. A plus (+) indicates a higher input and a minus (-) indicates a lower input. When you start to transmit, your transmitter should automatically go to the proper input frequency. Some repeaters also require a sub-audible tone as part of your input transmission. Ask the local operators how to engage the tone signal on your ham radio set.

T9A09 What is the usual input/output frequency separation for repeaters in the 2-meter band?
A. 600 kHz
B. 1.0 MHz
C. 1.6 MHz
D. 5.0 MHz

ANSWER A: The two most popular bands for new Technician class beginner operators are 2 meters and 70 cm. On the *2-meter band,* the usual input and output *frequency separation* for repeater use *is 600 kHz.* If you choose a handheld or mobile radio with "automatic repeater shifts," these will automatically be preset as you dial around the band. ➡ **www.artscipub.com**

T9A10 What is the usual input/output frequency separation for repeaters in the 70-centimeter band?
A. 600 kHz
B. 1.0 MHz
C. 1.6 MHz
D. 5.0 MHz

ANSWER D: *70 centimeters* (0.70 meters) is the 450-MHz band, and input and output repeater *separation usually is 5.0 MHz.* ➡ **www.rfparts.com**

T8A01 What two bands are most commonly used by "dual band" hand-held transceivers?
A. 6 meters and 2 meters
B. 2 meters and 1.25 meters
C. 2 meters and 70 cm
D. 70 cm and 23 cm

ANSWER C: The *2 most common bands* throughout the United States in a dual-band handheld *are 2 meters and 70 cm.* Another name for 70 cm is the "440 band." ➡ **www.alinco.com**

T9B20 What does it mean if you are told that a tone is required to access a repeater?

A. You must use keypad tones like your phone system to operate it
B. You must wait to hear a warbling two-tone signal to operate it
C. You must wait to hear a courtesy beep tone at the end of another's transmission before you can operate it
D. You must use a subaudible tone-coded squelch with your signal to operate it

ANSWER D: Since *most repeaters now require subaudible tone,* you will need a local listing of repeaters in your area along with the subaudible tone frequency. You must use the subaudible tone in order to bring the repeater up on the air. No tone, no repeater access! All ham radio handhelds come with a subaudible tone encode capability built in. ➡ **www.aesham.com**

T9B19 What is a continuous tone-coded squelch system (CTCSS) tone? (sometimes called PL – a Motorola trademark)

A. A special signal used for telecommand control of model craft
B. A sub-audible tone, added to a carrier, which may cause a receiver to accept the signal
C. A tone used by repeaters to mark the end of a transmission
D. A special signal used for telemetry between amateur space stations and Earth stations

ANSWER B: Every mountain top and skyscraper probably has a few ham repeaters atop a small tower. These repeaters are hearing so many signals coming in, including interfering signals, that they need a way of not accidentally self-triggering and turning on when it wasn't the real signal. What makes a signal into a ham repeater REAL? *The repeater may employ CTCSS tone decode,* and it will take the ham out there in radioland to ENCODE a subaudible tone *which causes the repeater receiver to accept the signal.* ➡ **www.eia.org**

EIA Standard Subaudible CTCSS (PL) Tone Frequencies								
Freq.	Tone No.	Tone Code	Freq.	Tone No.	Tone Code	Freq.	Tone No.	Tone Code
67.0	01	XZ	110.9	15	2Z	179.9	29	6B
71.9	02	XA	114.8	16	2A	186.2	30	7Z
74.4	03	WA	118.8	17	2B	192.8	31	7A
77.0	04	XB	123.0	18	3Z	203.5	32	M1
79.7	05	SP	127.3	19	3A	206.5		8Z
82.5	06	YZ	131.8	20	3B	210.7	33	M2
85.4	07	YA	136.5	21	4Z	218.8	34	M3
88.5	08	YB	141.3	22	4A	225.7	35	M4
91.5	09	ZZ	146.2	23	4B	229.2		9Z
94.8	10	ZA	151.4	24	5Z	233.6	36	
97.4	11	ZB	156.7	25	5A	241.8		M5
100.0	12	1Z	162.2	26	5B	250.3		M6
103.5	13	1A	167.9	27	6Z	256.3		M7
107.2	14	1B	173.8	28	6A			

➡ **www.com-spec.com**

T5A08 What type of amateur station does not require the control operator to be present at the control point?
A. A locally controlled station
B. A remotely controlled station
C. An automatically controlled station
D. An earth station controlling a space station

ANSWER C: About the only time you will see a big rack of ham radio equipment with *no actual operator on duty* would be the *automatically controlled station.* This could be a repeater up on a mountain top, or a radio link atop a high rise. The law requires that all of the details indicating who is in charge be posted on the equipment in case of a malfunction during automatic control. [97.109(D)]
➡ www.limarc.org

T9A08 How could you determine if a repeater is already being used by other stations?
A. Ask if the frequency is in use, then give your call sign
B. If you don't hear anyone, assume that the frequency is clear to use
C. Check for the presence of the CTCSS tone
D. If the repeater identifies when you key your transmitter, it probably was already in use

ANSWER A: To determine if a repeater channel is in use, *first LISTEN!* I usually monitor for at least 30 seconds. Next, if I'm still not certain the repeater is available, I'll *key the mike push-to-talk button and say quickly, "channel clear?* WB6NOA." If all is clear, I will go ahead and place my call to the other station. If I'm just looking to chat, I may simply give my call sign phonetically and say, "monitoring for any call."

Before you start talking over any frequency, listen to make sure the frequency is open.

T1B09 What rule applies if two amateur stations want to use the same frequency?
A. The station operator with a lesser class of license must yield the frequency to a higher-class licensee
B. The station operator with a lower power output must yield the frequency to the station with a higher power output
C. Both station operators have an equal right to operate on the frequency
D. Station operators in ITU Regions 1 and 3 must yield the frequency to stations in ITU Region 2

ANSWER C: Hams must share the amateur frequencies. No ham owns a specific spot on the dial! *All hams have an equal right to operate on any frequency* that their class of license authorizes. [97.101b]

T9A06 Why should you pause briefly between transmissions when using a repeater?

A. To check the SWR of the repeater
B. To reach for pencil and paper for third-party communications
C. To listen for anyone wanting to break in
D. To dial up the repeater's autopatch

ANSWER C: A repeater is like a party line – there may be others who may wish to use the system. In an emergency, stations may break in saying "Break, Break, Break." Give up the channel immediately. *Always leave enough time* between picking up the conversation *for other stations to break in.* It's a pause that may refresh someone else's day in an emergency.

T9A02 What is a courtesy tone, as used in repeater operations?

A. A sound used to identify the repeater
B. A sound used to indicate when a transmission is complete
C. A sound used to indicate that a message is waiting for someone
D. A sound used to activate a receiver in case of severe weather

ANSWER B: Most repeaters have *a beep tone that lets you know when the other person has stopped transmitting.* Wait at least a second before continuing the conversation. ➡ **www.rad-comm.com**

T9A04 Which of the following is a proper way to break into a conversation on a repeater?

A. Wait for the end of a transmission and start calling the desired party
B. Shout, "break, break!" to show that you're eager to join the conversation
C. Turn on an amplifier and override whoever is talking
D. Say your call sign during a break between transmissions

ANSWER D: If you tune into a repeater transmission between 2 hams, and they are talking about something YOU really know about and want to share with them, too, *quickly drop your call sign in between the time one station releases their push-to-talk button and the few seconds before the other station begins* to return onto the airwaves. Usually stations leave about a 2-second gap for this type of call sign drop-in. They will usually immediately recognize you, and welcome you to the conversation. Never enter a conversation with the word "break" unless it is a priority or emergency call. Stay away from the word "break" at all times on ham frequencies except for very important matters that just can't wait.

T9A07 Why should you keep transmissions short when using a repeater?

A. A long transmission may prevent someone with an emergency from using the repeater
B. To see if the receiving station operator is still awake
C. To give any listening non-hams a chance to respond
D. To keep long-distance charges down

ANSWER A: During peak traffic hours, *keep your transmissions short.* Repeaters are a great way to find out traffic reports and *for reporting traffic accidents or emergencies.*

T9A17 What is the purpose of a repeater time-out timer?

A. It lets a repeater have a rest period after heavy use
B. It logs repeater transmit time to predict when a repeater will fail
C. It tells how long someone has been using a repeater
D. It limits the amount of time a repeater can transmit continuously

ANSWER D: Repeater timers keep operators from getting long-winded. *The repeater cycles off the air (times-out) if it doesn't get a few seconds break during one long transmission.* Some timers are as short as 30 seconds. It's always good practice to keep your transmissions shorter than a half-minute period. If you need to talk longer, announce, "Reset," release the mike button, and let the repeater reset its time-out timer.

T9A03 During commuting rush hours, which type of repeater operation should be discouraged?

A. Mobile stations
B. Low-power stations
C. Highway traffic information nets
D. Third-party communications nets

ANSWER D: It's *not a good idea to let a friend (third party) talk* over your microphone as a third party *during heavy repeater use time.* During rush hours, most repeaters are used for traffic advisories and traffic accident reports.
➡ www.w6yx.stanford.edu

T8B11 What device could boost the low power output from your hand-held radio up to 100 watts?

A. A voltage divider
B. A power amplifier
C. A impedance network
D. A voltage regulator

ANSWER B: As a new Technician class operator, you will probably choose a handheld, dual-band as your first radio. You can run this in your vehicle using an outside antenna with a magnetic mount and achieve great results! I would also suggest a headset speaker/mic, too. If you really need more than the 5 watts of power that comes out of the handheld, you also could purchase *a power amplifier that would boost the 5 watts to up to 100 watts power output.* But I think you'll find the outside antenna may be all you'll need for successful handheld operation from inside your vehicle. ➡ www.command1.com

This little 2-meter linear amplifier meets stringent FCC spurious emission standards.
2-Meter Power Amplifier

T5C09 If an amateur transmits to test access to a repeater without giving any station identification, what type of communication is this called?
  A. A test emission; no identification is required
  B. An illegal unmodulated transmission
  C. An illegal unidentified transmission
  D. A non-communication; no voice is transmitted

ANSWER C: Every now and then you may hear a repeater being "keyed up" by another station, but the other *station that is accessing the repeater* as a test *never gives its official FCC call sign.* This is sometimes called "kerchunking" a repeater, and without call letters, this is absolutely illegal and *is considered an unidentified transmission.* [97.119a]

T9A18 What should you do if you hear a closed repeater system that you would like to be able to use?
  A. Contact the control operator and ask to join
  B. Use the repeater until told not to
  C. Use simplex on the repeater input until told not to
  D. Write the FCC and report the closed condition

ANSWER A: Closed repeaters are available for membership. Most closed repeaters offer autopatch, paging, and sometimes remote high-frequency base functions. These exotic systems are supported by *club membership.* Listen to the repeater for announcements for their next general membership meeting. *Go to the meeting,* and they'll tell you how to join up. ➡ **www.nhrc.net**

T9A12 What is the most likely reason you might hear Morse code tones on a repeater frequency?
  A. Intermodulation   C. The repeater's identification
  B. An emergency request for help   D. A courtesy tone

ANSWER C: You are listening to your brand new handheld on the 2-meter band, and all of a sudden the stations talking on the repeater are accompanied by rapid-fire Morse code dots and dashes. What's this? Signals from the moon? Nope. The *Morse code* you hear *on a repeater* every 10 minutes *is the repeater's automatic call sign identification.* ➡ **www.liarsclub.tk**

T9A13 What is the common amateur meaning of the term "simplex operation"?
  A. Transmitting and receiving on the same frequency
  B. Transmitting and receiving over a wide area
  C. Transmitting on one frequency and receiving on another
  D. Transmitting one-way communications

ANSWER A: *Simplex means same frequency.* Operate simplex on VHF or UHF when the other station is within a few miles of your station. The opposite of simplex is duplex, a type of repeater operation. ➡ **www.juns.com**

T9A14 When should you use simplex operation instead of a repeater?
  A. When the most reliable communications are needed
  B. When a contact is possible without using a repeater
  C. When an emergency telephone call is needed
  D. When you are traveling and need some local information

ANSWER B: If you are communicating with a station that is located within 10 miles of you, *go "simplex" (or direct) rather than through a repeater.* This localizes your transmissions and *frees the repeater for more distant contacts.*

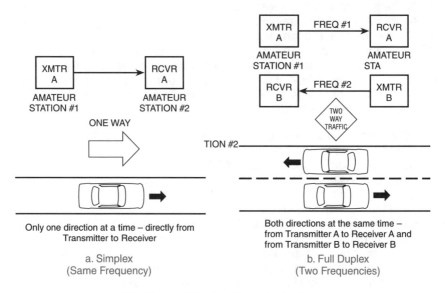

Simplex and Duplex Communications

T9A15 If you are talking to a station using a repeater, how would you find out if you could communicate using simplex instead?
  A. See if you can clearly receive the station on the repeater's input frequency
  B. See if you can clearly receive the station on a lower frequency band
  C. See if you can clearly receive a more distant repeater
  D. See if a third station can clearly receive both of you

ANSWER A: Almost all portable, mobile, and base VHF/UHF FM equipment have a small button marked *"REV". Momentarily push the button,* and it *causes your receiver to quickly shift to the input frequency of the repeater.* This allows you *to see if you can pick up the other station direct.* If so, suggest that you switch over to simplex for the remainder of the communications.

T9B13 What is an autopatch?
  A. An automatic digital connection between a US and a foreign amateur
  B. A digital connection used to transfer data between a hand-held radio and a computer
  C. A device that allows radio users to access the public telephone system
  D. A video interface allowing images to be patched into a digital data stream

ANSWER C: One benefit of becoming an amateur operator is using an *autopatch to access the public telephone system.* There are autopatches on the 2-meter band, and on the 70-cm (440-MHz) band. Most autopatches are offered through club and organization participation. If you are operating on an open repeater, and hear someone making a phone call over it, ask that person how to join the club for the additional benefit of autopatch. Most clubs include local dialing autopatch privileges as part of their $15 to $30 yearly dues. If the autopatch has long-distance capabilities, you will pay for the long-distance calls just like you do when dialing from home. You may not use your autopatch to stay in touch with your own business. However, rules now allow you to use autopatch to order a pizza, make dinner reservations, or to call an auto parts store to see whether or not they have that specific auto part in stock. Autopatch is a fringe benefit of ham radio operating, and under no circumstances should you rely on an autopatch solely to beat long-distance charges or substitute for your cellular phone. ➡ **www.dxer.com**

T9B14 Which of the following statements about Amateur Radio autopatch usage is true?
    A. The person called using the autopatch must be a licensed radio amateur
    B. The autopatch will allow only local calls to police, fire and ambulance services
    C. Communication through the autopatch is not private
    D. The autopatch should not be used for reporting emergencies
ANSWER C: When you are communicating through an *autopatch,* keep in mind that *everybody on frequency is listening,* too. It is definitely not a private conversation!

T1A16 Which of the following is a prohibited amateur radio transmission?
    A. Using an autopatch to seek emergency assistance
    B. Using an autopatch to pick up business messages
    C. Using an autopatch to call for a tow truck
    D. Using an autopatch to call home to say you are running late
ANSWER B: Many 2-meter repeaters offer autopatch access to the "land line" telephone service. The autopatch might be a great way to call home and tell them you're going to be running a little bit late for dinner. You could also use the autopatch to call for a tow truck, or place a call to a police agency in an emergency, and it is also permissible to call a restaurant for dinner reservations or to call a parts store and see if they have that little widget to get you back on the road again. But one thing *taboo for an autopatch call would be dialing up your office answering machine to retrieve business messages* or calling work and discussing business appointments with your secretary. [97.113a3]

T6B06 What is a band plan?
    A. A voluntary guideline beyond the divisions established by the FCC for using different operating modes within an amateur band
    B. A guideline from the FCC for making amateur frequency band allocations
    C. A plan of operating schedules within an amateur band published by the FCC
    D. A plan devised by a club to best use a frequency band during a contest
ANSWER A: Every amateur radio band is sliced up into specific operating band plans. Many of the *band plans are voluntary guidelines that hams have established for specific* data *signals*, voice operation, automatic position reporting system operation, weak signal work, DX-ing, slow-scan amateur television, propagation beacons, and specific areas for working satellites, the International Space Station and the Space Shuttle. It takes time to understand where the 2-meter and 70 cm band plans are, so when you get your new equipment, let a fellow ham help you program it to insure you operate within the voluntary band plan. In other words, don't just buy a brand new handheld and start talking with your class buddy on the frequency that just happens to come up on the display when you first turn it on. Get some local help to make sure you begin operating within the voluntary band plan. ➡ **www.dxer.com**

T9A16 What is it called if the frequency coordinator recommends that you operate on a specific repeater frequency pair?
A. FCC type acceptance
B. FCC type approval
C. Frequency division multiplexing
D. Repeater frequency coordination

ANSWER D: *Repeater input and output frequency pairs are coordinated* throughout the United States by amateur operators volunteering as repeater frequency coordinators. This is not a pleasant volunteer job because there are few frequencies left that are open for repeaters in most major metropolitan areas. Some frequencies have waiting lists, and frequency coordinators are constantly being asked for more repeater pairs that simply are not available. However, away from major cities, many frequencies may still be available for repeater coordination. If you are thinking of putting up your own VHF, UHF, or microwave repeater system, check with local hams in your area and ask them who the local frequency coordinators are and how you can contact them in writing to obtain the proper forms. ➡ www.artscipub.com

T9A20 If a repeater is causing harmful interference to another amateur repeater and a frequency coordinator has recommended the operation of both repeaters, who is responsible for resolving the interference?
A. The licensee of the repeater that has been recommended for the longest period of time
B. The licensee of the repeater that has been recommended the most recently
C. The frequency coordinator
D. Both repeater licensees

ANSWER D: If *both repeater stations are coordinated, both repeater licensees* must mutually *work out the interference problem.* [97.205c]

T9A19 Who pays for the site rental and upkeep of most repeaters?
A. All amateurs, because part of the amateur license examination fee is used
B. The repeater owner and donations from its users
C. The Federal Communications Commission
D. The federal government, using money granted by Congress

ANSWER B: *Repeater owners* have a huge job of maintaining the repeater and *are not allowed to charge* ham operators for using the repeater. However, ham operators would certainly donate a few dollars for the repeater upkeep if they regularly use the repeater. If you regularly use a repeater, help support it financially. The amount is up to you.

T9B21 What is the term that describes a repeater that receives signals on one band and retransmits them on another band?

A. A special coordinated repeater	C. An auxiliary station
B. An illegally operating repeater	D. A crossband repeater

ANSWER D: If you are into emergency communications, you may find that rigging up your *dual-band* mobile radio as a *cross-band repeater* is a good way to extend the range of a small portable nearby. But remember the control operator requirements – your crossband mobile repeater must have a licensed ham sitting in the front seat of the vehicle to satisfy the control operator requirement.

T5A10 If you own a dual-band mobile transceiver, what requirement must be met if you set it up to operate as a crossband repeater?

A. There is no special requirement if you are licensed for both bands
B. You must hold an Amateur Extra class license
C. There must be a control operator at the system's control point
D. Operating a crossband mobile system is not allowed

ANSWER C: When you get started as a new Technician class operator, chances are you'll begin with dual-band equipment. This might give you one radio for both 2 meters and 440 MHz. Most of this equipment may be configured to act as a quasi-repeater, sometimes nicknamed a crossband repeater. Signals come in on 70 cm, and are simultaneously retransmitted on 2 meters. Signals on 2 meters could be retransmitted on 70 cm. But the rules are clear – and often ignored – if you set up a station in *crossband repeat, there must be a control operator right at that station* to meet the rules. Not down the street – not a half mile away – but right there at the controls of your little mobile radio acting as a crossband repeater. It's the law. ➡ **www.kenwood.net/ amateur/commindex.cfm**

You can set up your dual-band mobile to work as a crossband repeater. This one is receiving on 144MHz and transmitting 447MHz.

T9B16 When may slow-scan television be transmitted through a 2-meter repeater?

A. At any time, providing the repeater control operator authorizes this unique transmission
B. Never; slow-scan television is not allowed on 2 meters
C. Only after 5:00 PM local time
D. Never; slow-scan television is not allowed on repeaters

ANSWER A: *Slow-scan television* is yet another way that a ham may send another ham a freeze-frame, high-definition, color picture. You can operate slow-scan television through most 2-meter repeaters, but it's *best to check out ahead of time with the repeater control operator* what you are going to do so they better understand what the strange sounds are they will be listening to! ➡ **www.sstv.org**

Amateur slow-scan TV pictures can be displayed on a tube, or an LCD display like this one.

Can line-of-sight be out-of-sight?
Sometimes, weather makes a difference on how far our signals travel.

T3B06 Why should local amateur communications use VHF and UHF frequencies instead of HF frequencies?

- A. To minimize interference on HF bands capable of long-distance communication
- B. Because greater output power is permitted on VHF and UHF
- C. Because HF transmissions are not propagated locally
- D. Because signals are louder on VHF and UHF frequencies

ANSWER A: We use VHF and UHF frequencies for operating on the 6-meter, 2-meter, 222-MHz, 450-MHz, and 1270-MHz FM ham bands. These bands are so high in frequency that they are line-of-sight to repeaters. We *use worldwide frequencies below 30 MHz for longer sky-wave range*. If we wish *to talk locally*, we go to local *VHF and UHF band frequencies*. ➡ **www.dxzone.com**

T3B01 When a signal travels in a straight line from one antenna to another, what is this called?

- A. Line-of-sight propagation
- B. Straight line propagation
- C. Knife-edge diffraction
- D. Tunnel ducting

ANSWER A: As a new Technician class operator, you will enjoy *line-of-sight propagation on all of the VHF and UHF bands* from 2 meters and higher. But keep in mind that the international space station and overhead space shuttles are also line-of-sight, so many times line-of-sight transmissions can take place over hundreds and even thousands of miles! ➡ **www.wswss.org**

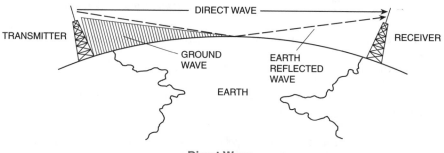

Direct Wave

Source: *Antennas — Selection and Installation*, © 1986, Master Publishing, Inc., Lincolnwood, Illinois

T3B02 What can happen to VHF or UHF signals going towards a metal-framed building?

- A. They will go around the building
- B. They can be bent by the ionosphere
- C. They can be reflected by the building
- D. They can be polarized by the building's mass

ANSWER C: Up on these frequencies, you'll be surprised how signals behave when they strike a *metal-framed building* or aircraft – *they are easily reflected* by the building, and this is what gives us some exciting 2-meter and 440 MHz operation with a handheld actually INSIDE a building where our signals somehow bounce around and reflect OUTSIDE.

T3B04 What causes VHF radio waves to be propagated several hundred miles over oceans?
- A. A polar air mass
- B. A widespread temperature inversion
- C. An overcast of cirriform clouds
- D. A high-pressure zone

ANSWER B: Have you ever seen a mirage? Out on the desert, it looks like blue water instead of sand ahead. Actually, that's the blue sky you are looking at. Light waves that normally travel in straight lines bounce off the super-heated, windless sand and pavement and are reflected back to your eyes. Same concept *during a tropospheric duct* – but just backwards. Typically straight-line *VHF and UHF signals* begin to travel up and away, but *are bent back by* a sharp boundary layer of warm, moist air overlying cool, dry air below and above – *a temperature inversion.* In the city, this is what traps the smog and gives us one of those unbearable days. Get on the radio – it is unbelievable!

➡ **www.ukradioamateur.org**

T3B03 Ducting occurs in which region of the atmosphere?

A. F2	C. Troposphere
B. Ecosphere	D. Stratosphere

ANSWER C: The key word in this question is *"ducting."* In your home you use ducts to direct that warm or cool air around the house. Out in radioland, natural atmospheric ducts form that can direct VHF and UHF radio waves well beyond line-of-sight range. *Tropospheric ducting* occurs most often during the summer months, and sometimes occurs in the presence of large storm systems. I happen to be one of the record holders in tropospheric ducting on VHF line-of-sight frequencies between my home near Los Angeles all the way over to Hawaii. This is not a skip wave off the ionosphere, but rather tropospheric ducting several hundred feet above the water traveling thousands of miles away! ➡ **www.grc.nasa.gov**

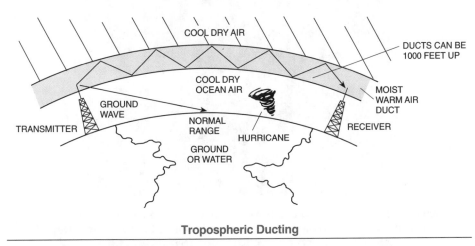

Tropospheric Ducting

T1C10 To what distance limit may Technician class licensees communicate?
- A. Up to 200 miles
- B. There is no distance limit
- C. Only to line of sight contacts distances
- D. Only to contacts inside the USA

ANSWER B: *There is absolutely no range limitation* on how far you might communicate as a new Technician class operator. You could even bounce signals off the moon for the ultimate in long-range contacts with your Tech license. There is plenty of great range available to you as a Technician class operator on frequencies above 50 MHz. Don't think for a second that your Tech license is just for local contacts – under the right conditions, your Technician class license gives you access for worldwide communications. ➡ **www.ssbusa.com**

T3A10 How does the signal loss for a given path through the troposphere vary with frequency?
- A. There is no relationship
- B. The path loss decreases as the frequency increases
- C. The path loss increases as the frequency increases
- D. There is no path loss at all

ANSWER C: Bouncing signals within tropospheric layers of warm and cool air is a popular sport among no-code Technician class operators. Remember, your no-code license allows unlimited privileges within the VHF and UHF Amateur Radio bands – microwave too. But *the higher you go in frequency, the greater the path loss.* Half loss (a decrease in signal levels to one-half of that at the antenna) increases as the frequency increases. If you are talking 500 miles away, simplex, with a station on 2 meters, up on the 70-cm (440-MHz) band, your signals will be much weaker. ➡ **www.ham-shack.com**

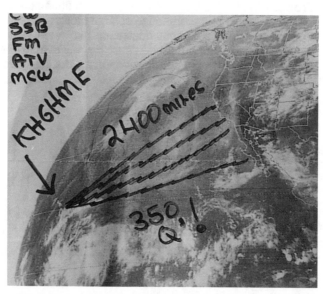

When a widespread temperature inversion creates a tropospheric duct over the Pacific, you can use line-of-sight frequencies to talk to California from Hawaii.
➡ **www.hiloweb.com/kh6foo/bbs/subduct.html**

Can I talk to the astronauts?

Talking to the International Space Station or NASA Shuttle on Technician frequencies – or around the world on amateur satellites!

T1A08 What is an amateur space station?
A. An amateur station operated on an unused frequency
B. An amateur station awaiting its new call letters from the FCC
C. An amateur station located more than 50 kilometers above the Earth's surface
D. An amateur station that communicates with the International Space Station

ANSWER C: Special rules pertain to amateur operation in a space station. *A space station is* considered *any amateur station located more than 50 kilometers above the Earth's surface.* Remote control of a model aircraft flying at 1000 feet is not considered a space station. [97.3a40] ➡ **www.amsat.org**

T9B03 The control operator of a station communicating through an amateur satellite must hold what class of license?
A. Amateur Extra or Advanced
B. Any class except Novice
C. Any class
D. Technician with satellite endorsement

ANSWER C: *Any class of Amateur Radio license may operate through Orbiting Satellites Carrying Amateur Radio (OSCAR).* You may operate on the bands for which you have privileges. As a Technician class operator, with or without the code, the VHF and UHF bands are full of amateur satellite uplink and downlink frequencies. A no-code Technician class operator could regularly work worldwide through Orbiting Satellites Carrying Amateur Radio. The new AMSAT Phase 3D satellite program will bring you all of the excitement of worldwide satellite communications with relatively small antennas and satellite radio equipment within your budget for a worldwide system. [97.209a] ➡**www.amsat.org.**

My Space Shuttle QSL Card Contacts

T1A09 Who may be the control operator of an amateur space station?
A. An amateur holding an Amateur Extra class operator license grant
B. Any licensed amateur operator
C. Anyone designated by the commander of the spacecraft
D. No one unless specifically authorized by the government

ANSWER B: It doesn't take any special grade of amateur operator license to be the licensee of an amateur space station. Years ago, only Extra class amateur operators could go into space. Now, *any licensed amateur operator may receive space station authorization.* Shall we beam you up? [97.207a]

T9B10 What is the typical amount of time an amateur has to communicate with the International Space Station?

A. 4 to 6 minutes per pass

B. An hour or two per pass

C. About 20 minutes per pass

D. All day

ANSWER A: The *International Space Station* travels around the earth approximately every 100 minutes. This gives us a line-of-sight view of the space station of only *about 4 to 6 minutes per pass.* We might only get 2 or 3 passes per day, and sometimes only one when the ISS is within view.

The International Space Station has a big ham station on board.
Photo courtesy of N.A.S.A.

T9B05 Why do many amateur satellites operate on the VHF/UHF bands?

A. To take advantage of the skip zone

B. Because VHF/UHF equipment costs less than HF equipment

C. To give Technician class operators greater access to modern communications technology

D. Because VHF and UHF signals easily pass through the ionosphere

ANSWER D: Almost all amateur and commercial satellites transmit on the *VHF and UHF* bands because these signals *easily pass through the ionosphere.*

T9B07 What does the term "apogee" refer to when applied to an Earth satellite?

A. The closest point to the Earth in the satellite's orbit

B. The most distant point from the Earth in the satellite's orbit

C. The point where the satellite appears to cross the equator

D. The point when the Earth eclipses the satellite from the sun

ANSWER B: When working satellites, any satellite at the *apogee* is at the point in its orbit when it is *farthest away from the Earth.* You will have to apologize to friends listening in that your signal is so faint.

T9B08 What does the term "perigee" refer to when applied to an Earth satellite?

A. The closest point to the Earth in the satellite's orbit

B. The most distant point from the Earth in the satellite's orbit

C. The time when the satellite will be on the opposite side of the Earth

D. The effect that causes the satellite's signal frequency to change

ANSWER A: *Perigee* is the PERFECT time to work a satellite because it is at the point in its orbit when it is *closest to the Earth* and signals will be strongest!

➡ www.spaceflight.nasa.gov

T9B04 How does the Doppler effect change an amateur satellite's signal as the satellite passes overhead?

A. The signal's amplitude increases or decreases
B. The signal's frequency increases or decreases
C. The signal's polarization changes from horizontal to vertical
D. The signal's circular polarization rotates

ANSWER B: *Doppler effect will change a satellite CW or SSB signal frequency either higher or lower,* or both if it approaches you, goes overhead, and then goes further away. This is the same Doppler effect you hear when the train whistle sounds high as it approaches you, and then sounds lower as it passes and goes away. The Doppler principle applies to signals coming in from a satellite, too. As the satellite is moving toward the receiver, the frequency is higher than the transmitted signal; and as the satellite is moving away from the receiver, the frequency is lower than the transmitted signal. This frequency change is called Doppler shift. ➡ **www.qsl.net/k1uhf**

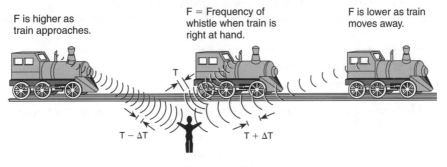

F is higher as train approaches.

F = Frequency of whistle when train is right at hand.

F is lower as train moves away.

T

T − ΔT

T + ΔT

Doppler Effect

T9B09 What mathematical parameters describe a satellite's orbit?

A. Its telemetry data
B. Its Doppler shift characteristics
C. Its mean motion
D. Its Keplerian elements

ANSWER D: Hams are able to *determine a satellite's specific orbit by its Keplerian elements,* which normally are published on the internet at satellite web pages. ➡ **www.heavensabove.com/ amateursats.asp**

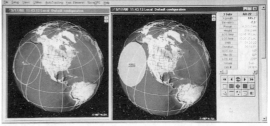

Computer programs and websites can show you where and when an amateur satellite or the Space Station will be in range of your ham station.

T9B17 What is the definition of telecommand?

A. All communications using the telephone or telegraphy with space stations
B. A one way transmission to initiate conversation with astronauts aboard a satellite or space station
C. A one way transmission to initiate, modify or terminate functions of a device at a distance
D. Two way transmissions to initiate, modify or terminate functions of a device at a distance

ANSWER C: *Telecommand is a one-way transmission to initiate, modify, or turn off functions,* usually on orbiting satellites or special equipment aboard the International Space Station. [97.3a43] ➡ **www.downeastmicrowave.com**

T9B18 What provisions must be in place for the legal operation of a telecommand station?
- A. The station must have a wire line or radio control link
- B. A photocopy of the station license must be posted in a conspicuous location
- C. The station must be protected so that no unauthorized transmission can be made
- D. All of these choices are correct

ANSWER D: The *Telecommand station is controlled by* either a *wire line or a radio link.* Although there may not be a control operator sitting right in front of the equipment, a *photocopy of the station license must be posted* inside the radio equipment rack. There must also be a *locked door to keep unauthorized,* non-hams from picking up a local mic and placing unauthorized *radio transmissions* in the ham radio service. [97.213a, b, c] ➡ **www.comdac.com**

Can I talk to the Moon?
No. But you can bounce your signals off the Moon!

T9B11 Which of the following would be the best emission mode for two-way EME contacts?

A. CW	C. FM
B. AM	D. Spread spectrum

ANSWER A: Earth-Moon-Earth *(EME)* contacts are relatively faint, and usually *CW* is the best mode to handle such a weak signal. ➡ **www.directivesystems.com**

T9B06 Which antenna system would NOT be a good choice for an EME (moonbounce) station?
- A. A parabolic-dish antenna
- B. A multi-element array of collinear antennas
- C. A ground-plane antenna
- D. A high-gain array of Yagi antennas

ANSWER C: *You're never going to hear* a station or work a station off *the Moon* if all you have is a *simple ground-plane antenna.* Really, you knew that!

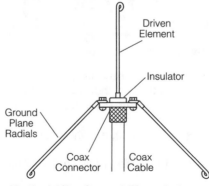

Vertical 1/4 λ Ground-Plane Antenna

Do computers and ham radio mix?
Sending wireless data, or sending your voice over the internet to distant repeaters, and more!

T2B03 What name does the FCC use for telemetry, telecommand or computer communications emissions?

A. CW
B. Image
C. Data
D. RTTY

ANSWER C: The FCC name *"data"* may be used for indicating *telemetry* communications, *telecommand* communications, or sending radio signals from your laptop or home *computer.* [97.3c2] ➡ **www.tapr.org**

Emission Definitions
CW – International Morse code telegraphy emissions.
Data – Telemetry, telecommand and computer communications commissions.
RTTY (Radioteletype) – Narrow-band, direct-printing telegraphy emissions.
Phone – Speech and other sound emissions.

T7B02 What type of electric circuit uses signals that have voltage or current values only in specific steps over a certain range?

A. An analog circuit
B. A digital circuit
C. A step modulator circuit
D. None of these choices is correct

ANSWER B: Think of a *digital circuit* as one with *specific steps,* like the steps leading down to the basement. These would be steps similar to what is found in a digital circuit made up of ones and zeroes. ➡ **www.marex-na.org**

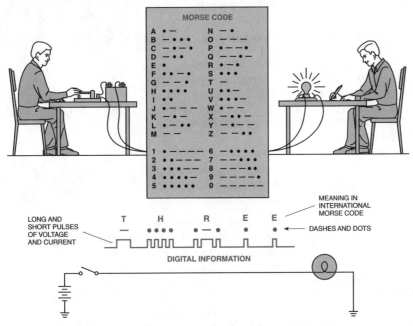

Telegraph Circuit – Digital systems send information as patterns of switched signals, similar to a telegraph circuit.

Source: *Basic Electronics, McWhorter & Evans,* © 2000, Master Publishing, Inc., Lincolnwood, Illinois

T8A03 Which of the following devices would you need to conduct Amateur Radio communications using a data emission?

A. A telegraph key
B. A computer

C. A transducer
D. A telemetry sensor

ANSWER B: To operate *data communications* over Amateur Radio, you will need to *tie your* present laptop or home *computer to your world wide or VHF/UHF ham radio transceiver.* You also will need a special radio modem that goes between your present computer and your ham set to send data.
➡ www.bark2m.com/packet.htm

T7B04 Which of the following is an example of a digital communications method?

A. Single-sideband (SSB) voice
B. Amateur Television (ATV)

C. FM voice
D. Radioteletype (RTTY)

ANSWER D: *Radioteletype is a digital mode.* It has all but been replaced by PSK 31, another digital mode. So for this question, radioteletype is the correct answer. All of the other answers are analog modes. ➡ www.westmountainradio.com

---

T8A10 What would you connect to a transceiver for RTTY operation?

A. A modem and a teleprinter or computer system
B. A computer, a printer and a RTTY refresh unit
C. A data-inverter controller
D. A modem, a monitor and a DTMF keypad

ANSWER A: *"RTTY"* stands for radioteleprinting, and it's a rather old way of sending and receiving data over the airwaves. Nonetheless, it IS a data transmission, and this means you would need to *hook up a modem and a printer to your transceiver* to make it work – or since I know you already have a computer, you would hook up a computer system for RTTY operation, plus a host of other data signals that your present computer tied into a modem and printer will receive and send quite nicely. If you are into computers, you will love your new amateur radio privileges!
➡ www.associatedradio.com

You can connect a PSK-31 and RTTY data reader to your radio to decode messages.

T8A13 What is one common method of transmitting RTTY on VHF/UHF bands?

A. Frequency shift the carrier to indicate mark and space at the receiver
B. Amplitude shift the carrier to indicate mark and space at the receiver
C. Key the transmitter on to indicate space and off for mark
D. Modulate a conventional FM transmitter with a modem

ANSWER D: Your 100-year-old neighbor who is a good friend of Marconi comes over to your house and wants you to *transmit RTTY* on your VHF/UHF radio. We haven't transmitted RTTY on VHF/UHF for many years, but to do so you would *modulate a conventional two-way FM transmitter WITH A MODEM.* Make this a brief test because no one on the air likes hearing RTTY anymore on VHF/UHF. ➡ www.vdazone.org/hamlines.html

---

T8A12 What might happen if you set your receiver's signal squelch too low while attempting to receive packet mode transmissions?
    A. Noise may cause the TNC to falsely detect a data carrier
    B. Weaker stations may not be received
    C. Transmission speed and throughput will be reduced
    D. The TNC could be damaged
ANSWER A: When setting up a mobile or home station for *packet mode* transmission, be sure to *adjust the squelch well into the silence* to minimize the squelch continuously triggering from stray noise. ➡ **www.aorusa.com**

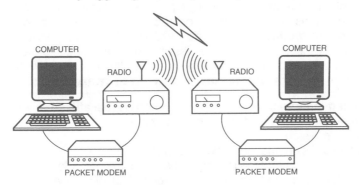

A Packet Radio System

T2B04 What does "connected" mean in a packet-radio link?
    A. A telephone link is working between two stations
    B. A message has reached an amateur station for local delivery
    C. A transmitting station is sending data to only one receiving station; it replies that the data is being received correctly
    D. A transmitting and receiving station are using a digipeater, so no other contacts can take place until they are finished
ANSWER C: Your packet radio system gives you many winking lights that indicate *your station is interacting with another station – one receiving station only.* ➡ **www.tapr.org**

T6B05 What name is given to an amateur radio station that is used to connect other amateur stations with the Internet?
    A. A gateway
    B. A repeater
    C. A digipeater
    D. FCC regulations prohibit such a station
ANSWER A: Imagine the excitement with your new Technician class license talking over your little radio through the Internet to another station halfway around the world! When you hear the letters IRLP (Internet Radio Linking Project), they refer to the capabilities of dialing up hundreds of *gateway stations* through the *internet* for some mighty impressive communications. How do you find out who has a gateway within range? Join your local amateur radio club and see whether or not there are members who have IRLP recommendations. ➡ **www.irlp.net**

Are you into radio-controlled models?

Get off the garage-door-opener frequencies and use ham bands to operate your models.

T5C02 What is one example of one-way communication that Technician class control operators are permitted by FCC rules?
A. Transmission for radio control of model craft
B. Use of amateur television for surveillance purposes
C. Retransmitting National Weather Service broadcasts
D. Use of amateur radio as a wireless microphone for a public address system

ANSWER A: The transmission for *radio control of model craft is considered a one-way communication* that is perfectly allowed by the Technician class operator. Usually these one-way transmissions take place on the 6-meter band, and you identify your band of operation by flying a black flag on the antenna.
[97.111(B) (3)] ➡ **www.hamtv.com** and **www.atn-tv.org**

T9B12 What minimum information must be on a label affixed to a transmitter used for telecommand (control) of model craft?
A. Station call sign
B. Station call sign and the station licensee's name
C. Station call sign and the station licensee's name and address
D. Station call sign and the station licensee's class of license

ANSWER C: With your Technician class license, you get to fly the coveted black flag. The black flag indicates 6-meter ham operation. Just make sure you have a label with *all of your license information on your transmitter.* [97.215a]

T5B10 What are the station identification requirements for an amateur transmitter used for telecommand (control) of model craft?
A. Once every ten minutes
B. Once every ten minutes, and at the beginning and end of each transmission
C. At the beginning and end of each transmission
D. Station identification is not required if the transmitter is labeled with the station licensee's name, address and call sign

ANSWER D: Are you into radio control of model planes, boats, or cars? If so, your Technician class license now gives you *model control frequencies* on 6 meters. You *don't need to station identify* because it would be mighty tough with a sail plane. However, your transmitter must have a label on it with your name, address, and call sign. Also, to further identify that you are a ham on 6 meters, your transmitter normally flies the black flag indicating ham radio 6-meter operation. [97.215a]

Radio Control Channels				
Old Channels			New Channels	
Freq. (MHz)	Channel I.D.		Freq. (MHz)	Channel I.D.
53.1	Black	Brown	50.80	00
53.2	Black	Red	50.82	01
53.3	Black	Orange	50.84	02
53.4	Black	Yellow	50.86	03
53.5	Black	Green	50.88	04
53.6	Black	Blue	50.90	05
53.7	Black	Violet	50.92	06
53.8	Black	Grey	50.94	07
53.9	Black	White	50.96	08
			50.98	09

What are radio waves, anyway?
A look at how we use electromagnetic signals to communicate.

T2A13 What is the basic principle of radio communications?

A. A radio wave is combined with an information signal and is transmitted; a receiver separates the two

B. A transmitter separates information to be received from a radio wave

C. A DC generator combines some type of information into a carrier wave so that it may travel through space

D. The peak-to-peak voltage of a transmitter is varied by the sidetone and modulated by the receiver

ANSWER A: When we *transmit a voice radio signal,* our *voice is combined with a radio wave (called the carrier)* and off it goes to a distant receiver. The *receiver* at the other end of the radio circuit *separates the two.* The technical name for combining a radio wave with an information signal is modulation.

➡ **www.twysted-pair.com**

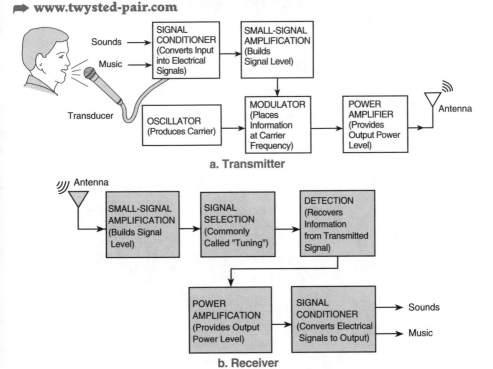

Block Diagram of a Basic Radio Communications System
Source: *Basic Communications Electronics,* Hudson & Luecke,
© 1999, Master Publishing, Inc., Lincolnwood, Illinois

T2A06 What is a radio frequency wave?

A. Wave disturbances that take place at less than 10 times per second

B. Electromagnetic oscillations or cycles that repeat between 20 and 20,000 times per second

C. Electromagnetic oscillations or cycles which that repeat more than 20,000 times per second

D. None of these answers are correct

ANSWER C: The FREQUENCY of a radio wave is how many times it oscillates over one second. Since they ask for *radio frequencies,* this always is *higher than 20,000 times per second.*

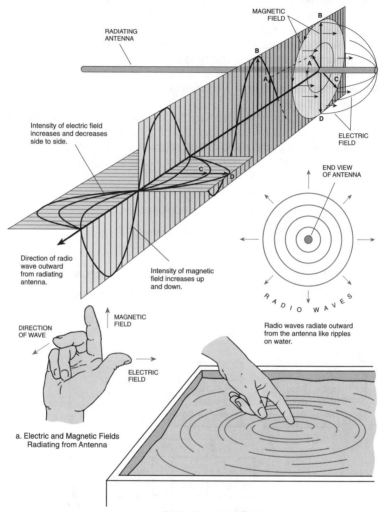

Radio Waves

Source: *Basic Electronics* © 1994, 2000 Master Publishing, Inc., Lincolnwood, Illinois

T2A11 How fast does a radio wave travel through space (in a vacuum)?
A. At the speed of light
B. At the speed of sound
C. Its speed is inversely proportional to its wavelength
D. Its speed increases as the frequency increases

ANSWER A: *Radio waves travel through a vacuum at the speed of light* (approximately 300,000,000 meters per second). They slow down just a bit when they get into air, clouds, smoke, haze, and smog. But you wouldn't know it!

T2A10 How is a radio frequency wave identified?
A. By its wavelength, the length of a single radio cycle from peak to peak
B. By its corresponding frequency
C. By the appropriate radio band in which it is transmitted or received
D. All of these choices are correct

ANSWER D: In this question, *ALL CHOICES are correct* when telling someone where you might want to meet them on the radio dial. It could be *wavelength* for the band, *frequency* for the specific spot, or just a specific *radio band* and you two can go hunting trying to find each other! ➡ **www.dxzone.com**

T2A16 What is the basic unit of frequency?
A. The hertz
B. The watt
C. The ampere
D. The ohm

ANSWER A: The basic unit of *frequency* is the *HERTZ.*

T2A12 What is the standard unit of frequency measurement?
A. A megacycle
B. A hertz
C. One thousand cycles per second
D. EMF, electromagnetic force

ANSWER B: *We measure frequencies in hertz.* When we abbreviate kilohertz (1,000 cycles), the designator is a little "k" for kilo, a capital "H" for the proper name Hertz, and the small letter "z" for the last letter of Hertz. For megahertz, the letter "M" is always capital "M," capital "H," and small "z." If you write articles for books about ham radio, be sure to get these letters correct, especially remembering whether they are a small "k" or the capital letter "M," along with the capital letter "H."

T2A15 What term means the number of times per second that an alternating current flows back and forth?
A. Pulse rate
B. Speed
C. Wavelength
D. Frequency

ANSWER D: When we measure frequencies, we count *the number of times per second that current flows back and forth*. And do you remember the name of the word *FREQUENCY*? Cycles per second, but now we officially call it hertz. ➡ **www.hfradio.org**

T2A03 What does 60 hertz (Hz) mean?
A. 6000 cycles per second
B. 60 cycles per second
C. 6000 meters per second
D. 60 meters per second

ANSWER B: *60 Hz means* the same thing as *60 cycles per second.* Frequency is measured in cycles per second, called hertz. Counting the number of alternating cycles in one second gives the frequency in hertz. The unit of frequency is named after Heinrich Hertz, who developed horizontal antennas. When spelled out, it is written as "hertz" with a lowercase "h"; but when abbreviated, it is written as "Hz" with an uppercase "H." (Old-timers remember when the unit was "cycles per second" and the abbreviation was CPS.)

T7B07 What is the lowest frequency of electrical energy that is usually known as a radio frequency?
A. 20 Hz
B. 2,000 Hz
C. 20,000 Hz
D. 1,000,000 Hz

ANSWER C: *Radio frequencies are above 20 kHz (20,000 Hz)* and audio frequencies are below 20 kHz.

T2A14 How is the wavelength of a radio wave related to its frequency?
A. Wavelength gets longer as frequency increases
B. Wavelength gets shorter as frequency increases
C. There is no relationship between wavelength and frequency
D. The frequency depends on the velocity of the radio wave, but the wavelength depends on the bandwidth of the signal

ANSWER B: The higher we go in frequency, the shorter the distance between each wave. The LOWER we go in frequency, the LONGER the distance between each wave. Now say this out loud – *LOWER LONGER, HIGHER SHORTER.* Got it? Now look around and see who is staring at you wondering what in the world you are saying! ➡ **www.df5ai.net**

T2A04 What is the name for the distance an AC signal travels during one complete cycle?
A. Wave speed   C. Wavelength
B. Waveform   D. Wave spread

ANSWER C: The key word here is *DISTANCE* that an AC signal travels over one complete cycle. We measure distance of ham radio signals as *WAVELENGTH.*

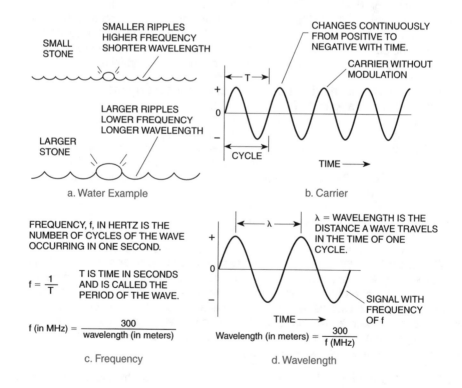

Carrier, Frequency, Cycle and Wavelength

T2A01 What happens to a signal's wavelength as its frequency increases?
- A. It gets shorter
- B. It gets longer
- C. It stays the same
- D. It disappears

ANSWER A: The *higher* we go in *frequency*, the more cycles per second. This means *wavelength* gets *shorter*. ➡ **www.spacetoday.org**

T2A09 Which of the following choices is often used to identify a particular radio wave?
- A. The "frequency" or their "wavelength of the wave"
- B. The length of the magnetic curve of wave
- C. The time it takes for the wave to travel a certain distance
- D. The free-space impedance of the wave

ANSWER A: When we want to meet a pal on a specific ham band, we usually say which band it is in meters. The most popular ham band for Technician class operators is the 2-meter band. Your pal says that she has a 2-meter radio, so the next question is, what exact FREQUENCY? So it's really a toss up on whether or not you want to tell someone to meet you at a specific frequency, or ask them whether or not they have a 2-meter radio which describes the WAVELENGTH of the band you plan to operate. So if you asked ME, I would first determine what *wavelength band* we were going to operate on, and then indicate the *specific frequency* we should try to make contact on.

T7A18 How many hertz are in a kilohertz?
- A. 10
- B. 100
- C. 1000
- D. 1,000,000

ANSWER C: *Kilo means one thousand* (1×10^3). *A kilohertz is 1000 Hz.*

T7B09 If a radio wave makes 3,725,000 cycles in one second, what does this mean?
- A. The radio wave's voltage is 3725 kilovolts
- B. The radio wave's wavelength is 3725 kilometers
- C. The radio wave's frequency is 3725 kilohertz
- D. The radio wave's speed is 3725 kilometers per second

ANSWER C: First, replace the 000 with kilohertz. *3725 kHz is* also *the same* thing *as 3.725 MHz.* We keep moving the decimal point 3 places to the left to go from Hz to kHz to MHz. Remember, cycles per second is the definition of frequency.

T7B08 Electrical energy at a frequency of 7125 kHz is in what frequency range?
- A. Audio
- B. Radio
- C. Hyper
- D. Super-high

ANSWER B: Is *7,125 kHz* above 20,000 hertz? You bet it is, so it must be *radiofrequency.*

T7A19 If a dial marked in megahertz shows a reading of 3.525 MHz, what would it show if it were marked in kilohertz?
- A. 0.003525 kHz
- B. 35.25 kHz
- C. 3525 kHz
- D. 3,525,000 kHz

ANSWER C: *Move the decimal point 3 places to the right* to convert MHz to kHz. *3.525 MHz is 3525 kHz.*

T7B05 Most humans can hear sounds in what frequency range?
- A. 0 - 20 Hz
- B. 20 - 20,000 Hz
- C. 200 - 200,000 Hz
- D. 10,000 - 30,000 Hz

ANSWER B: I'm not sure that I can still hear all the way up to 20,000 hertz (20 kHz). However, my dogs and cats can! *Humans hear audio frequencies from 20 Hz to 20 kHz.*

T7B06 Why do we call electrical signals in the frequency range of 20 Hz to 20,000 Hz audio frequencies?
A. Because the human ear cannot sense anything in this range
B. Because the human ear can sense sounds in this range
C. Because this range is too low for radio energy
D. Because the human ear can sense radio waves in this range

ANSWER B: *Audio frequencies are those that you can hear with your ear.* Among the radio frequencies, above 20,000 hertz, are those that you can pick up with your ham receiver.

T2A07 What is an audio-frequency signal?
A. Wave disturbances that cannot be heard by the human ear
B. Electromagnetic oscillations or cycles that repeat between 20 and 20,000 times per second
C. Electromagnetic oscillations or cycles that repeat more than 20,000 times per second
D. Electric energy that is generated at the front end of by an AM or FM radio receiver

ANSWER B: Now they ask us about AUDIO frequencies. These are always BELOW 20,000 times per second, and audio *frequencies between 20 to 20,000 cycles per second (hertz) are audio frequencies* – those within the range of human hearing. The term "hertz" is just another fancy name for cycles per second.

Now, for a clarification. Sound waves (audio) are transmitted as a pressure differential in air or other media. Radio waves travel as electromagnetic energy through free space (even a vacuum). It just happens that audio waves are measured in frequency (hertz), just like radio waves. There also are radio frequencies all the way down to 20 Hz or less. The Navy uses very low radio frequencies like these to communicate with submarines under water. You can hear sound in the range of audio frequencies. You cannot hear electromagnetic waves at any frequency.

Do I need the dots and dashes?

No. But you'll get more ham radio privileges if you pass that 5-wpm Morse code test.

T5B06 On which band(s) may a Technician licensee who has passed a Morse code exam use up to 200 watts PEP output power?

A. 80, 40, 15, and 10 meters	C. 1.25 meters
B. 80, 40, 20, and 10 meters	D. 23 centimeters

> **Question deleted by QPC – will NOT be on exam**

ANSWER A: If you pass your Element 1 *Morse code* 5-wpm exam when you also take and pass your Element 2 *Technician* written exam, you will be *allowed CW on 80-, 40-, 15-, and 10-meters,* and a little bit of 10-meter voice, sharing the sub-bands with grandfathered Novice operators. On these Novice CW and 10-meter voice sub-bands, a Technician class licensee holding code credit is limited to no more than 200 watts of peak envelope power output. But hey, gang, 200 watts is plenty of power to easily work the world. That's about all I run here at my station here in southern California. [97.313c] ➡ **www.gigaparts.com**

T1D05 If you are a Technician licensee who has passed a Morse code exam, what is one document you can use to prove that you are authorized to use certain amateur frequencies below 30 MHz?

A. A certificate from the FCC showing that you have notified them that you will be using the HF bands

B. A certificate showing that you have attended a class in HF communications

C. A Certificate of Successful Completion of Examination showing that you have passed a Morse code exam

D. No special proof is required

ANSWER C: When you successfully *pass your Morse code test,* you will be issued a *Certificate of Successful Completion of Examination (CSCE)* that is valid for 365 days as exam credit when you go for Element 3, the worldwide General class license. That CSCE also is permanent proof that you have passed the 5-wpm code test; and you may continue to operate on those 4 worldwide bands as a Technician class operator as long as you continue to renew your license. The CSCE conveys exam credit for only 365 days. But what the heck – once you get the code out of the way, the General class license is just one more simple written exam of just 35 questions found in my *General Class* test preparation book. [97.9b] ➡ **www.w5yi.org**

Don't Lose Your CSCE

T1D09 What is the purpose of the Element 1 examination?

A. To test Morse code comprehension at 5 words-per-minute
B. To test knowledge of block diagrams
C. To test antenna-building skills
D. To test knowledge of rules and regulations

ANSWER A: *Element 1 is a test for Morse code comprehension at 5-wpm.* You do NOT need to take a code test for your entry-level Technician class examination. Ultimately, after you have been on the air for a couple of years, you may wish to upgrade to General class. Then you begin to study for the code and take the Element 1 Morse code test, plus the Element 3 General class written exam. The Morse code examination may get phased out, but don't bother waiting – the elimination of CW as a requirement for the General class license is many years away! You will hear me describing CW in detail on my audio cassette tapes, and learning CW using my tapes is one of the fastest ways to pass the Morse Code test. ➡ **www.dxsoft.com**

T1D10 If a Technician class licensee passes only the 5 words-per-minute Morse code test at an exam session, how long will this credit be valid for license upgrade purposes?

A. 365 days
B. Until the current license expires
C. Indefinitely
D. Until two years following the expiration of the current license

ANSWER A: The Morse code Element 1 examination is probably most feared out of all the exam elements because it is a timed test. You will copy the code at the 5-wpm rate on the code test. The actual code character rate must be set between 13- to 15-wpm. This allows big spaces in between each letter, with just enough time for you to think of the sound that was sent, and what letter, number, or punctuation mark you will write down on your paper. Many hams prefer to take the code test before any written element, and this is perfectly acceptable with the *code credit lasting for 365 days for your license upgrade.* Most applicants first study and pass the Tech exam, then get on the air, and then about a year later prepare for the General class exam. Whether they pass the code or theory first, there is a 365-day limit for the code or theory credit. But don't let anyone pressure you to immediately go to the next upgrade – as a new Technician class operator, there is absolutely NO time limit on how long you want to wait until you next decide to upgrade. And will the Morse code requirement ultimately be dropped for the General class license and higher? Don't hold your breath – it's still several years off before this might happen. [97.505(A) (6)] ➡ **www.fists.com**

T1D08 How may an Element 1 exam be administered to an applicant with a physical disability?

A. It may be skipped if a doctor signs a statement saying the applicant is too disabled to pass the exam
B. By holding an open book exam
C. By lowering the exam's pass rate to 50 percent correct
D. By using a vibrating surface or flashing light

ANSWER D: Ham tests are administered by a team of 3 accredited licensed amateur operators. These 3 hams, usually assisted by up to 5 additional hams, may go to extraordinary efforts to accommodate the *physically handicapped* applicant. This could include reading them the examination, as well as offering an *Element 1*

Morse code test by starting and stopping between each character, or allowing the applicant to see a *flashing light or touch a vibrating surface* to see and feel the code as it is being sent at 5-wpm. ➡ **www.handiham.org**

T1D11 Question deleted from Element 2 pool by QPC.

T2B01 What are the frequency limits of the 80-meter band in ITU Region 2 for Technician class licensees who have passed a Morse code exam?

A. 3500 - 4000 kHz

B. 3675 - 3725 kHz

C. 7100 - 7150 kHz

D. 7000 - 7300 kHz

ANSWER B: Pass that simple 5-wpm Morse code test when you take your first Element 2 Technician class written exam. Passing the code test gives you exciting *CW* privileges *on the 80-meter band from 3675 to 3725 kHz.* [97.301e]

	3.675 MHz	N/T+	3.725 MHz	
75/80 m		200 WATTS		
3.500 MHz				4.000 MHz

75/80-Meter Wavelength Band Privileges

T2B05 What emission types are Technician control operators who have passed a Morse code exam allowed to use from 7100 to 7150 kHz in ITU Region 2?

A. CW and data

B. Phone

C. Data only

D. CW only

ANSWER D: As a Technician class operator having passed the Element 1 5-wpm Morse code test, you are allowed *CW ONLY from 7100 to 7150 kHz on the 40-meter band.* [97.305/.307f9]

T8A06 What would you connect to a transceiver to send Morse code?

A. A key-click filter

B. A telegraph key

C. An SWR meter

D. An antenna switch

ANSWER B: Since they're asking about *Morse code,* you would need a *telegraph key.*

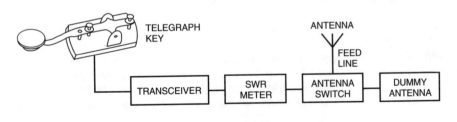

Morse Code Station

T8A07 What do many amateurs use to help form good Morse code characters?

A. A key-operated on/off switch

B. An electronic keyer

C. A key-click filter

D. A DTMF keypad

ANSWER B: If you enjoy the *Morse code,* you may wish to invest in an *electronic keyer* with side paddles. This lets you form *perfect dits and dahs.*

T8A08 Why is it important to provide adequate power supply filtering for a CW transmitter?
A. It isn't important, since CW transmitters cannot be modulated by AC hum
B. To eliminate phase noise
C. It isn't important, since most CW receivers can easily suppress any hum by using narrow filters
D. To eliminate modulation of the RF signal by AC hum

ANSWER D: If you decide to build your own power supply, be sure to use plenty of big *filter capacitors to reduce the amount of AC hum from the RF signal.* Remember, the rectifier only conducts in one direction, which creates pulsing DC that is then filtered to smooth DC by the filter capacitors. A bad cap can cause plenty of hum. ➡ **www.comm-pute.com**

T2B02 What are the frequency limits of the 10-meter band in ITU Region 2 for Technician class licensees who have passed a Morse code exam?
A. 28.000 - 28.500 MHz
B. 28.100 - 29.500 MHz
C. 28.100 - 28.500 MHz
D. 29.100 - 29.500 MHz

ANSWER C: *10 meters* is an exciting band for Technician class operators who also pass the Element 1 *Morse code* test. Your privileges will extend from *28.100 to 28.500 MHz*, and the region between 28.300 to 28.500 MHz is for single-sideband voice, too! Get that code test out of the way at the same time you take your Element 2 Technician written exam. Trust me, you will be glad you learned the code. [97.301e]

28.100 MHz	N/T + (200 WATTS)	28.500 MHz	
10 m	CODE	VOICE	
28.000 MHz	28.300 MHz		29.700 MHz

10-Meter Wavelength Band Privileges for Techs with Code Credit

---

T2B06 What emission types are Technician control operators who have passed a Morse code exam allowed to use on frequencies from 28.3 to 28.5 MHz?
A. All authorized amateur emission privileges
B. CW and data
C. CW and single-sideband phone
D. Data and phone

ANSWER C: I hope you pass the Morse code Element 1 test along with your Technician written Element 2 exam, because the *10-meter band* from *28.3 to 28.5 MHz allows* you not only *Morse code* but also exciting *SINGLE-SIDEBAND PHONE* transmissions, too. [97.305/ 307f10] ➡ **www.ten-ten.org**

T1B10 If you are operating on 28.400 MHz, in what amateur band are you operating?
A. 80 meters
B. 40 meters
C. 15 meters
D. 10 meters

ANSWER D: Look at the frequency privileges in the authorized frequency bands chart in the Appendix of this book, and memorize the MHz frequencies as they relate to the band in meters. To convert MHz to meters, simply divide 28.400 MHz into 300, and presto, you end up with 10 meters. The answer is rounded to 10 because the wavelength for a band is an average number broadly covering all the frequencies in the band. The meter band is the wavelength of the operating frequency. Wavelength is found by the equation:

$$\lambda(\text{wavelength in meters}) = 300 \div f(\text{MHz})$$

which says that the wavelength in meters is equal to 300 divided by the frequency in megahertz. With a calculator, the keystrokes are: CLEAR 300 ÷ 28.4 = 10.56, rounded to 10 meters. *28.400 MHz = 10 meter band.* [97.301e]

Converting Frequency to Wavelength	Converting Wavelength to Frequency
To find wavelength (λ) in meters, if you know frequency (f) in megahertz (MHz), Solve: $$\lambda(\text{meters}) = \frac{300}{f(\text{MHz})}$$	To find frequency (f) in megahertz (MHz), if you know wavelength (λ) in meters, Solve: $$f(\text{MHz}) = \frac{300}{\lambda(\text{meters})}$$

Conversions Between Wavelength and Frequency

T2B11 Which sideband is commonly used for 10-meter phone operation?
    A. Upper sideband   C. Amplitude-compandored sideband
    B. Lower sideband   D. Double sideband

ANSWER A: When you pass your Technician class exam, your privileges begin on the 6-meter 50 MHz band and higher. If you practice and pass the International Morse code test, Element 1, you gain privileges on additional bands BELOW 6 meters. The most exciting band for a Technician with code credit is the *10-meter band*, 28.300-28.500 MHz, where Technician operators with code credit run *UPPER SIDEBAND* radio equipment. Upper sideband is the mode for your privileges on the 10-meter band. Remember, you must pass the code test to get 10-meter upper sideband privileges.

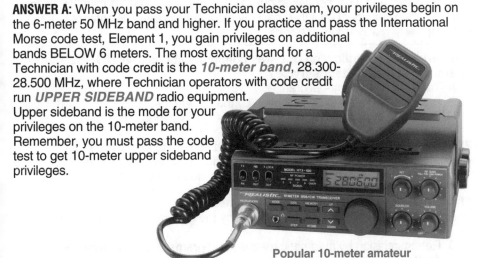

Popular 10-meter amateur radio SSB transceiver

T2B12 What is the most transmitter power a Technician control operator with telegraphy credit may use on the 10-meter band?
    A. 5 watts PEP output   C. 200 watts PEP output
    B. 25 watts PEP output   D. 1500 watts PEP output

ANSWER C: *PEP is Peak Envelope Power* – the amount of electrical energy emitted by your transmitting antenna. Although *200 watts output on 10 meters* is allowed, try to keep your power output to a minimum. This band could cause second harmonic interference to your neighbors on television Channel 2. [97.313c2]

How do I stay on the straight and narrow?

The ham rules and regs are straight-forward. Here are some important topics to remember when you're on the air!

T1A01 Who makes and enforces the rules for the amateur service in the United States?
- A. The Congress of the United States
- B. The Federal Communications Commission (FCC)
- C. The Volunteer Examiner Coordinators (VECs)
- D. The Federal Bureau of Investigation (FBI)

ANSWER B: The Federal Communications Commission *(FCC) makes and enforces all Amateur Radio rules* in the United States. [97]

T4B09 When is the FCC allowed to conduct an inspection of your amateur station?
- A. Only on weekends
- B. At any time
- C. Never, the FCC does not inspect stations
- D. Only during daylight hours

ANSWER B: It has only happened to me ONCE. It was a knock on the door and the Federal Communications Commission wanted to inspect my station. This was back in the days of CB radio, and regardless of what radio service it is, when the *FCC* comes knocking, they are allowed to conduct an *inspection of the radio station AT ANY TIME.* And, yes, I checked out fine – they just couldn't imagine how I had such a big monster signal until they saw my extra big monster CB antenna! [97.103c] ➡ **www.rainreport.com**

T1A07 Which of the following one-way communications may NOT be transmitted in the amateur service?
- A. Telecommand to model craft
- B. Broadcasts intended for reception by the general public
- C. Brief transmissions to make adjustments to the station
- D. Morse code practice

ANSWER B: This is one of those questions where you are to look for the "not" answer. No, *you may not broadcast* information intended *for the general public.* Only commercial broadcast stations may do that. [97.3a10, 97.113b]

T1A14 What does the term broadcasting mean?
- A. Transmissions intended for reception by the general public, either direct or relayed
- B. Retransmission by automatic means of programs or signals from non-amateur stations
- C. One-way radio communications, regardless of purpose or content
- D. One-way or two-way radio communications between two or more stations

ANSWER A: You may not operate your station like an AM or shortwave *broadcast* station. You cannot *transmit to the public directly.* [97.3a10]

T1A04 When is an amateur station authorized to transmit information to the general public?
- A. Never
- B. Only when the operator is being paid

C. Only when the broadcast transmission lasts less than 1 hour

D. Only when the broadcast transmission lasts longer than 15 minutes

ANSWER A: News bulletins broadcast over the ham radio airwaves must relate solely to Amateur Radio matters or be of interest to amateur operators who tune in, *never to the general public.* [97.113b] ➡ **www.arnewsline.org**

T1A05 When is an amateur station authorized to transmit music?

    A. Amateurs may not transmit music, except as an incidental part of an authorized rebroadcast of space shuttle communications

    B. Only when the music produces no spurious emissions

    C. Only when the music is used to jam an illegal transmission

    D. Only when the music is above 1280 MHz, and the music is a live performance

ANSWER A: Music is generally not allowed on the ham bands. No playing the violin or piano, and no singing happy birthday. However, a little-known rule COULD permit you to blow your trumpet for reveille when sending up an authorized signal to the space shuttle or international space station. Answer A calls this *"incidental music during authorized space shuttle communications."* You DO play the trumpet, right? [97.113a4, 113e]

Space Shuttle
Photo courtesy of N.A.S.A.

T1A06 When is the transmission of codes or ciphers allowed to hide the meaning of a message transmitted by an amateur station?

    A. Only during contests

    B. Only during nationally declared emergencies

    C. Codes and ciphers may not be used to obscure the meaning of a message, although there are special exceptions

    D. Only when frequencies above 1280 MHz are used

ANSWER C: *Secret codes are not allowed.* It's even considered poor practice to use police-type "ten codes" on the air. [97.113a4, .211b, .217]

T1A10 When may false or deceptive signals or communications be transmitted by an amateur station?

    A. Never

    B. When operating a beacon transmitter in a "fox hunt" exercise

    C. When playing a harmless "practical joke"

    D. When you need to hide the meaning of a message for secrecy

ANSWER A: Going on the air using someone else's call sign, or reporting a *false* emergency, is strictly *forbidden!* [97.113a4]

T5C08 If an amateur pretends there is an emergency and transmits the word "MAYDAY," what is this called?
A. A traditional greeting in May
B. An emergency test transmission
C. False or deceptive signals
D. Nothing special; "MAYDAY" has no meaning in an emergency

ANSWER C: It's wise not to even utter the word "MAYDAY" in the course of your conversation. Reserve this word for the highest of emergencies over the worldwide bands. On local VHF and UHF repeaters, the equivalent of the worldwide word "MAYDAY" is the phrase "Break, break, break." A triple break signifies a local emergency. *NEVER send false or deceptive emergency calls!* [97.113a4]

T5B11 Why is transmitting on a police frequency as a "joke" called harmful interference that deserves a large penalty?
A. It annoys everyone who listens
B. It blocks police calls that might be an emergency and interrupts police communications
C. It is in bad taste to communicate with non-amateurs, even as a joke
D. It is poor amateur practice to transmit outside the amateur bands

ANSWER B: Many dual-band Amateur Radio sets are frequency agile after modifications have been made. *It is illegal to transmit on a police frequency,* and it could block a police call for an emergency broadcast. Never play games with a ham radio transceiver. [97.3a22]

T1A12 What is an amateur communication called that does NOT have the required station identification?
A. Unidentified communications or signals
B. Reluctance modulation
C. Test emission
D. Tactical communication

ANSWER A: Although not required, it's common practice to use your call sign at the beginning of a transmission. The law does allow you to begin communicating without your call sign for up to 10 minutes. While it's not required at the beginning of a transmission, it's required when you sign off. If you *fail to give your call sign, it's an unidentified signal.* [97.119a]

T1A11 When may an amateur station transmit unidentified communications?
A. Only during brief tests not meant as messages
B. Only when they do not interfere with others
C. Only when sent from a space station or to control a model craft
D. Only during two-way or third-party communications

ANSWER C: Normally we would NEVER transmit communications without giving our FCC call sign. However, transmissions from a space station or transmitting up to a 6-meter model aircraft may take place *without station I.D.* So look for the answer says *"space station" and "model aircraft."* [97.119a]

T1A13 What is a transmission called that disturbs other communications?
A. Interrupted CW
B. Harmful interference
C. Transponder signals
D. Unidentified transmissions

ANSWER B: Amateur operators regularly conduct organized round-table gatherings on a specific frequency. This is called a "net," and "nets" are a fun way to meet new friends and get started on ham radio. If another amateur operator repeatedly transmits on a frequency that is already in use by members of the net, and if that operator does not stop transmitting when requested to do so by the net control, this would be considered *harmful or malicious interference* and is absolutely illegal. Luckily, occurrences like this bad behavior are relatively rare on the ham bands. And the very best procedure to discourage harmful interference is simply to ignore the interfering station and make absolutely no reference that someone is out there trying to break up the net. Without recognition, they will probably go away. [97.3a22, 23]

T5C10 When may you deliberately interfere with another station's communications?
A. Only if the station is operating illegally
B. Only if the station begins transmitting on a frequency you are using
C. Never
D. You may expect, and cause, deliberate interference because it can't be helped during crowded band conditions

ANSWER C: Ham radio operators pride themselves on being polite. *Deliberate interference* is rare, and *will not be tolerated.* The FCC will respond to jamming complaints from the amateur community. You could lose your amateur operator/primary station license permanently if found guilty of intentional interference. [97.101d]

T5C11 If an amateur repeatedly transmits on a frequency already occupied by a group of amateurs in a net operation, what type of interference is this called?
A. Break-in interference
B. Harmful or malicious interference
C. Incidental interference
D. Intermittent interference

ANSWER B: Hams take pride in how they conduct their radio transmissions over the airwaves. Hams will not cause *harmful or malicious interference* because, when caught by the FCC, the FCC could take away their hard-earned license. [97.3a22]

T1A15 Why is indecent and obscene language prohibited in the Amateur Service?
A. Because it is offensive to some individuals
B. Because young children may intercept amateur communications with readily available receiving equipment
C. Because such language is specifically prohibited by FCC Rules
D. All of these choices are correct

ANSWER D: Bad language is OUT on amateur radio frequencies. If ever I encounter a ham using bad language, I politely and abruptly sign off, and hopefully they will get the message. *No bad language on ham frequencies!* [97.113a4]

T4B12 How could you best keep unauthorized persons from using your amateur station at home?
  A. Use a carrier-operated relay in the main power line
  B. Use a key-operated on/off switch in the main power line
  C. Put a "Danger - High Voltage" sign in the station
  D. Put fuses in the main power line
ANSWER B: You are responsible for unauthorized use of your station even though the use may be without your approval. Most hams remove the microphone and *shut off the main power line with a key-operated switch* to protect a station from being operated without permission. (Before you can go on the air again, you must remember where you hid the mike!)

T4B13 How could you best keep unauthorized persons from using a mobile amateur station in your car?
  A. Disconnect the microphone when you are not using it
  B. Put a "do not touch" sign on the radio
  C. Turn the radio off when you are not using it
  D. Tune the radio to an unused frequency when you are done using it
ANSWER A: One good way to keep unauthorized persons from using a mobile amateur station is to *disconnect the microphone.* Lock it up in the glove compartment.

Can I help?

In an emergency, hams are often first on the scene. Here's what to do when someone calls for help!

T4C09 What are messages called that are sent into or out of a disaster area concerning the immediate safety of human life?

    A. Tactical traffic   C. Formal message traffic
    B. Emergency traffic   D. Health and welfare traffic

ANSWER B: Any *communications relating to the safety* of human life or the immediate protection of property *are considered emergency traffic.* They deserve the highest priority.

T4C05 If you are in contact with another station and you hear an emergency call for help on your frequency, what should you do?

    A. Tell the calling station that the frequency is in use
    B. Direct the calling station to the nearest emergency net frequency
    C. Call your local Civil Preparedness Office and inform them of the emergency
    D. Stop your QSO immediately and take the emergency call

ANSWER D: An emergency call always has the highest priority. *Stop your communications!* Do what you can to *take down the message* accurately, and then *call the proper authorities.* The letters "QSO" mean a communication in progress between two stations. ➡ **www.cq-amateur-radio.com**

T5B09 If you are helping in a communications emergency that is being handled by a net control operator, how might you best minimize interference to the net once you have checked in?

    A. Whenever the net frequency is quiet, announce your call sign and location
    B. Move 5 kHz away from the net's frequency and use high power to ask for other emergency communications
    C. Do not transmit on the net frequency until asked to do so by the net operator
    D. Wait until the net frequency is quiet, then ask for any emergency traffic for your area

ANSWER C: Ham operators do an excellent job in handling big emergencies. If you are part of the actual emergency that is being handled by ham radio, ONLY respond to the net control after they ask for new check-ins or emergency reports. Keep your transmissions brief, and remember, *don't transmit on the net until specifically asked to do so by the net control operator.*

Hams are well-known for their work with the Red Cross, Salvation Army, and others providing emergency communications.

T4C01 If you hear a voice distress signal on a frequency outside of your license privileges, what are you allowed to do to help the station in distress?

A. You are NOT allowed to help because the frequency of the signal is outside your privileges

B. You are allowed to help only if you keep your signals within the nearest frequency band of your privileges

C. You are allowed to help on a frequency outside your privileges only if you use international Morse code

D. You are allowed to help on a frequency outside your privileges in any way possible

ANSWER D: *In an emergency, anything goes!* If you hear someone calling "MAYDAY" on a frequency outside of your normal operating privileges, it's perfectly okay to transmit on any frequency (except police) to save someone's life. [97.405a]

T4C02 When may you use your amateur station to transmit an "SOS" or "MAYDAY"?

A. Never

B. Only at specific times (at 15 and 30 minutes after the hour)

C. In a life- or property-threatening emergency

D. When the National Weather Service has announced a severe weather watch

ANSWER C: Don't even utter the word "MAYDAY" in the course of your conversation. *Only in the highest of emergencies would you "MAYDAY"* over the worldwide bands. The same applies, of course, for "SOS" when transmitting with CW. [97.403]

T4C03 If a disaster disrupts normal communication systems in an area where the FCC regulates the amateur service, what kinds of transmissions may stations make?

A. Those that are necessary to meet essential communication needs and facilitate relief actions

B. Those that allow a commercial business to continue to operate in the affected area

C. Those for which material compensation has been paid to the amateur operator for delivery into the affected area

D. Those that are to be used for program production or newsgathering for broadcasting purposes

ANSWER A: If you do take part in *emergency communications,* keep your transmissions as short as possible. To learn how, listen to airline pilots communications over the airwaves – you should adopt their brief style when taking part in emergency communications. [97.401a] ➡ **www.wavehunter.com**

T4C04 What information is included in an FCC declaration of a temporary state of communication emergency?

A. A list of organizations authorized to use radio communications in the affected area

B. A list of amateur frequency bands to be used in the affected area

C. Any special conditions and special rules to be observed during the emergency

D. An operating schedule for authorized amateur emergency stations

ANSWER C: If you are asked to *stop transmitting on a certain frequency* because it is *reserved only for emergency communications,* then by all means comply! Do listen in to see if there is anything that you might do to help – but avoid transmitting on the frequency unless directed to do so by the emergency net controller. Unless they are asking for outside help, don't transmit an offer for assistance. [97.401c]

T4C06 What is the proper way to interrupt a repeater conversation to signal a distress call?
A. Say "BREAK" once, then your call sign
B. Say "HELP" as many times as it takes to get someone to answer
C. Say "SOS," then your call sign
D. Say "EMERGENCY" three times

ANSWER A: *On repeater frequencies, the word "BREAK"* is spoken several times to indicate a priority or emergency distress call. Keep this in mind when operating routinely on a repeater – don't say the word "break" unless it's an emergency or something very, very important.

T4C07 What is one reason for using tactical call signs such as "command post" or "weather center" during an emergency?
A. They keep the general public informed about what is going on
B. They are more efficient and help coordinate public-service communications
C. They are required by the FCC
D. They increase goodwill between amateurs

ANSWER B: It's perfectly legal to use such *tactical words* as "command post," "triage team," or "disaster communicator" during an emergency. This *promotes efficiency* in the ham radio communications being provided.
➡ www.warn.org

Hams Operating from an Emergency
Communications Command Post.

T4C08 What type of messages concerning a person's well being are sent into or out of a disaster area?
A. Routine traffic
B. Tactical traffic
C. Formal message traffic
D. Health and welfare traffic

ANSWER D: This type of traffic deserves priority because we are talking about the *health and welfare of human lives.*

T4C10 Why is it a good idea to have a way to operate your amateur station without using commercial AC power lines?
A. So you may use your station while mobile
B. So you may provide communications in an emergency
C. So you may operate in contests where AC power is not allowed
D. So you will comply with the FCC rules

ANSWER B: Your author's station operates on solar panel power. The battery is located safely outside, and the solar panels keep the battery charged even though my ham station is used often. Even *in an emergency when the power is out, I can communicate.* ➡ www.batteriesamerica.com

T4C11 What is the most important accessory to have for a hand-held radio in an emergency?
A. An extra antenna
B. A portable amplifier
C. Several sets of charged batteries
D. A microphone headset for hands-free operation

ANSWER C: *Rechargeable* nickel cadmium *batteries* self-discharge up to 10 percent per week. This means a nickel-cadmium battery will need frequent charging. Alkaline batteries have long shelf life, but cannot be recharged. ➡ **www.ww-manufacturing.com**

In an emergency, it is important to have a back-up energy source such as rechargeable batteries.

T4C14 With what organization must you register before you can participate in RACES drills?
A. A local Amateur Radio club
B. A local racing organization
C. The responsible civil defense organization
D. The Federal Communications Commission

ANSWER C: *RACES* stands for Radio Amateur Civil Emergency Service. It is a division of the *civil defense organization.* You must be registered to take part in RACES drills. ➡ **www.gordonwestradioschool.com**

RACES Logo.

T4C13 How must you identify messages sent during a RACES drill?
A. As emergency messages
B. As amateur traffic
C. As official government messages
D. As drill or test messages

ANSWER D: To eliminate any misunderstanding of a drill message versus the real thing, *always announce messages for practice as drill or test messages.* You never know how many scanner monitor listeners are out there tuning in the ham bands!

T1C09 Under what conditions are amateur stations allowed to communicate with stations operating in other radio services?

    A. Never; amateur stations are only permitted to communicate with other amateur stations

    B. When authorized by the FCC or in an emergency

    C. When communicating with stations in the Citizens Radio Service

    D. When a commercial broadcast station is using Amateur Radio frequencies for newsgathering during a natural disaster

ANSWER B: You can spot the correct answer by looking for the words "in an emergency." Remember *in an emergency, communicating with any station is permitted.* You are also allowed to communicate with other radio services when specifically authorized by the FCC. [97.113a3]

In an emergency, authorized hams participating in a RACES organization may communicate from a police helicopter.

CQ? DE? 73?
What do I say when I'm looking for my first contact?
Different lingo for different bands - and the meaning behind some of those radio signal words and letters.

T6A03 What should you do before you transmit on any frequency?
A. Listen to make sure others are not using the frequency
B. Listen to make sure that someone will be able to hear you
C. Check your antenna for resonance at the selected frequency
D. Make sure the SWR on your antenna feed line is high enough

ANSWER A: *Always listen for a few seconds* before initiating a transmitted call. On worldwide, ask, "Is the frequency in use?" Always choose a frequency within your privileges, within the American Radio Relay League (ARRL) suggested band plan, and clear of an ongoing conversation. ➡**www.arrl.org**

T6A04 How do you call another station on a repeater if you know the station's call sign?
A. Say "break, break 79," then say the station's call sign
B. Say the station's call sign, then identify your own station
C. Say "CQ" three times, then say the station's call sign
D. Wait for the station to call "CQ," then answer it

ANSWER B: Before transmitting on any frequency, be sure to listen for a few seconds to insure the channel is clear. Then depress the microphone push-to-talk button and *say the call sign of the station you are wishing to hook up with, followed by your call sign,* and the optional word "over." If you are placing a repeater call to ANY station, state your call sign a couple of times phonetically, and just say the fact that you are on the air looking for a contact with anyone else monitoring. You will find plenty of friends responding to your call. ➡**www.qrz.com**

T2B16 Which of the following descriptions is used to describe a good signal through a repeater?
A. Full quieting
B. Over deviation
C. Breaking up
D. Readability zero

ANSWER A: The way we describe how well someone is coming in through a repeater is how strong their signal is to suppress normal band noise. *A signal that is "full quieting"* is one that *completely silences background noise* and is considered an excellent signal through the repeater.

A signal that is "full quieting" completely
silences background white noise.

T6A11 What is the meaning of: "Your signal is full quieting..."?

A. Your signal is strong enough to overcome all receiver noise
B. Your signal has no spurious sounds
C. Your signal is not strong enough to be received
D. Your signal is being received, but no audio is being heard

ANSWER A: When transmitting on VHF or UHF FM equipment, the S meter is simply a row of LCD bars that may illustrate relative signal strength. It's much easier to tell the sending station its signal strength by saying how well *the signal is quieting the background white noise.* ➡ www.amcominc.com

T6A01 What is the advantage of using the International Telecommunication Union (ITU) phonetic alphabet when identifying your station?

A. The words are internationally recognized substitutes for letters
B. There is no advantage
C. The words have been chosen to represent Amateur Radio terms
D. It preserves traditions begun in the early days of Amateur Radio

ANSWER A: When you get your new call sign, hardly anyone else on the repeater will be familiar with it, and you should *use the International Phonetic Alphabet to make your individual letters recognized by substituting a word for each letter.* Memorize the phonetic alphabet, and use it often. [97.119b2]

ITU Phonetic Alphabet
Adopted by the International Telecommunication Union

A - Alpha	F - Foxtrot	K - Kilo	P - Papa	U - Uniform	Z - Zulu
B - Bravo	G - Golf	L - Lima	Q - Quebec	V - Victor	
C - Charlie	H - Hotel	M - Mike	R - Romeo	W- Whiskey	
D - Delta	I - India	N - November	S - Sierra	X - X-Ray	
E - Echo	J - Juliette	O - Oscar	T - Tango	Y - Yankee	

T6A02 What is one reason to avoid using "cute" phrases or word combinations to identify your station?

A. They are not easily understood by non-English-speaking amateurs
B. They might offend English-speaking amateurs
C. They do not meet FCC identification requirements
D. They might be interpreted as codes or ciphers intended to obscure the meaning of your identification

ANSWER A: When communicating through satellites or to other operators who may not speak English well, always *stick with the International Phonetic Alphabet.* Some amateurs say the last three letters of my call sign as "Never-Out-of-Answers!" While this may be cute, November-Oscar-Alpha might be better *so a foreign station would know exactly my "NOA" call sign.* [97.119b2]

T8F09 What is used to measure relative signal strength in a receiver?

A. An S meter
B. An RST meter
C. A signal deviation meter
D. An SSB meter

ANSWER A: *An S meter measures signal strength.* All worldwide ham sets have one.

T6A05 What does RST mean in a signal report?

A. Recovery, signal strength, tempo
B. Recovery, signal speed, tone

C. Readability, signal speed, tempo

D. Readability, signal strength, tone

ANSWER D: We use the *RST signal reporting system* on the worldwide bands regularly. Sometimes we use the RST system when operating weak signal equipment on VHF and UHF frequencies. *Readability* is how well you can audibly make out the signal with your ears. *Signal strength* is usually indicated by an LCD bar graph scale or a needle movement signal strength meter on your radio. *Tone* is something that you judge with your own ears and brain when receiving a CW signal.

T6A06 What is the meaning of: "Your signal report is five nine plus 20 dB..."?

A. Your signal strength has increased by a factor of 100

B. Repeat your transmission on a frequency 20 kHz higher

C. The bandwidth of your signal is 20 decibels above linearity

D. A relative signal-strength meter reading is 20 decibels greater than strength 9

ANSWER D: *Any signal over S9 is an excellent one.* Most worldwide sets have well-calibrated S-meters that register 10, 20, 40, and 60 dB over S9. Your signal is plenty strong! Although the question and answer is worded technically correct, most hams would simply state that "your signal is 20 over 9." Same meaning, but less formal on the air. See Table.

Signal Reporting System

The RST System is a way of reporting on the quality of a received signal by using a three digit number. The first digit indicates Readability (R), the second digit indicates received Signal Strength (S), and the third digit indicates Tone (T).

READABILITY (R) Voice and CW

1 – Unreadable

2 – Barely readable, occasional words distinguishable

3 – Readable with considerable difficulty

4 – Readable with practically no difficulty

5 – Perfectly readable

SIGNAL STRENGTH (S) Voice and CW

1 – Faint and barely perceptible signals

2 – Very weak signals

3 – Weak signals

4 – Fair signals

5 – Fairly good signals

6 – Good signals

7 – Moderately strong signals

8 – Strong signals

9 – Extremely strong signals

*TONE (T) Use on CW only

1 – Very rough, broad signals, 60 cycle AC may be present

2 – Very rough AC tone, harsh, broad

3 – Rough, low pitched AC tone, no filtering

4 – Rather rough AC tone, some trace of filtering

5 – Filtered rectified AC note, musical, ripple modulated

6 – Slight trace of filtered tone but with ripple modulation

7 – Near DC tone but trace of ripple modulation

8 – Good DC tone, may have slight trace of modulation

9 – Purest, perfect DC tone with no trace of ripple or modulation.

* The TONE report refers only to the purity of the signal, and has no connection with its stability or freedom from clicks or chirps. If the signal has the characteristic steadiness of crystal control, add X to the report (e.g., RST 469X). If it has a chirp or "tail" (either on "make" or "break") add C (e.g., RST 469C). If it has clicks or other noticeable keying transients, add K (e.g., RST 469K). If a signal has both chirps and clicks, add both C and K (e.g., RST 469CK).

T6A07 What is the meaning of the procedural signal "CQ"?
- A. Call on the quarter hour
- B. New antenna is being tested (no station should answer)
- C. Only the called station should transmit
- D. Calling any station

ANSWER D: The 2 letters *"CQ" mean "calling any station,"* and we use this on all worldwide bands and weak signal calls over VHF and UHF frequencies. But the CQ is NOT EVER USED when operating on FM repeater and simplex frequencies because the presence of your FM carrier is strong enough to let everyone else know you are on the air. Instead of calling "CQ" over a repeater, you would simply announce your call letters, and indicate you are monitoring for a call. And if you're on the air for the very first time, tell them you are a Gordo grad, and that may be all that is necessary to bring back plenty of responses from the ham community welcoming you to the exciting airwaves. ➡ **www.universalradio.com**

T6A09 What is the correct way to call CQ when using voice?
- A. Say "CQ" once, followed by "this is," followed by your call sign spoken three times
- B. Say "CQ" at least five times, followed by "this is," followed by your call sign spoken once
- C. Say "CQ" three times, followed by "this is," followed by your call sign spoken three times
- D. Say "CQ" at least ten times, followed by "this is," followed by your call sign spoken once

ANSWER C: *Three's the magic number when calling CQ.* We use "CQ" as a general call only on the worldwide bands. On the FM, VHF and UHF bands, we are less formal, and simply announce ourselves as being on the air by just giving our call sign. ➡ **www.cq-amateur-radio.com**

T6A10 How should you answer a voice CQ call?
- A. Say the other station's call sign at least ten times, followed by "this is," then your call sign at least twice
- B. Say the other station's call sign at least five times phonetically, followed by "this is," then your call sign at least once
- C. Say the other station's call sign at least three times, followed by "this is," then your call sign at least five times phonetically
- D. Say the other station's call sign once, followed by "this is," then your call sign given phonetically

ANSWER D: If you hear a lively CQ call, then go ahead and respond to that station and enjoy a great conversation. If the station is coming in clear, you would only need to *call it once, followed by "This is," and then give your call sign,* slowly, and phonetically. I also like to give my location.

T6B09 What is a good way to call CQ when using Morse code?
- A. Send the letters "CQ" three times, followed by "DE," followed by your call sign sent once
- B. Send the letters "CQ" three times, followed by "DE," followed by your call sign sent three times
- C. Send the letters "CQ" ten times, followed by "DE," followed by your call sign sent twice
- D. Send the letters "CQ" over and over until a station answers

ANSWER B: Practice sending "CQ" on a Morse code oscillator before actually going on the air. Don't send it too fast. A response will be sent back at the same rate that you send "CQ." *Send your CQ call three times, along with your call sign.*

T6B07 At what speed should a Morse code CQ call be transmitted?
A. Only speeds below five WPM
B. The highest speed your keyer will operate
C. Any speed at which you can reliably receive
D. The highest speed at which you can control the keyer

ANSWER C: We use CQ for a general call to communicate with anyone, about anything, on worldwide frequencies. When using telegraphy, a fast CW CQ call will result in a very fast reply since it will be assumed that you can receive Morse code as fast as you can send it. *Don't transmit CW faster than you can receive it.*

T6B10 How should you answer a Morse code CQ call?
A. Send your call sign four times
B. Send the other station's call sign twice, followed by "DE," followed by your call sign twice
C. Send the other station's call sign once, followed by "DE," followed by your call sign four times
D. Send your call sign followed by your name, station location and a signal report

ANSWER B: Reply by *sending the other station's call sign followed by "DE", followed by your call sign twice.* When you respond to a Morse code "CQ," respond at the rate that the sending station was using. If they were sending fast, then it's okay to send code back to them fast. The letters "QRS" mean "please send more slowly."

T5B04 What emission type may always be used for station identification, regardless of the transmitting frequency?
A. CW   C. MCW
B. RTTY   D. Phone

ANSWER A: *CW* stands for continuous wave. We use an interrupted continuous wave to transmit the dots and dashes of Morse code telegraphy. *Telegraphy may be used for all station identification.* [97.305a] ➡ www.eqf-software.com

T6B08 What is the meaning of the procedural signal "DE"?
A. "From" or "this is," as in "W0AIH DE KA9FOX"
B. "Directional Emissions" from your antenna
C. "Received all correctly"
D. "Calling any station"

ANSWER A: When working CW, it's much easier to send abbreviations than the whole word or phrase. Abbreviations are very important for you to know for both your written and code examinations. *"DE" means "this is."*

T6B11 What is the meaning of the procedural signal "K"?
A. "Any station transmit"   C. "End of message"
B. "All received correctly"   D. "Called station only transmit"

ANSWER A: Telegraphy means using code with a telegraph key. Don't confuse this word with telephony which means using a microphone, like a telephone. In telegraphy, the *"K" means the same as "over" or "go ahead."* The prosign "SK" indicates the sender is signing off or "goodbye."

T6B12 What is one meaning of the Q signal "QRS"?

A. "Interference from static"
B. "Send more slowly"
C. "Send RST report"
D. "Radio station location is"

ANSWER B: When you first start on the air, *"QRS"* can be very important because it *means "send more slowly."* Remember, in your CW transmissions, it's much easier to send abbreviations; so learn them well, especially for your examinations.

T6A13 What is the meaning of the term "73"?

A. Long distance
B. Best regards
C. Love and kisses
D. Go ahead

ANSWER B: *"73" means best regards,* and is an old railroad telegraph signature. Ladies sometimes sign "88." That is an affectionate way of saying their best regards. ➡ **www.dcace.com**

T6A12 What is meant by the term "DX"?

A. Best regards
B. Distant station
C. Calling any station
D. Go ahead

ANSWER B: When someone says they are working *"DX"*, this *means* they are working a *distant station* that may be many miles away.

T6A08 What is a QSL card in the amateur service?

A. A letter or postcard from an amateur pen pal
B. A Notice of Violation from the FCC
C. A written acknowledgment of communications between two amateurs
D. A postcard reminding you when your license will expire

ANSWER C: Hams exchange colorful *postcard QSLs to confirm contacts.* Always take a look at another ham's QSL card collection. You will find it fascinating! Here is my QSL card. ➡ **www.w4mpy.com**

See the full list of CW abbreviations and Q signals in the Appendix on pages 214 and 215.

The Effect of the Ionosphere on Radio Waves

To help you with the questions on radio wave propagation, here is a brief explanation on the effect the ionosphere has on radio waves.

The ionosphere is the electrified atmosphere from 40 miles to 400 miles above the Earth. You can sometimes see it as "northern lights." It is charged up daily by the sun, and does some miraculous things to radio waves that strike it. Some radio waves are absorbed during daylight hours by the ionosphere's D layer. Others are bounced back to Earth. Yet others penetrate the ionosphere and never come back again. The wavelength of the radio waves determines whether the waves will be absorbed, refracted, or will penetrate. Here's a quick way to memorize what the different layers do during day and nighttime hours:

The D layer is about 40 miles up. The D layer is a Daylight layer; it almost disappears at night. D for Daylight. The D layer absorbs radio waves between 1 MHz to 7 MHz. These are long wavelengths. All others pass through.

The E layer is also a daylight layer, and it is very Eccentric. E for Eccentric. Patches of E layer ionization may cause some surprising reflections of signals on both high frequency as well as very-high frequency. The E layer height is usually 70 miles.

The F1 layer is one of the layers farthest away. The F layer gives us those Far away signals. F for Far away. The F1 layer is present during daylight hours, and is up around 150 miles. The F2 layer is also present during daylight hours, and it gives us the Furthest range. The F2 layer is 250 miles high, and it's the best for the Farthest range on medium and short waves. At nighttime, the F1 and F2 layers combine to become just the F layer at 180 miles. This F layer at nighttime will usually bend radio waves between 1 MHz and 15 MHz back to earth. At night, the D and E layers disappear.

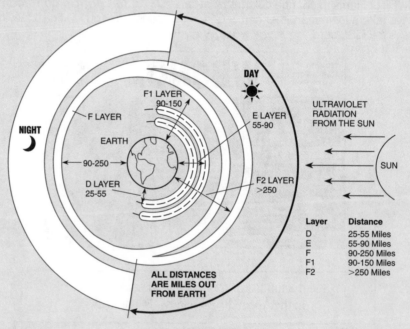

Layer	Distance
D	25-55 Miles
E	55-90 Miles
F	90-250 Miles
F1	90-150 Miles
F2	>250 Miles

Ionosphere Layers

Source: *Antennas — Selection and Installation,* © 1986, Master Publishing, Inc., Lincolnwood, Illinois

Signals from heaven?

How we use the ionosphere to communicate thousands of miles on 6-meters, and more!

T3A05 When a signal travels along the surface of the Earth, what is this called?

   A. Skywave propagation
   B. Knife-edge diffraction
   C. E-region propagation
   D. Ground-wave propagation

ANSWER D: All stations on all frequencies emit *radio waves that hug the earth, called ground waves.* They travel out from your transmitter antenna up to approximately 100 miles. The better the conductivity of the soil, the more intense your ground wave propagation.

T3A11 When a signal is returned to Earth by the ionosphere, what is this called?

   A. Skywave propagation
   B. Earth-Moon-Earth propagation
   C. Ground-wave propagation
   D. Tropospheric propagation

ANSWER A: *Skywaves are radio signals refracted back to Earth from the ionosphere.* During daylight hours at both of the stations working skywaves, the best frequencies are 5 MHz to 29 MHz. At night, expect skywave contacts from 1.8 MHz to 10 MHz. ➡ **www.dxer.com**

T3A12 How does the range of skywave propagation compare to ground-wave propagation?

   A. It is much shorter
   B. It is much longer
   C. It is about the same
   D. It depends on the weather

ANSWER B: *Ground waves have a much shorter range than skywaves* refracted off the ionosphere. It's quite common for skywave signals on 10 meters originating 3000 miles away to overpower local signals originating only a few miles away! You will be fascinated with 10-meter propagation. ➡ **http://oh2aq.kolumbus.com/dxs**

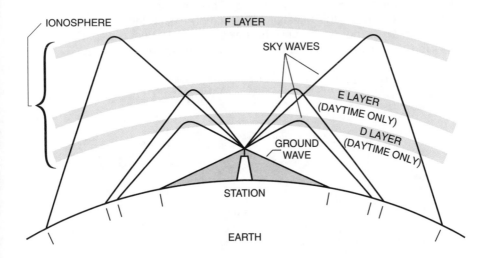

Radio Wave Propagation
Source: *Mobile 2-Way Radio Communications,* G. West, © 1993, Master Publishing, Inc.

T3A01 What is the name of the area of the atmosphere that makes long-distance radio communications possible by bending radio waves?

A. Troposphere
B. Stratosphere
C. Magnetosphere
D. Ionosphere

ANSWER D: When *radio waves* in the medium- and high-frequency range strike the ionosphere, they are often refracted, or simply bent back to Earth *traveling long distances*. This occurs *in the ionosphere.*
➡ www.ecjones.org/propag.html

T3A07 What is the usual cause of skywave propagation?

A. Signals are reflected by a mountain
B. Signals are reflected by the Moon
C. Signals are bent back to Earth by the ionosphere
D. Signals are retransmitted by a repeater

ANSWER C: As a new Technician class operator, the 6-meter band may offer plenty of excitement when it comes to skywave propagation. Many times, during the afternoon, 6-meter *signals are bent back to Earth by the ionosphere.* It's a common phenomenon during summertime, called sporadic E, and during the spring and fall months, longer F-layer ionospheric skip conditions may prevail. Your new Technician class privileges offer unlimited capabilities of 6 meters for skywave contacts throughout the world, so join in from your base station or mobile and have fun on 6!

T3B05 In which of the following frequency ranges does skywave propagation least often occur?

A. LF
B. UHF
C. HF
D. VHF

ANSWER B: You will *never find any skywave propagation on UHF* frequencies above 300 MHz. ➡ www.radioinc.com

T3A02 Which ionospheric region is closest to the Earth?

A. The A region
B. The D region
C. The E region
D. The F region

ANSWER B: Be careful on this question – they simply ask for the *lowest ionospheric layer,* not necessarily the lowest one that gives us skip. Since the *D layer is the lowest,* this is the correct answer. ➡ www.ac6v.com

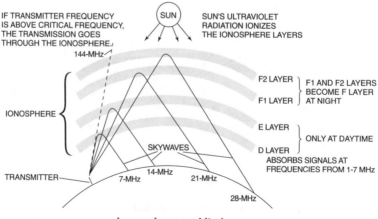

Ionosphere and Its Layers

T3A09 What effect does the D region of the ionosphere have on lower frequency HF signals in the daytime?
- A. It absorbs the signals
- B. It bends the radio waves out into space
- C. It refracts the radio waves back to earth
- D. It has little or no effect on 80-meter radio waves

ANSWER A: On the 80- and 100-meter bands, during daylight hours, *these HF skywaves are almost always absorbed by the D layer.*

T3A03 Which region of the ionosphere is mainly responsible for absorbing MF/HF radio signals during the daytime?
- A. The F2 region
- B. The F1 region
- C. The E region
- D. The D region

ANSWER D: The key word in this question is *"absorption."* Only one layer absorbs radio signals like a sponge, and that's the *D layer* during daylight hours. It absorbs medium- and low-frequency signals only. Higher frequencies pass through the D layer, and bounce off of other layers. ➡ **www.mem-amateur.com**

T3B09 Which of the following frequency bands is most likely to experience summertime sporadic-E propagation?
- A. 23 centimeters
- B. 6 meters
- C. 70 centimeters
- D. 1.25 meters

ANSWER B: As a no-code Technician, you can enjoy *skywave "skip" communications on the 6-meter band,* 50-54 MHz. That's right, no-code Tech is all that is required for unlimited excitement on the 6-meter band during summertime when skywaves regularly refract back to earth.
➡ **www.dxworld.com/50prop.html**

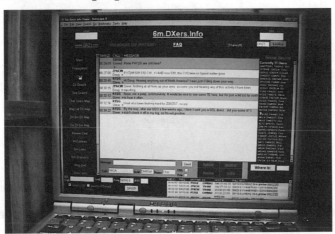

There are websites that provide skywave DX conditions.

T3A04 Which region of the ionosphere is mainly responsible for long-distance skywave radio communications?
- A. D region
- B. E region
- C. F1 region
- D. F2 region

ANSWER D: Since the *F2 layer is higher* than the F1 layer, it is mainly responsible for the *longest distance skywave* hop back to earth.

T3A08 What type of propagation has radio signals bounce several times between Earth and the ionosphere as they travel around the Earth?
- A. Multiple bounce
- B. Multi-hop
- C. Skip
- D. Pedersen propagation

ANSWER B: Your new Technician class privileges allow you to regularly enjoy skywave communications on the 6-meter band every summer. In the spring and fall, *6-meter signals often times "go long" and take multiple bounces* off the ionosphere. This is *called MULTI-HOP,* and the Technician class operator on 6 meters has full privileges and power levels for this band. Many Techs have worked hundreds of countries via multi-hop, which usually occurs from morning to late afternoon from March through November. ➡ http://6mt.com/beacon.htm

T3B13 In relation to skywave propagation, what does the term "maximum usable frequency" (MUF) mean?
- A. The highest frequency signal that will reach its intended destination
- B. The lowest frequency signal that will reach its intended destination
- C. The highest frequency signal that is most absorbed by the ionosphere
- D. The lowest frequency signal that is most absorbed by the ionosphere

ANSWER A: The Maximum Usable Frequency *(MUF) is the highest frequency that will be refracted by the ionosphere* to arrive back down to Earth to your ham pal half way around the world. During a daytime path, the MUF may be as high as 29 MHz. At night, it drops to around 14 MHz, Your best reception to a distant skywave station is just below the Maximum Usable Frequency.

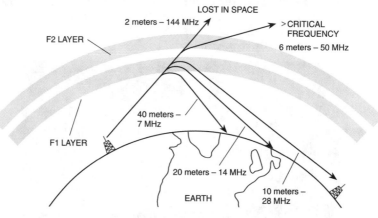

Critical Frequency
Source: *Antennas — Selection and Installation,* © 1986, Master Publishing, Inc.

T3B12 What happens to signals that take off vertically from the antenna and are higher in frequency than the critical frequency?
- A. They pass through the ionosphere
- B. They are absorbed by the ionosphere
- C. Their frequency is changed by the ionosphere to be below the maximum usable frequency
- D. They are reflected back to their source

ANSWER A: The critical frequency rises during local daylight hours, and falls in the nighttime. If you transmit well *above the critical frequency, your radio waves* penetrate the ionosphere and *don't refract back as a skywave.*

T3A06 What type of solar radiation is most responsible for ionization in the outer atmosphere?

A. Thermal
B. Non-ionized particle

C. Ultraviolet
D. Microwave

ANSWER C: It's the *ultraviolet* component of the sun's radiation that *creates* our *ionosphere*. More ultraviolet radiation on any one day will lead us to either improved or disturbed radio conditions. ➡ **www.hfradio.com**

T3B07 How does the number of sunspots relate to the amount of ionization in the ionosphere?

A. The more sunspots there are, the greater the ionization
B. The more sunspots there are, the less the ionization
C. Unless there are sunspots, the ionization is zero
D. Sunspots do not affect the ionosphere

ANSWER A: *The higher the solar activity, the greater the ionization.* Listen to WWV, 10 or 15 MHz, at 18 minutes past every hour. It broadcasts reports on the amount of solar activity, and you can many times predict whether 10 meters is going to be hot, or not, the next day. ➡ **www.radio-ware.com**

T3B08 How long is an average sunspot cycle?

A. 2 years
B. 5 years

C. 11 years
D. 17 years

ANSWER C: Our sun exhibits periods of *high solar activity, peaking every 11 years.* During the peak of the sunspot cycles, you will be able to reach out with your 6-meter station over thousands of miles. The next sunspot peak will occur in 2012. But if you learn the code at 5-wpm and get up to General class, you can operate all over the world OFF PEAK quite nicely by choosing the lower bands. There is always worldwide propagation on the high-frequency band as soon as you get your 5-wpm Morse code credit.

T3B11 What is the condition of the ionosphere above a particular area of the Earth just before local sunrise?

A. Atmospheric attenuation is at a maximum
B. The D region is above the E region
C. The E region is above the F region
D. Ionization is at a minimum

ANSWER D: The amount of *ionization* left in the ionosphere *is at a minimum just before sunrise* when the outside temperature is at its minimum.

How do I know what band will work?
Beacon stations tell you propagation conditions.

T9B01 What is an amateur station called that transmits communications for the purpose of observation of propagation and reception?

A. A beacon

B. A repeater

C. An auxiliary station

D. A radio control station

ANSWER A: You can *tune in radio beacons* on 14.100, 18.110, 21.150, 24.930, and 28.200 MHz. They use CW to send their call signs over and over again *for propagation phenomena information.* [97.3a9] ➡ **www.radioinc.com**

T9B02 Which of the following is true of amateur radio beacon stations?

A. Automatic control is allowed in certain band segments

B. One-way transmissions are permitted

C. Maximum output power is 100 watts

D. All of these choices are correct

ANSWER D: *Beacon stations* are a great way to *judge propagation conditions.* Beacon transmitters *operate under automatic control* in certain band segments, and are considered one-way transmissions. They *are limited to a maximum power of 100 watts output.* [97.203c, d, g]

Radio Beacon Stations								
Slot	Country	Call	14.100	18.110	21.150	24.930	28.200	Operator
1	United Nations	4U1UN	00:00	00:10	00:20	00:30	00:40	UNRC
2	Canada	VE8AT	00:10	00:20	00:30	00:40	00:50	RAC
3	USA	W6WX	00:20	00:30	00:40	00:50	01:00	NCDXF
4	Hawaii	KH6WO	00:30	00:40	00:50	01:00	01:10	UHRO
5	New Zealand	ZL	00:40	00:50	01:00	01:10	01:20	NZART
6	Australia	VK8	00:50	01:00	01:10	01:20	01:30	W1A
7	Japan	JA21CY	01:00	01:10	01:20	01:30	01:40	JARL
8	China	BY	01:10	01:20	01:30	01:40	01:50	CRSA
9	Russia	UA	01:20	01:30	01:40	01:50	02:00	TBO
10	Sri Lanka	4S7B	01:30	01:40	01:50	02:00	02:10	RSSL
11	South Africa	ZS6DN	01:40	01:50	02:00	02:10	02:20	ZS6DN
12	Kenya	5Z4B	01:50	02:00	02:10	02:20	02:30	RSK
13	Israel	4X6TU	02:00	02:10	02:20	02:30	02:40	U of Tel Aviv
14	Finland	OH2B	02:10	02:20	02:30	02:40	02:50	U oh Helsinki
15	Madeira	CS3B	02:20	02:30	02:40	02:50	00:00	ARRM
16	Argentina	LU4AA	02:30	02:40	02:50	00:00	00:10	RCA
17	Peru	OA4B	02:40	02:50	00:00	00:10	00:20	RCP
18	Venezuela	YV5B	02:50	00:00	00:10	00:20	00:30	RCV

The 10-second, phase-3, message format is: "W6WX dah-dah-dah-dah" — each "dah" lasts a little more than one second. W6WX is transmitted at 100 watts, then each "dah" is attenuated in order, beginning at 100 watts, then 10 watts, then 1 watt, and finally 0.1 watt. *Courtesy CQ Magazine*

➡ **www.ng3k.com/ohpadx/**

Where does all the power go?

A little understanding of basic electronics to get you on the airwaves with a great signal.

T8F01 Which instrument would you use to measure electric potential or electromotive force?
    A. An ammeter
    B. A voltmeter
    C. A wavemeter
    D. An ohmmeter
ANSWER B: Another name for *electromotive force is voltage.* We *measure voltage with a voltmeter.*

Parameter	Basic Unit	Measuring Instrument
Voltage	Volts	Voltmeter
Current	Amperes	Ammeter
Resistance	Ohms	Ohmmeter
Power	Watts	Wattmeter

T8F02 How is a voltmeter usually connected to a circuit under test?
    A. In series with the circuit
    B. In parallel with the circuit
    C. In quadrature with the circuit
    D. In phase with the circuit
ANSWER B: We *test for voltage* by hooking our meter across the voltage source without undoing any wires – *a parallel connection.* "VIP"–Voltage In Parallel.

T8F16 Where would you connect a voltmeter to a 12-volt transceiver if you think the supply voltage may be low when you transmit?
    A. At the battery terminals
    B. At the fuse block
    C. Midway along the 12-volt power supply wire
    D. At the 12-volt plug on the chassis of the equipment
ANSWER D: To make sure your brand new transceiver has enough voltage going into the equipment, *check for 12 volts right at the plug* where the red and black wire disappears into the back of the radio. If you check for 12 volts anywhere else, you are not really seeing exactly how much DC is actually making it up the line to your transmitter. Also, measure for 12 volts when you are transmitting into a dummy load.

T8F20 In Figure T8-9, what circuit quantity is meter A reading?
    A. Battery current
    B. Battery voltage
    C. Battery power
    D. Battery current polarity
ANSWER B: Meter A is across the battery, so it is measuring battery voltage.

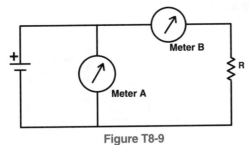

Figure T8-9

T7A06 How much voltage does an automobile battery usually supply?
A. About 12 volts
C. About 120 volts
B. About 30 volts
D. About 240 volts

ANSWER A: Most *automobile batteries* supply direct current at an electromotive force of *12 volts.*

T8B10 What device converts 120 VAC to 12 VDC?
A. A catalytic converter
C. A power supply
B. A low-pass filter
D. An RS-232 interface

ANSWER C: Your handheld transceiver may be charged at home from *a power supply that converts household current to 12 VDC.* Use only the charger supplied with the handheld. ➡**www.mfjenterprises.com**

T8A02 If your mobile transceiver works in your car but not in your home, what should you check first?
A. The power supply
C. The microphone
B. The speaker
D. The SWR meter

ANSWER A: Most ham radio sets run off of 12 volts for mobile applications. If you plan to run your equipment in your home, you will need a *power supply* that converts 110 VAC household power to 12 VDC.

T8B09 What might you use instead of a power supply for home operation of a mobile radio?
A. A filter capacitor
C. A 12-volt battery
B. An alternator
D. A linear amplifier

ANSWER C: An *alternate to the power supply* would be a sealed *12-volt battery.* I suggest a sealed battery to minimize the chance of spilling battery acid on that brand new Persian rug, or boiling off dangerous gases within the ham shack. ➡ **www.ham-central.com**

T0A13 When fuses are installed in 12-volt DC wiring, where should they be placed?
A. At the radio
B. Midway between voltage source and radio
C. Fuses aren't required for 12-volt DC equipment
D. At the voltage source

ANSWER D: When wiring your new ham set in your car or pickup, make sure you have the red lead positive fuse *as close to the battery terminal voltage source as possible.* This will protect the rest of your wire run against an accidental short circuit in case it should make contact with the metal fire wall. If the fuse is right next to the equipment, rather than at the battery, you don't protect that long red lead from a short.

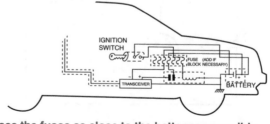

Place the fuses as close to the battery as possible

T8B08 A mobile radio may be operated at home with the addition of which piece of equipment?

A. An alternator
B. A power supply
C. A linear amplifier
D. A rhombic antenna

ANSWER B: A Technician class operator may wish to purchase a higher power *mobile radio* and run it *at home* before it ultimately gets installed in the car. This will work well with the necessary power supply that converts 110 volt AC household power to 12 volts DC. You *will need the power supply* for home operation.

T8F17 If your mobile transceiver does not power up, what might you check first?

A. The antenna feedpoint
B. The coaxial cable connector
C. The microphone jack
D. The 12-volt fuses

ANSWER D: If your mobile radio just won't power up, I would take a *look at both 12-volt fuses* and make sure they are conducting. Sometimes you need to do this with an ohmmeter because I have seen many blown fuses that actually look good.

T0A10 What type of electrical circuit is created when a fuse blows?

A. A closed circuit
B. A bypass circuit
C. An open circuit
D. A short circuit

ANSWER C: The purpose of a fuse in a radio circuit is to act as a weak link to protect that circuit from too much current. *When that* circuit becomes overloaded with excessive current, the *fuse element* gets warm, then gets hot, and then *melts*, creating *an open circuit.* With an open circuit, no further current will flow, thus protecting your equipment from high current.

T0A12 What safety equipment item should you always add to home built equipment that is powered from 110 volt AC lines?

A. A fuse or circuit breaker in series with the equipment
B. A fuse or circuit breaker in parallel with the equipment
C. Install Zener diodes across AC inputs
D. House the equipment in a plastic or other non-conductive enclosure

ANSWER A: Be sure to *put a fuse or circuit breaker in any homebrew ham radio equipment* that plugs into house power or 12 volts DC. The fuse always goes *in series* with the equipment power leads.

T0A03 What could happen to your transceiver if you replace its blown 5 amp AC line fuse with a 30 amp fuse?

A. The 30-amp fuse would better protect your transceiver from using too much current
B. The transceiver would run cooler
C. The transceiver could use more current than 5 amps and a fire could occur
D. The transceiver would not be able to produce as much RF output

ANSWER C: A fuse is installed in both the red and black power leads of your transceivers to protect the wires from overload. Pulling too much current through the wires could cause them to heat up, and for the insulation to give off toxic smoke and eventually burst into flames. If you *substitute a 30-amp fuse for a 5-amp fuse* on a small radio that is malfunctioning and blowing the 5-amp fuse, the 30-amp fuse might carry the load, *causing the wires to heat up and, POOF, you smoke your installation.* ➡ **www.iriamateurelectronics.com**

T0A01 What is the minimum voltage that is usually dangerous to humans?
A. 30 volts
B. 100 volts
C. 1000 volts
D. 2000 volts

ANSWER A: *30 volts is dangerous!* Even a couple of golf cart batteries could kill you if you aren't careful! This is why you must be especially careful not to touch any bare wires or connections when leaning across a bank of batteries because that would allow current to flow through your body accidentally.

T8F08 For which of the following measurements would you normally use a multimeter?
A. SWR and power
B. Resistance, capacitance and inductance
C. Resistance and reactance
D. Voltage, current and resistance

ANSWER D: Every amateur operator should own a *multimeter.* The multiple function meter *can measure voltage, current, and resistance,* and check continuity. Even an inexpensive multimeter is better than no meter when you are trying to check out a circuit in the field. You can buy an excellent multimeter for less than $25.00.

T8F07 What might damage a multimeter that uses a moving-needle meter?
A. Measuring a voltage much smaller than the maximum for the chosen scale
B. Leaving the meter in the milliamps position overnight
C. Measuring voltage when using the ohms setting
D. Not allowing it to warm up properly

ANSWER C: You're likely to *damage your* brand new needle *multimeter by measuring voltage* if you accidentally leave it *in the ohms reading setting.*

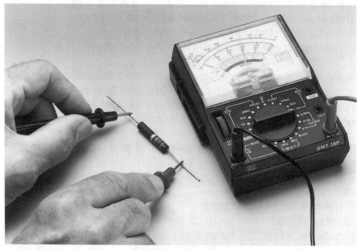

D'Arsonval-type Meter

T8F03 What happens inside a voltmeter when you switch it from a lower to a higher voltage range?
A. Resistance is added in series with the meter
B. Resistance is added in parallel with the meter
C. Resistance is reduced in series with the meter
D. Resistance is reduced in parallel with the meter

ANSWER A: As *more resistance is added in series with a voltmeter,* the meter can indicate a higher voltage range without exceeding the meter's maximum rating. This is why you must look carefully on a multimeter to see to which voltage range the range switch is set. Many digital voltmeters have an auto-ranging circuit so you don't have to set the range.

T8A09 Why is it important to provide adequate DC source supply filtering for a mobile transmitter or transceiver?
- A. To reduce AC hum and carrier current device signals
- B. To provide an emergency power source
- C. To reduce stray noise and RF pick-up
- D. To allow the use of smaller power conductors

ANSWER C: If you plan to run your mobile radio in the house, you will need a professional power supply with plenty of filtering. *Filtering will reduce stray noise coming in from the AC line cord* and also reduce any noise generated within the power supply itself. ➡ **www.astroncorp.com**

T7A01 What is the name for the flow of electrons in an electric circuit?
- A. Voltage
- B. Resistance
- C. Capacitance
- D. Current

ANSWER D: Think of the *flow of electrons* as the flow of water in a stream. If you get out there in midstream, you will feel the *current.*

T7A05 What is the basic unit of electric current?
- A. The volt
- B. The watt
- C. The ampere
- D. The ohm

ANSWER C: The flow of electrons in a conductor is called current. *Current is measured in amperes.* Amperes is often referred to as *"amps."*

Parameter	Basic Unit	Measuring Instrument
Voltage	Volts	Voltmeter
Current	Amperes	Ammeter
Resistance	Ohms	Ohmmeter
Power	Watts	Wattmeter

T7A02 What is the name of a current that flows only in one direction?
- A. An alternating current
- B. A direct current
- C. A normal current
- D. A smooth current

ANSWER B: Batteries generate direct current. Even though a current may vary in value, *if it always flows in the same direction, it is a direct current (DC).*

T8F05 Which instrument would you use to measure electric current?
- A. An ohmmeter
- B. A wavemeter
- C. A voltmeter
- D. An ammeter

ANSWER D: *Current is* measured in *amperes,* the unit of current. We use an *ammeter* to measure electrical current.

T8F04 How is an ammeter usually connected to a circuit under test?
- A. In series with the circuit
- B. In parallel with the circuit
- C. In quadrature with the circuit
- D. In phase with the circuit

ANSWER A: A ammeter measures current. To measure current, turn off the power, disconnect one lead of the load from its source voltage and *insert your ammeter in series* with that lead. If you are measuring DC current, you will need to connect the meter with the correct polarity, so the meter reads up scale when power is turned on. *AMPS – AMPs in Series* ➡ **www.eastcoastradio.com**

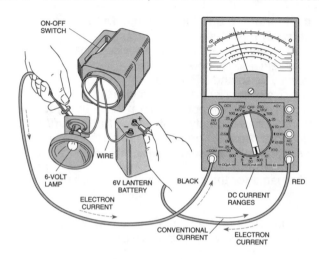

Using a Multimeter to Measure a Series Circuit
Source: *Basic Electronics* © 1994, 2000, Master Publishing, Inc., Lincolnwood, Illinois

T8F19 In Figure T8-9, what circuit quantity would meter B indicate?
A. The voltage across the resistor
B. The power consumed by the resistor
C. The power factor of the resistor
D. The current flowing through the resistor

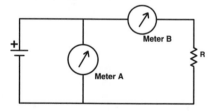

ANSWER D: *Meter B* is in series with the load, R, so it *is measuring current flowing through the resistor.*

Figure T8-9

T0A02 Which electrical circuit draws high current?
A. An open circuit   C. A closed circuit
B. A dead circuit   D. A short circuit

ANSWER D: Anytime you have a malfunction in a piece of equipment, and you hear a pop or smell something burning, chances are *a short circuit* has caused the malfunction. Some electrical connection has provided a much lower resistance path for current than is normal in the circuit.

T7A17 If an ammeter marked in amperes is used to measure a 3000-milliampere current, what reading would it show?
A. 0.003 amperes   C. 3 amperes
B. 0.3 amperes   D. 3,000,000 amperes

ANSWER C: One milliampere equals one one-thousandth of an ampere (1 x 10^{-3}); therefore, one ampere equal 1000 milliamperes. Divide milliamperes by 1000 to convert to amperes. Or *move the decimal point 3 places to the left.* Calculator keystrokes are: CLEAR 3000 ÷ 1000 = and *the answer is 3.*

T0A04 How much electrical current flowing through the human body will probably be fatal?
- A. As little as 1/10 of an ampere
- B. Approximately 10 amperes
- C. More than 20 amperes
- D. Current through the human body is never fatal

ANSWER A: *One-tenth of an ampere (amp)* is the same as 100 milliamperes. One-tenth of an amp is as little as the small current drawn by a tiny dial light. It *is enough to zap you for good if it travels through your body and heart* in the right path. Never, never, never work without shoes on a concrete garage floor. Never let any metal electrical appliance get near a bathtub.

T0A05 Which body organ can be fatally affected by a very small amount of electrical current?
- A. The heart
- B. The brain
- C. The liver
- D. The lungs

ANSWER A: *Your heart* is a pump that is powered by your own electricity. If you disturb the natural flow of electricity driving the heart, it could be fatal. This is why you never work on electrical equipment in the garage with a cement floor when you are not wearing shoes. Electricity could flow through your hands, through your heart, and out of your feet to ground. Not good.

T7A07 What limits the current that flows through a circuit for a particular applied DC voltage?
- A. Reliance
- B. Reactance
- C. Saturation
- D. Resistance

ANSWER D: In a river, there is a *limit* as to how much current will flow downstream. Logs and rocks offer *"resistance"* to the river current. Similarly, certain materials or small diameter wires in an electric circuit offer resistance to electric current.

T7A08 What is the basic unit of resistance?
- A. The volt
- B. The watt
- C. The ampere
- D. The ohm

ANSWER D: *The basic unit of resistance is the "ohm."* If one volt DC is applied to a circuit and one ampere of current results, the circuit has one ohm of resistance.

T8F06 What test instrument would be useful to measure DC resistance?
- A. An oscilloscope
- B. A spectrum analyzer
- C. A noise bridge
- D. An ohmmeter

ANSWER D: We *use an ohmmeter to check for* ohms of *resistance.*

T7A12 What formula shows how voltage, current and resistance relate to each other in an electric circuit?
- A. Ohm's Law
- B. Kirchhoff's Law
- C. Ampere's Law
- D. Tesla's Law

ANSWER A: *The relationship between voltage, current, and resistance* in an electric circuit *is called "Ohm's Law."*

T7A13 If a current of 2 amperes flows through a 50-ohm resistor, what is the voltage across the resistor?

    A. 25 volts   C. 100 volts

    B. 52 volts   D. 200 volts

ANSWER C: The relationship between voltage (E), current (I), and resistance (R) in an electronic circuit is described by Ohm's Law, which states: *the applied electromotive force, E, in volts, is equal to the circuit current, I, in amperes, times the circuit resistance, R, in ohms.* It is expressed by the equation $E = I \times R$.

    A simple way to remember how to calculate Ohm's Law is to use the magic circle. The magic circle shows E, I, and R in position so that it provides the correct equation for your problem. *In this question, they ask you to solve for E (voltage), which is equal to I (current) times R (resistance).*

    To use the magic circle, cover the letter that you are solving for with your finger. Now, plug in the other two values that they give you in the examination question. Solve the problem by performing the mathematical operation indicated by the position of the remaining letters, as shown here:

      $E = I \times R$ $I = E \div R$ $R = E \div I$

   Finding Voltage   Finding Current   Finding Resistance

Since we are looking for E, the applied voltage, cover E with your finger, and you now have *I (2 amps) times R (50 ohms)*. Multiply these two to obtain your *answer of 100 volts*. The calculator keystrokes are: CLEAR 2 x 50 =.

    T7A14 If a 100-ohm resistor is connected to 200 volts, what is the current through the resistor?

    A. 1 ampere   C. 300 amperes

    B. 2 amperes   D. 20,000 amperes

ANSWER B: In this problem, you are looking for I. Using the Ohm's Law magic circle in question T7A13, *cover I with your finger. You now have E over R, or 200 over 100.* Do the division, and you will end up with 2 amps. See how simple this is! Calculator *keystrokes are: CLEAR 200 ÷ 100 = and your answer is 2.*

T7A15 If a current of 3 amperes flows through a resistor connected to 90 volts, what is the resistance?

A. 3 ohms   C. 93 ohms
B. 30 ohms   D. 270 ohms

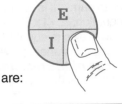

ANSWER B: Again, use the magic circle in question T7A13. In this problem, you want to find R. *Covering R with your finger leaves E over I. 90 divided by 3 gives 30* ohms. See how simple it is to use Ohm's Law. Calculator keystrokes are: CLEAR 90 ÷ 3 =. Your answer is 30.

T7A03 What is the name of a current that flows back and forth, first in one direction, then in the opposite direction?

A. An alternating current   C. A rough current
B. A direct current   D. A steady state current

ANSWER A: If you have been shocked by household current, chances are you felt the "buzz." Be careful, it is very dangerous! Direct current (DC) flows in one direction; *alternating current (AC) changes direction.* Initially it flows in one direction, then it reverses and flows in the opposite direction.

T7A04 What is the basic unit of electrical power?

A. The ohm   C. The volt
B. The watt   D. The ampere

ANSWER B: Power is energy, and you all have one of those energy meters on the side of your house. You know, that's the meter that keeps turning after you've turned just about everything off! *Volts times amps equals watts.* There is a "magic circle" for power calculation that is similar to the one for Ohm's Law. Here it is:

POWER CIRCLE

Power Calculation

As shown, P = power in watts, E = voltage in volts, and I = current in amperes. Use it in the same way as you use the Ohm's Law magic circle; that is, cover the unknown quantity with your finger and perform the mathematical operation represented by the remaining quantities.

T8F21 In Figure T8-9, how would the power consumed by the resistor be calculated?

A. Multiply the value of the resistor times the square of the reading of meter B
B. Multiply the value of the resistor times the reading of meter B

C. Multiply the reading of meter A times the value of the resistor

D. Multiply the value of the resistor times the square root of the reading of meter B

ANSWER A: The relationship between voltage (E), current (I), and resistance (R) in an electronic circuit is described by Ohm's Law which states: The applied electromotive force, E, in volts, is equal to the circuit current, I, in amperes, times the circuit resistance, R, in ohms. It is expressed by the equation: $E = I \times R$. In THIS problem, power also is equal to current squared times resistance, so we *multiply the value of the resistor times the square of the current reading in meter B,* and this is the answer they are looking for. (Not the square root!)

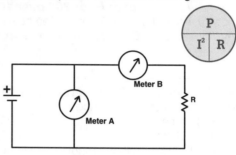

Figure T8-9

T7C01 Which of the following lists include three good electrical conductors?

A. Copper, gold, mica

B. Gold, silver, wood

C. Gold, silver, aluminum

D. Copper, aluminum, paper

ANSWER C: Most *wire is copper,* and this is a good conductor. Some *relays use gold-* or silver-plated contacts, and these are also good conductors. You can use *aluminum foil as a ground* plane; it also is a good conductor. Always read all answers completely – mica, wood and paper are insulators!

T7C02 What is one reason resistors are used in electronic circuits?

A. To block the flow of direct current while allowing alternating current to pass

B. To block the flow of alternating current while allowing direct current to pass

C. To increase the voltage of the circuit

D. To control the amount of current that flows for a particular applied voltage

ANSWER D: *Resistors* are found in electronic circuits to *control the amount of current that flows* for a particular applied voltage.

R

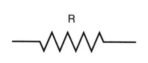

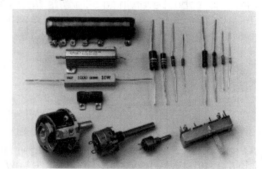

a. Symbol

b. Physical Part

Resistor

T7C11 Which symbol of Figure T7-1 represents a fixed resistor?

A. Symbol 1

B. Symbol 2

C. Symbol 3

D. Symbol 5

ANSWER C: If this were a stream of water, all those bends would present resistance to the current; likewise, a *resistor* presents resistance to an electric current. *Symbol 3.*

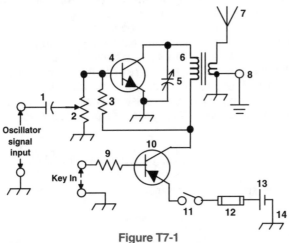

Figure T7-1

T7C03 If two resistors are connected in series, what is their total resistance?
- A. The difference between the individual resistor values
- B. Always less than the value of either resistor
- C. The product of the individual resistor values
- D. The sum of the individual resistor values

ANSWER D: *Resistors in series simply add up.* If you had a 5-ohm and 7-ohm resistor, in series, the total resistance would be 5 + 7 = 12 ohms. If you had a 3-ohm and 2-ohm resistor in series, your total resistance would be 5 ohms.

T7C12 In Figure T7-1, which symbol represents a variable resistor or potentiometer?
- A. Symbol 1
- B. Symbol 2
- C. Symbol 3
- D. Symbol 12

ANSWER B: A *variable resistor* is component *Symbol 2.* Notice the *wiper contact* on this adjustable resistor *indicated as an arrow* in the diagram.

T7C06 What does a capacitor do?
- A. It stores energy electrochemically and opposes a change in current
- B. It stores energy electrostatically and opposes a change in voltage
- C. It stores energy electromagnetically and opposes a change in current
- D. It stores energy electromechanically and opposes a change in voltage

ANSWER B: *Capacitors store their energy in an electrostatic field,* not a magnetic field, as in a coil.

T7A10 What is the basic unit of capacitance?
- A. The farad
- B. The ohm
- C. The volt
- D. The henry

ANSWER A: It is the *farad,* but because the farad is a fairly large unit, we measure *capacitance* in one millionths of a farad (microfarad) or one million millionths of a farad (picofarad).(See the scientific notation tables in the Appendix on page 216.)

➡**www.surplussales.com**

T7C04 What is one reason capacitors are used in electronic circuits?
 A. To block the flow of direct current while allowing alternating current to pass
 B. To block the flow of alternating current while allowing direct current to pass
 C. To change the time constant of the applied voltage
 D. To change alternating current to direct current

ANSWER A: Remember that noise eliminator filter you just bought? That filter contains a *capacitor* that freely *allows the alternating current to pass* to ground but *blocks the flow of direct current* so things don't short out. That simple filter to minimize alternator noise on your new automobile radio is a coil and a capacitor, which does the job nicely because the coil blocks AC and passes DC, and the *capacitor passes the AC to ground but blocks DC*.

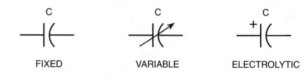

a. Symbols

b. Physical Parts
Capacitors

T7C15 Which symbol of Figure T7-1 represents a fixed-value capacitor?
 A. Symbol 1   C. Symbol 5
 B. Symbol 3   D. Symbol 13

ANSWER A: *Symbol 1 is a fixed-value capacitor.*

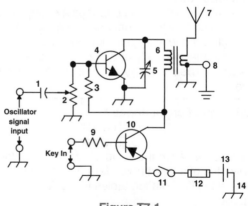

Figure T7-1

T7C05 If two equal-value capacitors are connected in parallel, what is their total capacitance?
   A. Twice the value of one capacitor
   B. Half the value of one capacitor
   C. The same as the value of either capacitor
   D. The value of one capacitor times the value of the other
ANSWER A: Treat capacitors just the opposite of how you treat resistors. *Capacitors in parallel add up to make larger value capacitors— Caps Add Parallel.*

T7A20 How many microfarads is 1,000,000 picofarads?
   A. 0.001 microfarads
   B. 1 microfarad
   C. 1000 microfarads
   D. 1,000,000,000 microfarads
ANSWER B: *A picofarad is one millionth (1×10^{-6}) of a microfarad* or one million millionth ($1 \times 10^{-6} \times 1 \times 10^{-6} = 1 \times 10^{-12}$) of a farad. Move the decimal point 6 places to the left to convert to microfarads or 12 places to the left to convert to farads. 1,000,000 picofarads = $1 \times 10^{6} \times 1 \times 10^{-12} = 1 \times 10^{-6}$ of a farad, *or 1 microfarad*, and 1 microfarad = 0.000001 farad.

T0A11 Why would it be unwise to touch an ungrounded terminal of a high voltage capacitor even if it's not in an energized circuit?
   A. You could damage the capacitor's dielectric material
   B. A residual charge on the capacitor could cause interference to others
   C. You could damage the capacitor by causing an electrostatic discharge
   D. You could receive a shock from a residual stored charge
ANSWER D: *High-voltage capacitors will* many times *store a charge for several minutes* after the equipment has been turned off. Keep your fingers well away from any power supply until you have metered it for lethal voltages still present, *even though it has been unplugged* from the wall for many hours.

T7C07 Which of the following best describes a variable capacitor?
   A. A set of fixed capacitors whose connections can be varied
   B. Two sets of insulating plates separated by a conductor, which can be varied in distance from each other
   C. A set of capacitors connected in a series-parallel circuit
   D. Two sets of rotating conducting plates separated by an insulator, which can be varied in surface area exposed to each other

ANSWER D: *A variable capacitor has two or more sets of conducting plates, separated by an insulator,* which can be varied in surface area exposed to each other. Older radios used big variable capacitors with many plates, with air as the separator. Modern digital signal processing is getting away from variable capacitors.

Variable Capacitor

T7C08 What does an inductor do?
    A. It stores energy electrostatically and opposes a change in voltage
    B. It stores energy electrochemically and opposes a change in current
    C. It stores energy electromagnetically and opposes a change in current
    D. It stores energy electromechanically and opposes a change in voltage
ANSWER C: Remember that coils *(inductors)* develop a magnetic field which is indicated by a magnetic compass held near the energized coil. *Energy is stored in the magnetic field.*

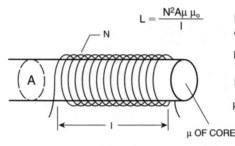

$$L = \frac{N^2 A \mu \, \mu_o}{l}$$

L = Inductance in henries
A = Cross-sectional area of coil core (m²)
N = Number of turns on coil
l = Length of coil (m)
μ = Permeabiltiy of core material (1000 for iron)
μ_o = Permeabiltiy of air (1.26 × 10⁻⁸ henries/m)

μ OF CORE

Inductance Equation

T7A09 What is the basic unit of inductance?
    A. The coulomb   C. The henry
    B. The farad   D. The ohm
ANSWER C: It is *the henry,* but because the henry is a fairly large unit, we measure inductance in one thousandths of a henry (millihenry) and one millionths of a henry (microhenry).

T7C17 In Figure T7-1, which symbol represents a fixed-value iron-core inductor?
    A. Symbol 6   C. Symbol 11
    B. Symbol 9   D. Symbol 12
ANSWER A: The *two lines next to the coil in Symbol 6 indicate an iron core.* Don't confuse the coil symbol with a resistor symbol.

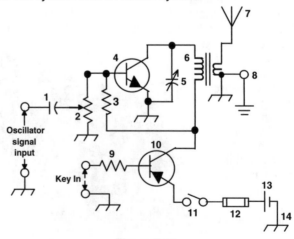

Figure T7-1

Basic Electronics

T7C09 What component controls current to flow in one direction only?
A. A fixed resistor
B. A signal generator
C. A diode
D. A fuse

ANSWER C: A *diode is like a one-way check valve.* In an electronic circuit, the diode only allows alternating current to flow in one direction. A popular place to find diodes is in power supplies that change AC to DC. But be careful – anytime you are inside a power supply, keep in mind there may be high voltages hanging around on those big capacitors. The capacitors help smooth out the pulsating DC that the diode creates from AC as it allows current to flow in only one direction.

T7A11 Which of the following circuits changes an alternating current signal into a varying direct current signal?
A. Transformer
B. Rectifier
C. Amplifier
D. Director

ANSWER B: It is the job of *the rectifier diode* to pass alternating current in only one direction, but block it in the other direction. This *changes the AC current into a pulsing direct current* that is then filtered by capacitors. If the rectifier goes bad, this gives you hum on both transmit as well as receive. Also, if the power supply capacitors go bad, this, too, will lead to hum.

T7C13 In Figure T7-1, which symbol represents a single-cell battery?
A. Symbol 1
B. Symbol 6
C. Symbol 12
D. Symbol 13

ANSWER D: *Battery plates never touch. Symbol 13* looks almost like a capacitor symbol. Ordinarily, the positive side (the long line) is indicated by a plus sign, and the negative side (the short line) is indicated by a minus sign.

T7B10 Which component can amplify a small signal using low voltages?
A. A PNP transistor
B. A variable resistor
C. An electrolytic capacitor
D. A multiple-cell battery

ANSWER A: A *transistor can amplify a small signal using a low-voltage* power supply. (A vacuum tube amplifier requires a high-voltage power supply.)

T7C14 In Figure T7-1, which symbol represents an NPN transistor?
A. Symbol 2
B. Symbol 4
C. Symbol 10
D. Symbol 12

ANSWER B: An easy way to identify an *NPN transistor* is to first identify base (B), collector (C), and emitter (E). Then look and see which way the arrow is pointing. If the arrow is *NOT POINTING IN*, as in *symbol 4*, then it's an NPN transistor.

T7C16 In Figure T7-1, which symbol represents an antenna?
A. Symbol 5
B. Symbol 7
C. Symbol 8
D. Symbol 14

ANSWER B: *Symbol 7 looks like an antenna*, doesn't it? (See the Schematic Symbols table in the Appendix on page 216.) ➡ **www.gapantenna.com**

T7C19 In Figure T7-2, which symbol represents a double-pole, single-throw switch?

A. Symbol 1   C. Symbol 3
B. Symbol 2   D. Symbol 4

ANSWER C: In *Symbol 3,* we see a *double-pole, single-throw switch* with its contacts shown in the open position. The *dashed line* between the two throw arms *indicates that the throw arms are linked* together so they will move in unison.

Figure T7-2

T7C18 In Figure T7-2, which symbol represents a single-pole, double-throw switch?

A. Symbol 1   C. Symbol 3
B. Symbol 2   D. Symbol 4

ANSWER D: If you had a double antenna system, such as a 10-meter dipole, and a 10-meter vertical, you would use a *single pole, double-throw switch* to allow a single radio to work from either antenna of your double antenna system. Look at *Symbol 4* and notice a single "throw" arm and two contacts, one at a time.

T7B11 Which component can amplify a small signal but normally uses high voltages?

A. A transistor   C. A vacuum tube
B. An electrolytic capacitor   D. A multiple-cell battery

ANSWER C: The *vacuum tube* does a nice job of amplifying small signals, but tubes require relatively *high voltage* for their operation. (A transistor can amplify a small signal using a low-voltage power supply.)

T7C10 What is one advantage of using ICs (integrated circuits) instead of vacuum tubes in a circuit?

A. ICs usually combine several functions into one package
B. ICs can handle high-power input signals
C. ICs can handle much higher voltages
D. ICs can handle much higher temperatures

ANSWER A: The IC also draws little current and does not require high voltages. It also runs cool. *Some ICs have more than 1 million transistor functions on the inside!* ➡ **www.alltronics.com**

Cut-away rendering of an integrated circuit.
Photo courtesy of Texas Instruments.

How does this thing work, anyway?

A look "under the hood" of your ham radio shows how your voice is transformed into a radio signal.

T2B08 What term describes the process of combining an information signal with a radio signal?

A. Superposition

B. Modulation

C. Demodulation

D. Phase-inversion

ANSWER B: *Combining an information signal with the carrier of a radio signal is called modulation.* Think of modulation as information. An RF modulated carrier "carries" information.

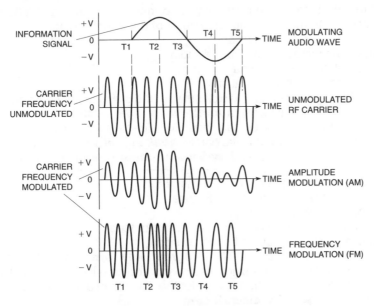

Modulation of RF Carrier

T2B10 What does the term "phone transmissions" usually mean?

A. The use of telephones to set up an amateur contact

B. A phone patch between amateur radio and the telephone system

C. AM, FM or SSB voice transmissions by radiotelephony

D. Placing the telephone handset near a transceiver's microphone and speaker to relay a telephone call

ANSWER C: Don't get "phone transmissions" mixed up with "phone patch." *Phone transmissions refer to voice transmissions by radiotelephony* where you actually speak over a microphone to communicate with another ham radio operator. The term "phone patch" refers to a hook-up into your regular "Ma Bell" land-line phone system, as indicated in incorrect answers A, B and D. Go for answer C, "transmissions by radiotelephony." ➡ **www.communication-concepts.com**

T8A05 What would you connect to a transceiver for voice operation?

A. A splatter filter

B. A terminal-voice controller

C. A receiver audio filter

D. A microphone

ANSWER D: To transmit your *voice*, you need a *microphone.* ➡**www.heilsound.com**

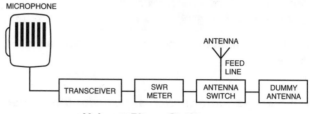

Voice or Phone Station

T8B01 Can a transceiver designed for FM phone operation also be used for single sideband in the weak-signal portion of the 2-meter band?
A. Yes, with simple modification
B. Only if the radio is a "multimode" radio
C. Only with the right antenna
D. Only with the right polarization

ANSWER B: When you are ready to pick out your radio system for home on the Technician class bands, look into a *multi-mode radio system.* This will allow you to *work not only FM* repeater, data, and FM voice to other common FM mobile and handheld radios, *but also* take part in *weak signal* activity on the 2-meter band using upper sideband or CW. ➡**www.amateuraccessories.com**

T8B02 How is a CW signal usually transmitted?
A. By frequency-shift keying an RF signal
B. By on/off keying an RF signal
C. By audio-frequency-shift keying an oscillator tone
D. By on/off keying an audio-frequency signal

ANSWER B: *CW is Morse code. The telegraph key turns on and off the radiofrequency signal.* This signal has no modulation – it's just interrupted carrier continuous wave (CW). The carrier is on for the duration of a "dit" or "dah" and is off the rest of the time. ➡**www.elecraft.com**

T8B03 What purpose does block 1 serve in the simple CW transmitter pictured in Figure T8-1?
A. It detects the CW signal
B. It controls the transmitter frequency
C. It controls the transmitter output power
D. It filters out spurious emissions from the transmitter

ANSWER B: *Block 1* in Figure T8-1 *is the oscillator circuit,* and the oscillator *controls the transmitter frequency.* ➡**www.ohr.com**

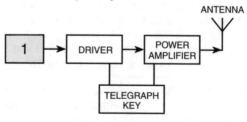

Figure T8-1

T8B04 What circuit is pictured in Figure T8-1 if block 1 is a variable-frequency oscillator?

    A. A packet-radio transmitter
    B. A crystal-controlled transmitter
    C. A single-sideband transmitter
    D. A VFO-controlled transmitter

ANSWER D: *A variable frequency oscillator is abbreviated "VFO."*

T8B05 What circuit is shown in Figure T8-2 if block 1 represents a reactance modulator?

    A. A single-sideband transmitter
    B. A double-sideband AM transmitter
    C. An FM transmitter
    D. A product transmitter

ANSWER C: Whenever you see the wording *"reactance modulator"* remember that this is part of a frequency modulation *(FM) transmitter.* ➡ **www.kenwood.net**

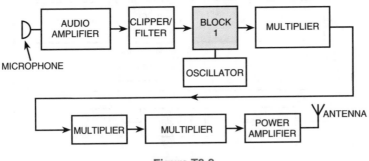

Figure T8-2

T2B18 What emissions do a transmitter using a reactance modulator produce?

    A. CW   C. Single-sideband, suppressed-carrier phone
    B. Test   D. Phase-modulated phone

ANSWER D: Some VHF transceivers use *phase modulation from a reactance modulator,* as opposed to frequency modulation. They sound a little bit different on the air. ➡ **www.yaesu.com/amateur**

T7B01 What type of electric circuit uses signals that can vary continuously over a certain range of voltage or current values?

    A. An analog circuit   C. A continuous circuit
    B. A digital circuit   D. A pulsed modulator circuit

ANSWER A: Think of *an analog circuit* like a roller coaster with smooth bends and dips. It *varies continuously* as you zip up and down and around the coaster tracks.

T7B03 Which of the following is an example of an analog communications method?

    A. Morse code (CW)   C. Frequency-modulated (FM) voice
    B. Packet Radio   D. PSK31

ANSWER C: *FM voice is an analog* transmission that varies continuously as you speak into the microphone. Things like Morse code, packet radio, and PSK 31 are all digital modes. ➡ **www.icomamerica.com**

T8B06 How would the output of the FM transmitter shown in Figure T8-2 be affected if the audio amplifier failed to operate (assuming block 1 is a reactance modulator)?
   A. There would be no output from the transmitter
   B. The output would be 6-dB below the normal output power
   C. The transmitted audio would be distorted but understandable
   D. The output would be an unmodulated carrier

ANSWER D: In this FM transmitter, you accidentally miswired your new microphone, and *blew the reactance modulator* integrated circuit. The transmitter would still put out power, but *the output would be an unmodulated carrier* because your microphone output is not being processed by the reactance modulator that you accidentally toasted. Since many 2-meter/440-MHz transceivers have voltage coming out of the microphone socket to drive keypad functions on the mike, make absolutely sure you don't cross the wires because the reactance modulator is usually the first thing to go.

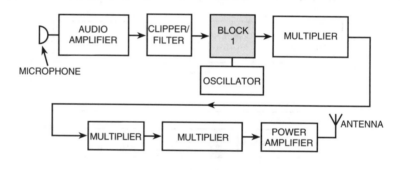

Figure T8-2

T8B12 What is the result of over deviation in an FM transmitter?
   A. Increased transmitter power   C. Increased transmitter range
   B. Out-of-channel emissions   D. Poor carrier suppression

ANSWER B: If you overdrive the audio stage of an FM transceiver, you will create *over-deviation* that *creates interference to adjacent channel users.*

T8B13 What can you do if you are told your FM hand-held or mobile transceiver is over deviating?
   A. Talk louder into the microphone
   B. Let the transceiver cool off
   C. Change to a higher power level
   D. Talk farther away from the microphone

ANSWER D: If your set is *over-deviating*, it means that too much modulation is driving your signal beyond its normal bandwidth. If you *talk farther away from the microphone,* you will minimize or even eliminate the over-deviation.

2-meter hand-held VHF ham transceiver

T8B14 In Figure T8-3, if block 1 is a transceiver and block 3 is a dummy antenna, what is block 2?

A. A terminal-node switch
B. An antenna switch
C. A telegraph key switch
D. A high-pass filter

ANSWER B: In Figure T8-3, *block 2 is an antenna switch* used to switch between the antenna on top of block 2 or to the dummy load, which is block 3.
➡ www.therfc.com

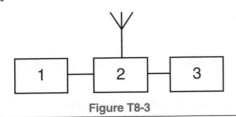

Figure T8-3

T8B15 In Figure T8-3, if block 1 is a transceiver and block 2 is an antenna switch, what is block 3?

A. A terminal-node switch
B. An SWR meter
C. A telegraph key switch
D. A dummy antenna

ANSWER D: Occasionally you may need to test your transmitter on full-power output, but you don't want to radiate a signal out on the airwaves from your antenna. You would switch the antenna selector over to the *dummy antenna*, and your transmitter output now goes into a noninductive resistor. The power output won't travel more than a couple hundred feet from your ham shack because it is absorbed by the dummy load.

T8B16 In Figure T8-4, if block 1 is a transceiver and block 2 is an SWR meter, what is block 3?

A. An antenna switch
B. An antenna tuner
C. A key-click filter
D. A terminal-node controller

ANSWER B: There is *only one antenna system* in Figure T8-4, therefore *block 3 is an antenna tuner.* ➡ www.sgcworld.com

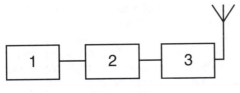

Figure T8-4

T8B17 In Figure T8-4, if block 1 is a transceiver and block 3 is an antenna tuner, what is block 2?

A. A terminal-node switch
B. A dipole antenna
C. An SWR meter
D. A high-pass filter

ANSWER C: When we incorporate a manual or automatic antenna tuner in series with the antenna connection, there is always a standing wave ratio meter in between the transceiver, block 1, and the automatic antenna tuner, block 3. The *SWR meter, block 2,* tells us that block 3 equipment is properly tuning the antenna system.

T8B18 In Figure T8-4, if block 2 is an SWR meter and block 3 is an antenna tuner, what is block 1?

A. A terminal-node switch   C. A telegraph key switch
B. A power supply   D. A transceiver

ANSWER D: Here we see a typical Amateur Radio installation. *Block 1 is the necessary transceiver* to drive block 2, the SWR meter, and block 3, the antenna tuner. ➡**www.icomamerica.com**

T2B19 What other emission does phase modulation most resemble?

A. Amplitude modulation   C. Frequency modulation
B. Pulse modulation   D. Single-sideband modulation

ANSWER C: *Frequency modulation* and *phase modulation* sound almost the same on the air, unless you listen very carefully.

T8C01 What type of circuit does Figure T8-5 represent if block 1 is a product detector?

A. A simple phase modulation receiver
B. A simple FM receiver
C. A simple CW and SSB receiver
D. A double-conversion multiplier

ANSWER C: A *product detector* is necessary in a simple Morse code *CW and single-sideband (SSB) receiver.* ➡**www.alinco.com**

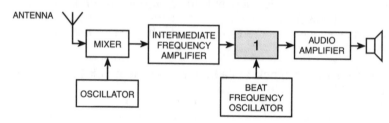

Figure T8-5

T8C02 If Figure T8-5 is a diagram of a simple single-sideband receiver, what type of circuit should be shown in block 1?

A. A high pass filter   C. A low pass filter
B. A ratio detector   D. A product detector

ANSWER D: Since Figure T8-5 is considered a simple single-sideband receiver *(SSB), block 1 would be a product detector.*

T8C03 What circuit is pictured in Figure T8-6, if block 1 is a frequency discriminator?

A. A double-conversion receiver   C. A superheterodyne receiver
B. A variable-frequency oscillator   D. An FM receiver

ANSWER D: Did you spot the words *"frequency discriminator"* in this question? This means we are looking at a frequency modulation *(FM) receiver.*

T8C04 What is block 1 in the FM receiver shown in Figure T8-6?

A. A frequency discriminator   C. A frequency-shift modulator
B. A product detector   D. A phase inverter

ANSWER A: *Block 1 is a frequency discriminator.* You find a frequency discriminator in all FM receivers. When you see the letters FM always go for the answer "frequency discriminator" if it is a receiver.

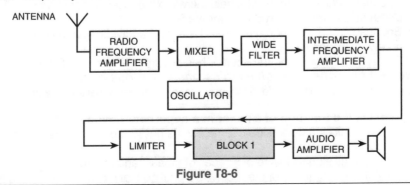

Figure T8-6

T8C05 What would happen if block 1 failed to function in the FM receiver diagram shown in Figure T8-6?
A. The audio output would sound loud and distorted
B. There would be no audio output
C. There would be no effect
D. The receiver's power supply would be short-circuited
ANSWER B: If *Block 1 in Figure T8-6 failed,* the signal would not pass to the audio amplifier, so you would have *no audio output.*

T8C06 What circuit function is found in all types of receivers?
A. An audio filter   C. A detector
B. A beat-frequency oscillator   D. An RF amplifier
ANSWER C: *All receivers contain a detector.* Think of the detective work that a detector must do to find small signals out there on the air waves that come in from the antenna system.

T8C07 What is one accurate way to check the calibration of your receiver's tuning dial?
A. Monitor the BFO frequency of a second receiver
B. Tune to a popular amateur net frequency
C. Tune to one of the frequencies of station WWV or WWVH
D. Tune to another amateur station and ask what frequency the operator is using
ANSWER C: *There are few signals more accurate than WWV.* That's why they are there, on the air 24 hours-a-day. You can easily hear their distinctive once-a-second tick, and their every-one-minute time broadcast. Also, listen at 18 minutes past the hour for solar conditions. Tune to 5, 10, 15 or 20 MHz for WWV.

T8C08 What circuit combines signals from an IF amplifier stage and a beat-frequency oscillator (BFO), to produce an audio signal?
A. An AGC circuit   C. A power supply circuit
B. A detector circuit   D. A VFO circuit
ANSWER B: It is the task of *the detector circuit* to combine signals from an intermediate frequency *(IF) amplifier and a beat frequency oscillator* to detect (recover) the audio signal.

T8C10 Why do many radio receivers have several IF filters of different bandwidths that can be selected by the operator?
A. Because some frequency bands are wider than others
B. Because different bandwidths help increase the receiver sensitivity
C. Because different bandwidths improve S-meter readings
D. Because some emission types need a wider bandwidth than others to be received properly

ANSWER D: A better worldwide transceiver has several *different IF filters* that may be *selected to properly receive emissions of various bandwidths.* Look for this feature when buying a worldwide base station. ➡ **www.timewave.com**

T8C11 What is the function of a mixer in a superheterodyne receiver?
A. To cause all signals outside of a receiver's passband to interfere with one another
B. To cause all signals inside of a receiver's passband to reinforce one another
C. To shift the frequency of the received signal so that it can be processed by IF stages
D. To interface the receiver with an auxiliary device, such as a TNC

ANSWER C: The function of a *mixer* in a radio receiver is to *shift the frequency* of the received signal *so it can be processed by the intermediate frequency (IF) stages.*

T8C12 What frequency or frequencies could the radio shown in Figure T8-7 receive?
A. 136.3 MHz
B. 157.7 MHz and 10.7 MHz
C. 10.7 MHz
D. 147.0 MHz and 168.4 MHz

ANSWER D: The most common intermediate frequency in radio receivers is 10.7 MHz. Notice that the oscillator is working at 157.7 MHz, so *the radio ultimately receives 10.7 MHz plus or minus the 157.7 oscillator frequency.* This works out to be 147 MHz, the desired frequency, and 168.4 MHz, an image frequency that is undesired. *Simply add or subtract the 10.7 MHz IF amplifier frequency to or from the 157.7 MHz oscillator frequency* in this question.

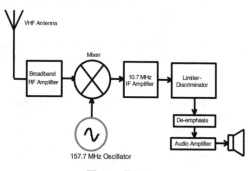

Figure T8-7

T8C13 What type of receiver is shown in Figure T8-7?
A. Direct conversion
B. Superregenerative
C. Single-conversion superhetrodyne
D. Dual conversion superhetrodyne

ANSWER C: This is a *single-conversion superheterodyne receiver.* You know it's single-conversion by the *single intermediate frequency (IF) amplifier.*

T8C14 What emission mode could the receiver in Figure T8-7 detect?
A. AM
B. FM
C. Single sideband (SSB)
D. CW

ANSWER B: In this figure, the *DISCRIMINATOR* gives it away – this is an *FM receiver.*

Skinny or wide?
A look at bandwidth and how we use it.

T6B01 Which list of emission types is in order from the narrowest bandwidth to the widest bandwidth?
A. RTTY, CW, SSB voice, FM voice
B. CW, FM voice, RTTY, SSB voice
C. CW, RTTY, SSB voice, FM voice
D. CW, SSB voice, RTTY, FM voice

ANSWER C: The more information you transmit, the more bandwidth you need. Modes that require more bandwidth are assigned higher frequencies. This gives you a clue why FM voice frequencies are usually found in the VHF and UHF spectrum – and the only place FM is found on worldwide frequencies is between 29.5 and 29.7 MHz. FCC rules do not permit FM repeater operation below 29.5 MHz. So from *narrowest to widest – CW, RTTY, SSB voice, and FM voice.*

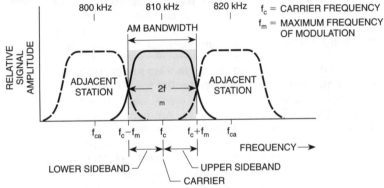

a. Full-Carrier, Double-Sideband AM Signal

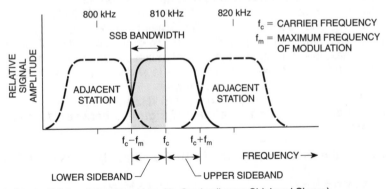

b. Single-Sideband Signal — Uses No Carrier (Lower Sideband Shown)

Carrier, Sidebands and Bandwidth
Source: *Mobile 2-Way Radio Communications,*
G. West, © 1993, Master Publishing, Inc., Lincolnwood, Illinois

T2B17 What is the typical bandwidth of PSK 31 digital communications?
A. 500 kHz
B. 31 Hz
C. 5 MHz
D. 600 kHz

ANSWER B: I hope all of you will join me on the VHF and UHF bands for weak signal work. This means transmitting the signal a lot further than it would normally travel to just a local repeater. How many of you are into computer communications? I see – a lot of you! One of the latest digital communications modes is called PSK 31, and occupies ONLY 31 Hz of bandwidth. Your computer's sound card and a Windows program, plus an interface box between your computer and ham radio, gets PSK 31 on the air big time. Phase shift keying (PSK) sounds like a whistle over the air with a multimode radio in CW or SSB. This audio signal phase shifts with the 31.25 bit-per-second datastream, with "Varicode" ones and zeroes representing specific letters of the alphabet. Start your study of this exciting mode at www.winpskse.com and stop by your local ham store to pick up additional reading materials on digital signaling. Remember, your new Technician class license gives you unrestricted digital capability on any frequencies you are authorized to use. And imagine – *PSK 31 occupies just 31 Hz of bandwidth.* ➡**www.packetradio.com**

T6B02 What is the usual bandwidth of a single-sideband amateur signal?
A. 1 kHz
B. 2 kHz
C. Between 3 and 6 kHz
D. Between 2 and 3 kHz
ANSWER D: A *single-sideband* Amateur Radio signal is typically *2 to 3 kHz wide.*

T3B10 Which of the following emission modes are considered to be weak-signal modes and have the greatest potential for DX contacts?
A. Single sideband and CW
B. Packet radio and RTTY
C. Frequency modulation
D. Amateur television
ANSWER A: If you enjoy experimenting with long-range VHF and UHF contacts, you will want to obtain a multi-mode transceiver that not only gives you the common FM, but also *CW (Morse code) and single sideband (SSB).* Most *weak signal* transmissions use upper sideband. ➡**www.tentec.com**

T6B03 What is the usual bandwidth of a frequency-modulated amateur signal?
A. Less than 5 kHz
B. Between 5 and 10 kHz
C. Between 10 and 20 kHz
D. Greater than 20 kHz
ANSWER C: In an amateur FM signal, the normal maximum deviation of the carrier frequency (f_c max) is +/-5 kHz; and the normal maximum deviation of the modulation frequency (f_m max) — your voice — is +/-3 kHz. We ues Carson's Rule to determine bandwidth of an FM signal. It says:
Bandwidth (BW) = 2 x (f_c max + f_m max) = 2 x (5 kHz + 3 kHz) = 16 kHz.
So, the usual *bandwidth of an amateur FM signal is between 10 and 20 kHz,* answer C.

T6B04 What is the usual bandwidth of a UHF amateur fast-scan television signal?
A. More than 6 MHz
B. About 6 MHz
C. About 3 MHz
D. About 1 MHz
ANSWER B: *Amateur TV on UHF* frequencies takes up a lot of room – *bandwidth of about 6 MHz.* But think of all the visual and audio information you are sending and receiving! ➡**www.atvresearch.com**

T9B15 Which of the following will allow you to monitor Amateur Television (ATV) on the 70-cm band?
A. A portable video camera
B. A cable ready TV receiver
C. An SSTV converter
D. A TV flyback transformer

ANSWER B: Another interesting area of Amateur Radio is ATV, amateur television. *You can preview all of the excitement in your local area! If you have a cable-ready television,* try this simple trick: Unplug the incoming cable from the back of the set, and plug in that old outside TV antenna that you may no longer be using. Turn to cable television Channel 58 or 59. NOT UHF Channel 58 or 59, but local cable Channel 58 and 59.

See what you might pick up in the evening when hams are most apt to be transmitting ATV on the 70-cm band.

➡ www.cris.com/gharlan

Amateur TV signals can be received on a variety of equipment – even a small hand-held monitor.

T8F18 What device produces a stable, low-level signal that can be set to a desired frequency?
    A. A wavemeter
    B. A reflectometer
    C. A signal generator
    D. An oscilloscope

ANSWER C: A *signal generator* with a digital readout is useful in troubleshooting scanner radios. You can *inject a tiny signal* into the "front end" of the set to check it's operation and to be sure that it is on frequency.

T8F14 What is the minimum FCC certification required for an amateur radio operator to build or modify their own transmitting equipment?
    A. A First-Class Radio Repair License
    B. A Technician class license
    C. A General class license
    D. An Amateur Extra class license

ANSWER B: To get started *building or modifying ham radio equipment,* you need the minimum of the amateur radio *Technician class license.*

➡ www.elecraft.com

T8F15 What safety step should you take when soldering?
    A. Always wear safety glasses
    B. Ensure proper ventilation
    C. Make sure no one can touch the soldering iron tip for at least 10 minutes after it is turned off
    D. All of these choices are correct

ANSWER D: When *soldering,* always make sure you have *plenty of fresh air, safety glasses ON,* and a *soldering iron holder* so no one can accidentally touch the tip for at least 10 minutes after turning off the soldering iron.

➡ www.solder-it.com

Are you getting that signal on your TV, too?
A look at what causes interference and how to prevent it.

T6C01 What is meant by receiver overload?
    A. Too much voltage from the power supply
    B. Too much current from the power supply
    C. Interference caused by strong signals from a nearby source
    D. Interference caused by turning the volume up too high

ANSWER C: *Receiver overload* may be *caused by your transmitting antenna being located too close to* your own or your neighbor's *hi-fi set.* Does the back of your own hi-fi cabinet look like a rat's nest of wires? If so, those wires might pick up a nearby signal and OVERLOAD your home entertainment electronics. Your TV might scramble, and your speakers now hear this mysterious voice giving brand new ham radio call letters. If you separate your antenna from the nearby hi-fi set-up, overload will probably disappear. You might also clean up all of those wires in back of your cabinet and add "clam shell" radio frequency interference filters, which may help minimize receiver overload. ➡**www.amidoncorp.com**

T6C07 If signals from your transmitter are causing front-end overload in your neighbor's television receiver, who is responsible for taking care of the interference?
    A. You alone are responsible, since your transmitter is causing the problem
    B. Both you and the owner of the television receiver share the responsibility
    C. The FCC must decide if you or the owner of the television receiver are responsible
    D. The owner of the television receiver is responsible

ANSWER D: This is an idealistic answer about who is responsible for taking care of interference when your neighbor's television receiver is overloading from your nearby transmitted signal. Although the correct answer reads, *"The owner of the television receiver is responsible,"* the GOOD Amateur Radio operator may also share some responsibility in assisting the neighbor with better shielded cable connections between the TV and VCR, as well as some bypass capacitors that might help reduce the problem. Although receiver overload is a fact of life that affects anything close to your transmitter antenna, the GOOD ham will do more than just cite Answer D as "You are the owner of the television, so you are responsible, not me." Go for this answer for the test, but in the real world of ham radio, work with your neighbors and be a good, responsible ham to resolve all forms of interference, whether it's your transmitter or their receiver.

T6C03 What type of filter should be connected to a TV receiver as the first step in trying to prevent RF overload from an amateur HF station transmission?

A. Low-pass	C. Band pass
B. High-pass	D. Notch

ANSWER B: The *TV band is higher than your worldwide radio* and your new voice privileges on 10 meters. *Putting a high-pass filter on the TV receiver,* if it's connected to an outside antenna, is a good start in cleaning up interference. Don't put a high-pass filter into a cable TV system. Cable television feeds will not work through a high-pass filter. ➡**www.pwdahl.com/hamcat.html**

T6C05 If you are told that your amateur station is causing television interference, what should you do?
- A. First make sure that your station is operating properly, and that it does not cause interference to your own television
- B. Immediately turn off your transmitter and contact the nearest FCC office for assistance
- C. Connect a high-pass filter to the transmitter output and a low-pass filter to the antenna-input terminals of the television
- D. Continue operating normally, because you have no reason to worry about the interference

ANSWER A: It's unlikely that VHF and UHF signals will cause television interference to your neighbors on an outside antenna, or on the dish or on cable. However, when you pass your 5-wpm code test and go on the worldwide bands, be aware that these frequencies could sneak into a television set and cause problems. First, *double check that your equipment is well grounded and operating properly,* and double check that your TV is working okay when you are transmitting over the air. If it is, chances are your neighbors may have some loose connections on their TV receivers, and this should be cured as a step to reducing the interference from your station when transmitting on high frequency.

T4B11 If you have been informed that your amateur radio station causes interference to nearby radio or television broadcast receivers of good engineering design, what operating restrictions can FCC rules impose on your station?
- A. Require that you discontinue operation on frequencies causing interference during certain evening hours and on Sunday morning (local time)
- B. Relocate your station or reduce your transmitter's output power
- C. Nothing, unless the FCC conducts an investigation of the interference problem and issues a citation
- D. Reduce antenna height so as to reduce the area affected by the interference

ANSWER A: As a new Technician class operator, your operations with handheld equipment and a modest 2-meter/440 MHz weak signal radio are not going to cause *interference to your neighbor's TV* or hi-fi. But ultimately, you will pass your General class license and go on the air with a major high-frequency station. Maybe it's not the most modern station in the world and has all sorts of harmonic problems and spurious emissions. If you don't clean up the problem at your end of the circuit, the *FCC might require that you stay off the air during certain evening hours and on Sunday mornings.* [97.121]

T6C12 What is the major cause of telephone interference?
- A. The telephone ringer is inadequate
- B. Tropospheric ducting at UHF frequencies
- C. The telephone was not equipped with interference protection when it was manufactured.
- D. Improper location of the telephone in the home

ANSWER C: Ultra-inexpensive wired telephone equipment and cheap analog cordless phones may sometimes pick up your ham radio transmissions. This interference could be licked if your neighbors would buy a more expensive telephone set, but first you may want to try interference filters that can be placed on each telephone jack. *The problem is caused by manufacturers making inexpensive telephones without these filters built in.* ➡ **www.amidon-inductive.com**

T2A02 How does the frequency of a harmonic compare to the desired transmitting frequency?
A. It is slightly more than the desired frequency
B. It is slightly less than the desired frequency
C. It is exactly two, or three, or more times the desired frequency
D. It is much less than the desired frequency

ANSWER C: *Harmonics are exact 2x or 3x multiples of your fundamental frequency,* and are not desirable.

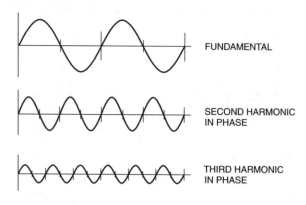

Fundamental Radio Wave and Harmonics

T2A05 What is the fourth harmonic of a 50.25 MHz signal?
A. 201.00 MHz
B. 150.75 MHz
C. 251.50 MHz
D. 12.56 MHz

ANSWER A: Every transmitter puts out harmonics that are multiples of the fundamental signal. These harmonics are generally suppressed so low that they don't become a problem to the higher frequencies. To *calculate the harmonic, simply multiply the harmonic indicated by the frequency. 4 x 50.25 MHz = 201 MHz.* You can do this one in your head.

T6C02 What type of filter might be connected to an amateur HF transmitter to cut down on harmonic radiation?
A. A key-click filter
B. A low-pass filter
C. A high-pass filter
D. A CW filter

ANSWER B: *Low-pass filters are designed for the worldwide transceivers* that you will use when you pass your Technician class exam plus pass the 5-wpm code test. Never put a low-pass filter on VHF or UHF equipment. Low-pass filters are only designed for the worldwide bands.
➡ www.ky-filters.com/cq.htm

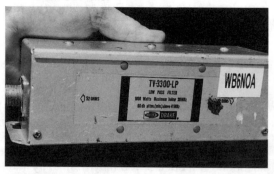

There are low-pass filters like this one, band-pass filters, and high-pass filters that can be used to solve interference problems.

T6C06 If harmonic radiation from your transmitter is causing interference to television receivers in your neighborhood, who is responsible for taking care of the interference?
A. The owners of the television receivers are responsible
B. Both you and the owners of the television receivers share the responsibility
C. You alone are responsible, since your transmitter is causing the problem
D. The FCC must decide if you or the owners of the television receivers are responsible

ANSWER C: A misaligned amateur transmitter may sometimes create harmonics of the fundamental frequency on the transmitter output. This usually occurs when someone gets inside the transmitter and starts adjusting things without looking at the output on a service monitor. If you are causing *harmonic interference to TV* receivers, you are putting out an illegal signal on the TV frequencies and *you alone are responsible* for solving the problem. With harmonics, it's your radio at fault.

T6C04 What effect might a break in a cable television transmission line have on amateur communications?
A. Cable lines are shielded and a break cannot affect amateur communications
B. Harmonic radiation from the TV receiver may cause the amateur transmitter to transmit off-frequency
C. TV interference may result when the amateur station is transmitting, or interference may occur to the amateur receiver
D. The broken cable may pick up very high voltages when the amateur station is transmitting

ANSWER C: When a cable TV *coaxial* cable line becomes nicked or *broken, amateur signals can sometimes leak into the cable causing television interference,* and TV signals will sometimes leak out of the cable causing interference on certain ham radio frequencies. You will notice this problem on the popular 2-meter band.

Make sure all coax connections are tight to help minimize interference.

T6C09 If someone tells you that signals from your hand-held transceiver are interfering with other signals on a frequency near yours, what may be the cause?
A. You may need a power amplifier for your hand-held
B. Your hand-held may have chirp from weak batteries
C. You may need to turn the volume up on your hand-held
D. Your hand-held may be transmitting spurious emissions

ANSWER D: If you receive a report from an amateur operator at least 5 miles away that your signals are interfering with signals on other frequencies near your transmitting frequency, *your handheld may be transmitting spurious emissions.* You will need to take your set in to an authorized equipment dealer for a quick checkout.

T6C10 What may happen if an SSB transmitter is operated with the microphone gain set too high?

A. It may cause digital interference to computer equipment

B. It may cause splatter interference to other stations operating near its frequency

C. It may cause atmospheric interference in the air around the antenna

D. It may cause interference to other stations operating on a higher frequency band

ANSWER B: All worldwide transceivers have a microphone gain control. Many base station microphones also offer audio compression and additional "mike" gain. Turning up the *mike gain too high will cause distortion, splatter, and interference* to stations on nearby frequencies. It's also bad Amateur Radio practice to operate with a "hot" mike setting. Read your instruction manual for proper microphone gain setting procedures while watching the ALC level on your transceiver's multimeter.

T6C11 What may cause a buzzing or hum in the signal of an HF transmitter?

A. Using an antenna that is the wrong length

B. Energy from another transmitter

C. Bad design of the transmitter's RF power output circuit

D. A bad filter capacitor in the transmitter's power supply

ANSWER D: If you find a 20-year-old power supply your dad used back in the good old days for his ham radio setup, better check its DC output power. Very old power supplies used big *electrolytic filter capacitors that dry out* and lose their capacity with age. The *result will be severe hum* on transmit and receive. Power supply technology has changed so rapidly that switching power supplies can easily deliver 12 volts at 20 amps in small and relatively lightweight packages. They have done away with the very heavy transformers needed in the older, conventional power supplies. The switching power supply also doesn't have those big filter capacitors that dry out. ➡**www.kjielectronics.com**

T6C08 What circuit blocks RF energy above and below certain limits?

A. A band-pass filter   C. An input filter

B. A high-pass filter   D. A low-pass filter

ANSWER A: Read this question carefully! Since it *blocks energy above and below* a certain frequency, it must be a *band-pass filter.* ➡**www.dci.ca**

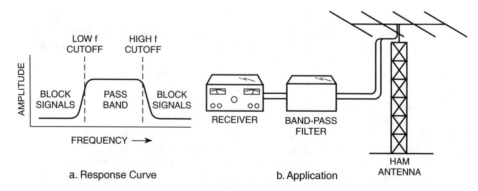

a. Response Curve   b. Application

Band-Pass Filter

So how much power do we really need?
A little bit of power can go a long, long way.

T5B05 What is the term for the average power supplied to an antenna transmission line during one RF cycle at the crest of the modulation envelope?
    A. Peak transmitter power
    B. Peak output power
    C. Average radio-frequency power
    D. Peak envelope power

ANSWER D: If we measure to *the crest of the modulation envelope,* this is at its peak, and *is called peak envelope power (PEP).* [97.3b6]
➡ **www.birdelectronic.com/home.htm**

A Professional Wattmeter

T5B07 What amount of transmitter power must amateur stations use at all times?
    A. 25 watts PEP output
    B. 250 watts PEP output
    C. 1500 watts PEP output
    D. The minimum legal power necessary to communicate

ANSWER D: Be careful of this one – the answer is not a numerical one, but rather a philosophical one. *Always run the minimum amount of power* necessary to make contact with another station. [97.313a]

T8F12 At what line impedance do most RF watt meters usually operate?
    A. 25 ohms
    B. 50 ohms
    C. 100 ohms
    D. 300 ohms

ANSWER B: Since *Amateur Radio transceivers all operate at a 50-ohm impedance,* our *wattmeter should also be rated at 50 ohms.* The impedance is kept the same for a perfect match.

T8B07 What minimum rating should a dummy antenna have for use with a 100-watt, single-sideband-phone transmitter?
    A. 100 watts continuous
    B. 141 watts continuous
    C. 175 watts continuous
    D. 200 watts continuous

ANSWER A: Your single-sideband phone *transmitter will put out about 100 watts.* This means you need a *dummy load* capable of handling that much power – *100 watts* continuous.

A Dummy Load

T7A16 If you increase your transmitter output power from 5 watts to 10 watts, what decibel (dB) increase does that represent?

A. 2 dB

B. 3 dB

C. 5 dB

D. 10 dB

ANSWER B: *Doubling the power* will lead to a *3 decibel increase.* Cutting the power in half will lead to a 3 decibel decrease.

± dB	Decimal Gain Value	Approx. ±Times Power Change	Decimal Loss Value
		dB Power Gain or Loss	
1 dB	1.259	1¼ X	0.794
2 dB	1.585	1½ X	0.633
3 dB	1.995	2 X	0.501
4 dB	2.511	2½ X	0.398
5 dB	3.162	3 X	0.316
6 dB	3.981	4 X	0.251
7 dB	5.011	5 X	0.200
8 dB	6.310	6¼ X	0.158
9 dB	7.943	8 X	0.126
10 dB	10.0	10 X	0.1

T7A21 If you have a hand-held transceiver with an output of 500 milliwatts, how many watts would this be?

A. 0.02

B. 0.5

C. 5

D. 50

ANSWER B: Remember *milli means* 1×10^{-3}, or *one thousandth,* so *divide 500 by 1000 to get 0.5 watt.* Most handhelds, on lower power, are rated in milliwatts. A unit rated at 500 mW puts out 0.5 watt. One-half watt is the same as 0.5 watt, and this is plenty of power for a handheld.

T0A08 What is an important consideration for the location of the main power switch?

A. It must always be near the operator

B. It must always be as far away from the operator as possible

C. Everyone should know where it is located in case of an emergency

D. It should be located in a locked metal box so no one can accidentally turn it off

ANSWER C: When you set up your ham station, *make sure everyone knows where the main power switch is located.* Tell your small children to turn off the circuit breaker if they ever smell smoke in mom or dad's radio room!

T0A09 What circuit should be controlled by a safety interlock switch in an amateur transceiver or power amplifier?

A. The power supply

B. The IF amplifier

C. The audio amplifier

D. The cathode bypass circuit

ANSWER A: One of the jobs of the transmitter power amplifier power supply is to develop high voltage to run the power amplifier tube. This is why the power amplifier *power supply is always controlled by a safety interlock switch,* usually mounted on the cabinet access door. Always turn off the amplifier and wait at least 15 minutes before opening up the access door to insure that all high voltages in the capacitors have dissipated through the bleeder resistor networks. Be very careful of high voltage power supplies even when they are unplugged! ➡ **www.ameritron.com**

What does an antenna do, anyway?
Sending your signal far and wide on a tiny wire or piece of aluminum.

T4C12 Which type of antenna would be a good choice as part of a portable HF amateur station that could be set up in case of an emergency?
A. A three-element quad
B. A three-element Yagi
C. A dipole
D. A parabolic dish
ANSWER C: A simple antenna for high-frequency *worldwide emergency communications is the dipole.* The dipole can be easily deployed up a tree with each side of the dipole's one-quarter wavelength wire extending out and tied off with nonconducting line. The dipole is one-half wavelength long, and you can easily coil it up to fit inside a padded brown envelope. All good worldwide emergency communicators carry a dipole for each band of operation. ➡**www.bwantennas.com**

T8D15 If the ends of a half-wavelength dipole antenna (mounted at least a half-wavelength high) point east and west, which way would the antenna send out radio energy?
A. Equally in all directions
B. Mostly up and down
C. Mostly north and south
D. Mostly east and west
ANSWER C: If the *dipole is erected east to west,* the *energy* would go *out* mostly *north to south.* Slightly droop the dipole ends if you wish more energy in other directions. ➡**www.amateur-radio-toystore.com**

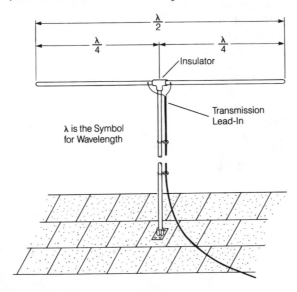

Dipole Antenna

T8D03 What would be the length, to the nearest inch, of a half-wavelength dipole antenna that is resonant at 147 MHz?
A. 19 inches
B. 37 inches
C. 55 inches
D. 74 inches
ANSWER B: Here are some halfwave and quarter-wavelength antenna formulas to work with. It is easy to figure out the math on any of these – *divide the frequency in MHz INTO 468 if you're looking for a halfwave antenna.* This comes out in

---

feet, and to go from feet to inches, *MULTIPLY your answer by 12.* Here are the steps using a calculator: *CLEAR 468 ÷ 147 =. 3.18 feet* is your answer. But they want it in inches, so *multiple (X) 3.2 by 12* and you end up with a half-wave dipole that is 38.16 inches long. The closest answer is Answer B, *37 inches.*

T8D04 How long should you make a half-wavelength dipole antenna for 223 MHz (measured to the nearest inch)?

A. 112 inches   C. 25 inches
B. 50 inches   D. 12 inches

ANSWER C: Use the formula 468 divided by the frequency in MHz for a half-wavelength antenna in feet. You must multiply your answer by 12 to arrive at 25 inches. Keystrokes are: *468 ÷ 223 =. Multiply the answer by 12 to convert feet to inches*, and select *answer C*, which is closest to the 25.183856 on your calculator screen. ➡**www.cq-amateur-radio.com**

T8D05 How long should you make a quarter-wavelength vertical antenna for 146 MHz (measured to the nearest inch)?

A. 112 inches   C. 19 inches
B. 50 inches   D. 12 inches

ANSWER C: Now let's see what it takes to get a good signal out with a little piece of welding rod on the top of your car roof on the 2-meter band. This time we are going for 146 MHz, and we are looking for the answer in inches. *Divide the frequency in MHz INTO 234 if you are looking for a quarterwave antenna.* Hit the CLEAR several times and then let's go: *2-3-4, the division sign, 1-4-6 = 1.6 feet* as an answer. But they want it in inches, so *multiple (X) 1.6 by 12* and you end up with a whip that is 19.232876 inches long, with the correct answer of *Answer C, 19 inches.* Now isn't that easy? Tell the kids to say goodbye to their calculator until after your exam. ➡**www.universal-radio.com**

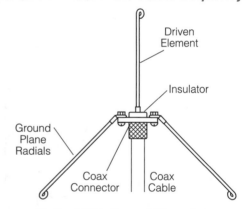

Vertical 1/4 λ Ground-Plane Antenna

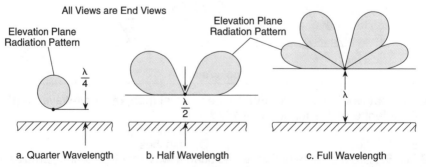

All Views are End Views

a. Quarter Wavelength   b. Half Wavelength   c. Full Wavelength

The Radiation Pattern of an Antenna Changes as Height Above Ground is Varied
Source: *Antennas,* A.J. Evans, K.E. Britain, ©1998, Master Publishing, Lincolnwood, Illinois

---

T8D06 How long should you make a quarter-wavelength vertical antenna for 440 MHz (measured to the nearest inch)?

A. 12 inches
B. 9 inches
C. 6 inches
D. 3 inches

ANSWER C: Oh-oh, time to find your kid's calculator. I know your math may be a little bit rusty, but a calculator can easily get you through this problem. And YES, you may bring the calculator to the test, too. *First hit the CLEAR button on the calculator, and then press 2-3-4, the division sign, 4-4-0 = for an antenna quarterwave length that is 0.5318181 feet long.* But wouldn't you know it – they want it in inches. No problem. Without removing those numbers from the screen, press the X *(multiply)* key and numbers 1-2, and then hit the equal button – and presto, you multiplied *your fraction of a foot by 12* (remember 12 inches to the foot) and came up with 6.3818172 inches. Answer C is the closest at *6 inches.* Easy, huh? ➡ **www.wb0w.com**

T8D20 What is one advantage to using a multiband antenna?

A. You can operate on several bands with a single feed line
B. Multiband antennas always have high gain
C. You can transmit on several frequencies simultaneously
D. Multiband antennas offer poor harmonic suppression

ANSWER A: Try to pass that 5-wpm code test to obtain Technician-Plus privileges. The "Plus" privileges will give you high-frequency access to 10-, 15-, 40-, and 80-meters. But how are you going to *get these four bands onto just one single high-frequency antenna*? You would operate a *multiband antenna*, which has most of the worldwide bands with just a single feed line going to your transceiver. Same thing on the 2-meter and 440 MHz bands for Technician no-code privileges – a single feed line can go to a single antenna that will operate on several bands. ➡**www.hy-gain.com**

T8D22 What device might allow use of an antenna on a band it was not designed for?

A. An SWR meter
B. A low-pass filter
C. An antenna tuner
D. A high-pass filter

ANSWER C: We sometimes will *use an antenna tuner* to allow us to use an antenna on a band for which it might not be specifically designed. ➡**www.sgcworld.com**

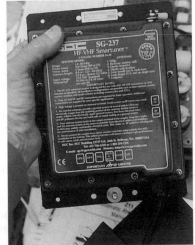

An Antenna Tuner

T8E05 What does an antenna tuner do?
A. It matches a transceiver output impedance to the antenna system impedance
B. It helps a receiver automatically tune in stations that are far away
C. It switches an antenna system to a transceiver when sending, and to a receiver when listening
D. It switches a transceiver between different kinds of antennas connected to one feed line

ANSWER A: An *antenna tuner will match your transceiver to an antenna system* that might not be perfectly tuned to the frequency on which you wish to operate.
➡ **www.ldgelectronics.com**

T8D21 What could be done to reduce the physical length of an antenna without changing its resonant frequency?
A. Attach a balun at the feed point
B. Add series capacitance at the feed point
C. Use thinner conductors
D. Add a loading coil

ANSWER D: We could *add a loading coil* at the base of a 6-meter antenna *to shorten its length* to get you into the garage. This is how General class operators on the worldwide bands operate on relatively long wavelengths with short antennas – they normally have some sort of a loading coil somewhere up the shaft. ➡ **www.hiqantennas.com**

A large loading coil on a mobile whip antenna.

T8D07 Which of the following factors has the greatest effect on the gain of a properly designed Yagi antenna?
A. The number of elements   C. Element spacing
B. Boom length   D. Element diameter

ANSWER B: The maximum possible gain of any type of *Yagi* directional beam antenna can be "guesstimated" by simply looking at how long the boom is. *Boom length is the greatest contributing factor to gain* – and to pick the highest gain antenna that will beam the signal in one direction, look for one with a major long boom! Don't worry about the number of elements, or how big they are, or how close or how far away they are spaced – look for boom length to determine the maximum amount of signal concentrated in one direction. The longer the boom, the greater your amount of effective radiated power.

T8D08 Approximately how long is the driven element of a Yagi antenna?
A. 1/4 wavelength   C. 1/2 wavelength
B. 1/3 wavelength   D. 1 wavelength

ANSWER C: Since the *Yagi antenna is a series of dipoles* affixed to a boom in the same plane, *the individual elements are about one-half wavelength long*, just like the driven element. The reflector is a little longer, the director a little shorter.

Antennas

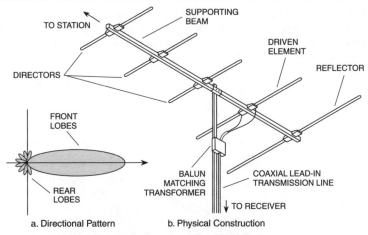

a. Directional Pattern b. Physical Construction

A Beam Antenna — The Yagi Antenna

Source: *Antennas – Selection and Installation,* ©1986, Master Publishing, Inc., Lincolnwood, Illinois

---

T8D11 In Figure T8-8, what is the name of element 1 of the Yagi antenna?
A. Director
B. Reflector
C. Boom
D. Driven element

ANSWER B: The *reflector is on the back of the beam.* A reflector is always longer than the driven element. Sometimes there are two or more reflectors.
➡ **www.associatedradio.com**

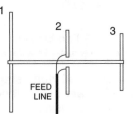

Figure T8-8

T8D09 In Figure T8-8, what is the name of element 2 of the Yagi antenna?
A. Director
B. Reflector
C. Boom
D. Driven element

ANSWER D: The *coaxial cable always connects to the driven element.* It is driven by the direct energy from the transmitter. ➡ **www.kwarc.org**

T8D10 In Figure T8-8, what is the name of element 3 of the Yagi antenna?
A. Director
B. Reflector
C. Boom
D. Driven element

ANSWER A: The *director is* usually the shortest element and is placed *in front* of the driven element. Directors help concentrate the signal into a tight radiation pattern.

T8D12 What is a cubical quad antenna?
A. Four straight, parallel elements in line with each other, each approximately 1/2-electrical wavelength long
B. Two or more parallel four-sided wire loops, each approximately one-electrical wavelength long
C. A vertical conductor 1/4-electrical wavelength high, fed at the bottom
D. A center-fed wire 1/2-electrical wavelength long. ➡ **www.m2inc.com**

ANSWER B: You can add reflectors and directors to your 1 wavelength *quad antenna system* to give it some real punch in just one direction. Just like the Yagi, the reflector element is slightly larger, and the director loop is slightly smaller.
➡ **www.cubex.com**

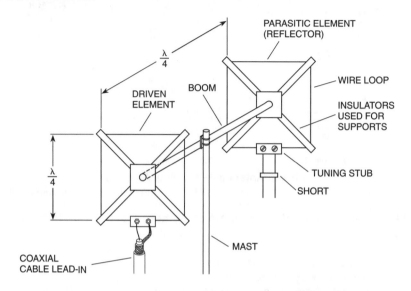

A Two-Element Cubical Quad Antenna — Horizontally Polarized
Source: *Antennas – Selection and Installation,* © 1986, Master Publishing, Inc., Lincolnwood, Illinois

T8D19 How will increasing antenna gain by 3 dB affect your signal's effective radiated power in the direction of maximum radiation?
A. It will cut it in half
B. It will not change
C. It will double it
D. It will quadruple it

ANSWER C: *Increasing antenna gain by 3 dB will double the effective radiated power.*

T8D13 What does horizontal wave polarization mean?
A. The magnetic lines of force of a radio wave are parallel to the Earth's surface
B. The electric lines of force of a radio wave are parallel to the Earth's surface
C. The electric lines of force of a radio wave are perpendicular to the Earth's surface
D. The electric and magnetic lines of force of a radio wave are perpendicular to the Earth's surface

ANSWER B: Radio waves are made up of electric and magnetic lines of force radiating at 90° to each other. Antenna polarization is determined by the direction of the electric field of the antenna. The key words are "electric lines." If the *electric lines* are *parallel to the Earth's surface*, then the antenna *polarization is horizontal.* ➡ **www.dxzone.com**

T8D14 What does vertical wave polarization mean?
A. The electric lines of force of a radio wave are parallel to the Earth's surface
B. The magnetic lines of force of a radio wave are perpendicular to the Earth's surface

C. The electric lines of force of a radio wave are perpendicular to the Earth's surface

D. The electric and magnetic lines of force of a radio wave are parallel to the Earth's surface

ANSWER C: For worldwide communications, polarization is not critical because sky-wave refraction will turn them every which way. However, for VHF propagation, almost everyone uses vertical polarization for best base-to-mobile range. If the *electric lines* are *perpendicular to the Earth's surface,* then the antenna polarization is vertical.

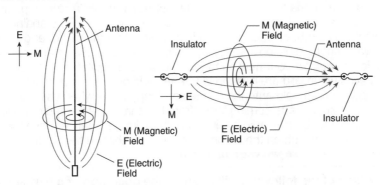

a. Vertically-Polarized Antenna   b. Horizontally-Polarized Antenna

Horizontal and Vertical Polarization

T8D16 What electromagnetic wave polarization do most repeater antennas have in the VHF and UHF spectrum?

A. Horizontal
B. Vertical

C. Right-hand circular
D. Left-hand circular

ANSWER B: Almost all *VHF and UHF FM repeaters operate vertically-polarized antennas.* This means you must hold your handheld straight up and down when you want best distance to a repeater. If you position your handheld with the antenna horizontal to the ground, you will lose many miles of communications range because the two antennas (yours and the repeater's) are cross-polarized.

T8D18 Which antenna polarization is used most often for weak signal VHF/UHF SSB operation?

A. Vertical
B. Horizontal

C. Right-hand circular
D. Left-hand circular

ANSWER B: *Weak signal SSB* operation on 6 meters, 2 meters, 222 MHz, 432 MHz, and 1296 MHz *is always HORIZONTAL.* We always use upper sideband for voice. ➡ **www.wswss.com**

T8D17 What electromagnetic wave polarization is used for most satellite operation?

A. Only horizontal
B. Only vertical

C. Circular
D. No polarization

ANSWER C: *Satellites operate circular polarization* because they are slowly rotating in space, and circular polarization best minimizes the fading in and out. You can spot a home satellite antenna as either a crossed-element Yagi, or an antenna that looks a little bit like a corkscrew! ➡ **www.amsat.com**

T8D02 Which is true of "rubber duck" antennas for hand-held transceivers?
A. The shorter they are, the better they perform
B. They are much less efficient than a quarter-wavelength telescopic antenna
C. They offer the highest amount of gain possible for any hand-held transceiver antenna
D. They have a good long-distance communications range

ANSWER B: When you pass your ham radio license test, you're probably going to make a bee line to the radio store. Most likely, your first radio will be a portable transceiver. They come with a little *"rubber-duck" antenna.* This is a small, rubber-coated antenna that is quite flexible, but *not very efficient* in putting out a good signal to a distant repeater. Sure, they'll do the job if you're standing out in the open, but the little rubber-duck antenna is no match to a much higher gain, one quarter-wavelength telescopic antenna. For more gain, purchase an accessory telescopic antenna for your new handheld. But a word of caution – watch out for people's eyes when you are running your handheld on a telescopic whip, and don't overstress your handheld antenna connector. Many times when using a telescopic whip, the connector starts coming loose from the chassis of the radio. If your antenna connector on the radio begins to wobble, immediately remove the telescopic whip and tighten the antenna connector either on the outside or the inside of the chassis. ➡ www.qrparci.com

T8D01 Which of the following will improve the operation of a hand-held radio inside a vehicle?
A. Shielding around the battery pack
B. A good ground to the belt clip
C. An external antenna on the roof
D. An audio amplifier

ANSWER C: Any *handheld operated inside a vehicle needs an external antenna on the roof.* Putting it on the roof gets the signal up and out of the vehicle, and minimizes RF radiation to you and the passengers by using the metal roof to shield the inside of the vehicle. Now, if you're driving a convertible, that's another story. ➡ www.antennaworld.com

T8A14 What would you use to connect a dual-band antenna to a mobile transceiver that has separate VHF and UHF output connectors?
A. A dual-needle SWR meter
B. A full-duplex phone patch
C. Twin high-pass filters
D. A duplexer

ANSWER D: Mobile transceivers for *dual-band operation* may have two separate antenna outputs. But you only want one antenna on your vehicle. You would use a *duplexer* to connect your dual-band antenna to the double antenna outputs on your transceiver.
➡ www.hammall.com

Duplexer

T8A11 What might you connect between your transceiver and an antenna switch connected to several antennas?

A. A high-pass filter
C. A key-click filter
B. An SWR meter
D. A mixer

ANSWER B: Use an SWR meter as a check of your antenna system and your antenna switch for a proper match. The *SWR meter goes between your transceiver and the switch.* ➡ **www.ww-manufacturing.com**

T8E14 What point in an antenna system is called the feed point?

A. The antenna connection on the back of the transmitter
B. Halfway between the transmitter and the feed line
C. At the point where the feed line joins the antenna
D. At the tip of the antenna

ANSWER C: The *antenna feedpoint is* up there at the antenna *where your feedline* – usually coax –*attaches to the* actual *antenna radiating element.*

T8E06 What is a coaxial cable?

A. Two wires side-by-side in a plastic ribbon
B. Two wires side-by-side held apart by insulating rods
C. Two wires twisted around each other in a spiral
D. A center wire inside an insulating material covered by a metal sleeve or shield

ANSWER D: Coaxial cable is similar to water pipes in that it doesn't leak and carries the good stuff inside while keeping everything else out. To maintain high water pressure at the output end requires large diameter pipes. Same thing with coaxial cable – if you plan to run a lot of power, or if you have an extremely long cable run, use a large-diameter coaxial cable. *Coax has a center conductor surrounded by insulation that is covered by a metal shield* to keep out interfering signals. ➡ **www.cablexperts.com**

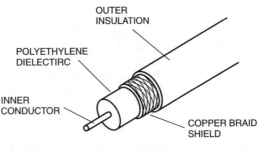

Coaxial Cable

T8E12 What happens to radio energy when it is sent through a poor quality coaxial cable?

A. It causes spurious emissions
B. It is returned to the transmitter's chassis ground
C. It is converted to heat in the cable
D. It causes interference to other stations near the transmitting frequency

ANSWER C: Experienced hams can tell how good an antenna match is by feeling the *coaxial cable* feed line after a few minutes of transmitting. A *warm feedline indicates high SWR.* If your transmitter is getting red hot, that's also an indication of high SWR. This condition needs to be corrected before meltdown.

T8E13 What is an unbalanced line?
A. A feed line with neither conductor connected to ground
B. A feed line with both conductors connected to ground
C. A feed line with one conductor connected to ground
D. All of these answers are correct

ANSWER C: *Coaxial cable is an unbalanced feedline.* Your radio waves travel along the center conductor. The grounded outside braid keeps interference out.

T8E10 What does "balun" mean?
A. Balanced antenna network
B. Balanced unloader
C. Balanced unmodulator
D. Balanced to unbalanced

ANSWER D: We use a balun to match balanced twin-lead to unbalanced 50-ohm coaxial cable. *Balun* receives its name from *BALanced to UNbalanced.* A balun is an impedance-matching transformer. ➡ www.aaradio.com

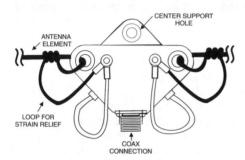
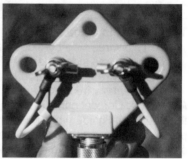

Using a Balun to Feed Dipole

T8E11 Where would you install a balun to feed a dipole antenna with 50-ohm coaxial cable?
A. Between the coaxial cable and the antenna
B. Between the transmitter and the coaxial cable
C. Between the antenna and the ground
D. Between the coaxial cable and the ground

ANSWER A: We *put a balun at the feedpoint* of an antenna to optimize the transfer of energy coming up the coax and into the antenna wires. It goes right at the point where the coaxial cable meets the actual radiating antenna.
➡ www.rad-comm.com

T8E07 Why should you use only good quality coaxial cable and connectors for a UHF antenna system?
A. To keep RF loss low
B. To keep television interference high
C. To keep the power going to your antenna system from getting too high
D. To keep the standing-wave ratio of your antenna system high

ANSWER A: When you begin operating at satellite frequencies with your new no-code license, coaxial cable and antenna connectors become important components for maximum transfer of signal and minimum loss. Low-quality coaxial cable can cause some of your signal to get lost. *Always use top-quality coaxial cable* connectors and feed lines, especially at ultra-high-frequency satellite bands where *signal loss must be kept at an absolute minimum.*
➡ www.burghardt-amateur.com

T8E08 What is parallel-conductor feed line?
A. Two wires twisted around each other in a spiral
B. Two wires side-by-side held apart by insulating material
C. A center wire inside an insulating material that is covered by a metal sleeve or shield
D. A metal pipe that is as wide or slightly wider than a wavelength of the signal it carries

ANSWER B: A less-used feedline is *"ladder line."* It's similar to *TV twin-lead*, which has *two parallel wires, separated by an insulator.* Ladder line can be used with certain types of wire antenna systems. Ladder line cannot be connected directly to any ham set; it must have an additional antenna tuning device.

➡ **www.texasparadise.com/hars**

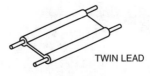

INSULATOR PARALLEL-CONDUCTOR "LADDER LINE" TWIN LEAD

Parallel Conductor and Twin Lead

T8E09 Which of the following are some reasons to use parallel-conductor, open-wire feed line?
A. It has low impedance and will operate with a high SWR
B. It will operate well even with a high SWR and it works well when tied down to metal objects
C. It has a low impedance and has less loss than coaxial cable
D. It will operate well even with a high SWR and has less loss than coaxial cable

ANSWER D: There was a ham that lived in a valley who put a wire antenna several thousand feet away on the top of a hill. He used *parallel conductor feedline* to connect his set with the hilltop antenna *because there is less loss* in this type of open-wire feed system than in coaxial cable. ➡ **www.norad.com**

How do I know if my antenna is working well?
Know which way your signals are traveling along your feedline.

T8E01 What does standing-wave ratio mean?
A. The ratio of maximum to minimum inductances on a feed line
B. The ratio of maximum to minimum capacitances on a feed line
C. The ratio of maximum to minimum impedances on a feed line
D. The ratio of maximum to minimum voltages on a feed line

ANSWER D: *Standing wave ratio (SWR) is the ratio of maximum voltage to minimum voltage along a transmission line.* It also is a ratio of the maximum current to minimum current along a transmission line. It also is the ratio of the power fed forward along a transmission line to the power accepted by the load.

*SWR Reading	Antenna Condition
1:1	Perfectly Matched
1.5:1	Good Match
2:1	Fair Match
3:1	Poor Match
4:1	Something Definitely Wrong

*Constant Frequency
SWR Meter and Readings

T8E02 What instrument is used to measure standing wave ratio?
A. An ohmmeter
B. An ammeter
C. An SWR meter
D. A current bridge

ANSWER C: We use an *SWR meter* to measure the relative match between an antenna and the coaxial cable feedline. I like the battery-operated SWR analyzer because it allows me to measure the match between the antenna and the feedline without needing to go back and forth between the radio and my SWR bridge.

T8F10 With regard to a transmitter and antenna system, what does "forward power" mean?
A. The power traveling from the transmitter to the antenna
B. The power radiated from the top of an antenna system
C. The power produced during the positive half of an RF cycle
D. The power used to drive a linear amplifier

ANSWER A: You should strive for maximum forward power and minimum reflected power. This will give you a perfect match. *Forward power is the power traveling from your transmitter to your antenna.*

T8F11 With regard to a transmitter and antenna system, what does "reflected power" mean?
A. The power radiated down to the ground from an antenna
B. The power returned towards the source on a transmission line
C. The power produced during the negative half of an RF cycle
D. The power returned to an antenna by buildings and trees

ANSWER B: If you have high amounts of reflected power, better check out what's happening at the antenna. Your antenna is either cut to the wrong frequency or has an impedance mismatch. Hopefully, your reflected power will always be less than one watt. *Reflected power is the power returned to your transmitter from your antenna.*

T8F13 If a directional RF wattmeter reads 90 watts forward power and 10 watts reflected power, what is the actual transmitter output power?

A. 10 watts   C. 90 watts

B. 80 watts   D. 100 watts

ANSWER B: Simply *subtract the wasted reflected power from the forward output* power, and you can see what's actually reaching the antenna feedpoint.

Forward Power–Reflected Power = Actual Power Output

$$90\ W - 10\ W = 80\ W$$

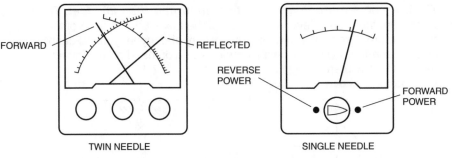

TWIN NEEDLE   SINGLE NEEDLE

Directional Wattmeter

T8E03 What would an SWR of 1:1 indicate about an antenna system?

A. That the antenna was very effective

B. That the transmission line was radiating

C. That the antenna was reflecting as much power as it was radiating

D. That the impedance of the antenna and its transmission line were matched

ANSWER D: An *SWR of 1:1 indicates a good antenna impedance match.*

T8E04 What does an SWR reading of 4:1 mean?

A. An impedance match that is too low

B. An impedance match that is good, but not the best

C. An antenna gain of 4

D. An impedance mismatch; something may be wrong with the antenna system

ANSWER D: A *4:1 reading is a sure indication that something is wrong* with your antenna system. Here, the SWR surely indicates you won't get many contacts. Find out what's wrong and correct it.

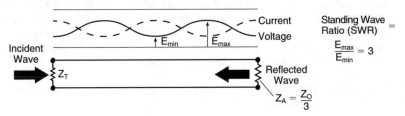

Impedance Mismatch Causes Reflected Wave

You're going to climb up on what?!!
Staying safe around towers, and more.

T4A09 What is the height restriction the FCC places on Amateur Radio Service antenna structures without registration with the FCC and FAA?
A. There is no restriction by the FCC
B. 200 feet
C. 300 feet
D. As permitted by PRB-1

ANSWER B: *An amateur antenna must be no higher than 200 feet.* This is measured from the ground level at the base of the tower up to the top of the antenna structure. Even if you live deep in a valley or canyon, you still cannot exceed the base-to-tip 200-feet height restriction. If you need more elevation, reconsider where you are going to locate your tower. [97.15b]
➡ www.xxtowers.com

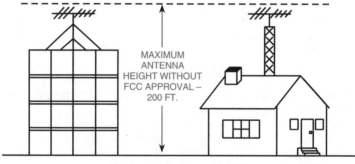

Maximum Antenna Height

T4A07 What do FCC rules require you to do if you plan to erect an antenna whose height exceeds 200 feet?
A. Notify the Federal Aviation Administration and register with the FCC
B. FCC rules prohibit antenna structures above 200 feet
C. Alternating sections of the supporting structure must be painted international airline orange and white
D. The antenna structure must be approved by the FCC and DOD

ANSWER A: Do you mean to say you're going to put up an antenna *OVER 200 feet?* If you're planning on it, you'll need to *notify the Federal Aviation Administration* as well as *register* your antenna structure *with the Federal Communications Commission.* You are also going to need all of those red flashing lights plus tower painting, and I don't think your neighbors will take kindly to this proposition. [97.15(A)] ➡ www.glenmartin.com

T4A08 Which of the following is NOT an important consideration when selecting a location for a transmitting antenna?
A. Nearby structures
B. Height above average terrain
C. Distance from the transmitter location
D. Polarization of the feed line

ANSWER D: How and where you route your feedline should not be a consideration for RF safety. If your SWR is low (reflected waves), *the polarization of your feedline is not critical to the antenna.* [97.13c] ➡ www.alumatower.com

T0B01 How can an antenna system best be protected from lightning damage?
A. Install a balun at the antenna feed point
B. Install an RF choke in the antenna feed line
C. Ground all antennas when they are not in use
D. Install a fuse in the antenna feed line

ANSWER C: Always *use a* good quality amateur-grade *grounded antenna selector switch for lightning protection.* You also can install lightning arrestors.
➡ **www.alphadelta.com**

T0A06 For best protection from electrical shock, what should be grounded in an amateur station?
A. The power supply primary
B. All station equipment connected to a common ground
C. The antenna feed line
D. The AC power mains

ANSWER B: *All of your equipment should be properly grounded!* When you add new gear to your ham station setup, always connect the chassis to the other gear with a good common braid or foil connection. Be certain all connections are tight! You will have less ground noise interference, and you will *protect yourself from electrical shock* in case of a short circuit. ➡ **www.metal-cable.com**

Copper Foil Ground Strap Provides Good
Surface Area Ground

T0A07 Which potential does the green wire in a three-wire electrical plug represent?
A. Neutral
B. Hot
C. Hot and neutral
D. Ground

ANSWER D: Remember *green for ground.* The 3-wire electrical plug should always have the ground connector in place to provide safety.

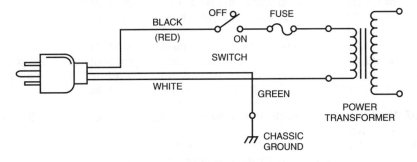

AC Line Connections

T0B02 How can amateur station equipment best be protected from lightning damage?
  A. Use heavy insulation on the wiring
  B. Never turn off the equipment
  C. Disconnect the ground system from all radios
  D. Disconnect all equipment from the power lines and antenna cables

ANSWER D: If you suspect a *lightning storm approaching, unplug everything,* and actually remove the set from other grounded equipment in your ham shack.

T0B03 Why should you wear a hard hat and safety glasses if you are on the ground helping someone work on an antenna tower?
  A. So you won't be hurt if the tower should accidentally fall
  B. To keep RF energy away from your head during antenna testing
  C. To protect your head from something dropped from the tower
  D. So someone passing by will know that work is being done on the tower and will stay away

ANSWER C: Local hams may invite you to an *"antenna party."* As a group, you may help another ham put the antenna up atop a tower. If you are on the ground, make sure you *wear a hard hat and safety glasses.*
➡ www.lentinicomm.com

Always wear a hard hat and safety glasses when working on an antenna tower.

T0B05 Which of the following is the best way to install your antenna in relation to overhead electric power lines?
  A. Always be sure your antenna wire is higher than the power line, and crosses it at a 90-degree angle
  B. Always be sure your antenna and feed line are well clear of any power lines
  C. Always be sure your antenna is lower than the power line, and crosses it at a small angle
  D. Only use vertical antennas within 100 feet of a power line

ANSWER B: Be particularly careful of the two wires atop power poles. These are bare wires and can carry as much as 15,000 volts. *Make sure your antenna and feedlines are well clear of all power lines!* ➡ www.cushcraft.com

T0B07 What is the most important safety precaution to take when putting up an antenna tower?
  A. Install steps on your tower for safe climbing
  B. Insulate the base of the tower to avoid lightning strikes
  C. Ground the base of the tower to avoid lightning strikes
  D. Look for and stay clear of any overhead electrical wires

Antenna Safety

ANSWER D: Anytime you're *working on an antenna system, look all over the place for any overhead electrical wires,* and steer clear of these fatal attraction conductors. Normally those wires on the top of a power pole are uncovered, bare wire, and a brush with those 2 top wires will be your last days in ham radio. Watch out for overhead electrical wires!

T0B06 What should you always do before attempting to climb an antenna tower?
  A. Turn on all radio transmitters that use the tower's antennas
  B. Remove all tower grounding to guard against static electric shock
  C. Put on your safety belt and safety glasses
  D. Inform the FAA and the FCC that you are starting work on a tower
ANSWER C: *Before climbing* any tower, first *inspect what condition it is in,* and check specifically how well it is held in place with guy wires or a base mounting system. When you are ready to climb the tower, *put on your safety belt and safety glasses,* and I also recommend a hard hat, too.
➡ www.onvsafetybelt.com

T0B10 What should you do before you do any work on top of your tower?
  A. Tell someone that you will be up on the tower
  B. Bring a variety of tools with you to minimize your trips up and down the tower
  C. Inspect the tower before climbing to become aware of any antennas or other obstacles that you may need to step around
  D. All of these choices are correct
ANSWER D: Oh yes, *don't forget to bring a bucket of tools* with you so you don't have to keep coming back down for more stuff that you needed aloft.

T0B08 What should you consider before you climb a tower with a leather climbing belt?
  A. If the leather is old, it is probably brittle and could break unexpectedly
  B. If the leather is old, it is very tough and is not likely to break easily
  C. If the leather is old, it is flexible and will hold you more comfortably
  D. An unbroken old leather belt has proven its holding strength over the years
ANSWER A: Years ago hams were dropping like flies from towers. We investigated why, and it was all of those old World War II leather lineman belts purchased at the army surplus stores that were failing. When the *leather dried out,* it became *brittle,* and would *begin to break apart* at the most inopportune time. For me, I go with my brand new nylon safety harness. ➡ www.mfjenterprises.com

T0B09 What should you do before you climb a guyed tower?
  A. Tell someone that you will be up on the tower
  B. Inspect the tower for cracks or loose bolts
  C. Inspect the guy wires for frayed cable, loose cable clamps, loose turnbuckles or loose guy anchors
  D. All of these choices are correct
ANSWER D: Anytime I climb a tower, I *let everyone know that I'm going up*, and I look all over the place to *make sure that nothing is going to break loose* when I'm way up there in the air, and I *inspect* to make sure *the associated guy wires* are in great shape.

T0B04 What safety factors must you consider when using a bow and arrow or slingshot and weight to shoot an antenna-support line over a tree?

    A. You must ensure that the line is strong enough to withstand the shock of shooting the weight

    B. You must ensure that the arrow or weight has a safe flight path if the line breaks

    C. You must ensure that the bow and arrow or slingshot is in good working condition

    D. All of these choices are correct

ANSWER D: Amateur operators have some ingenious ways of getting antenna support lines up and over a tall tree. I like the *sling shot* as my best tool for this job, making sure my *line is nice and strong* – and if it should break, *the weight* out of the sling shot *does not go through my next door neighbor's window* Be careful not to allow the bare antenna wire to be pulled up into the tree limbs because your neighbor is really not going to like that tree catching on fire as soon as you transmit over high frequency. ➡ **www.ezhang.com**

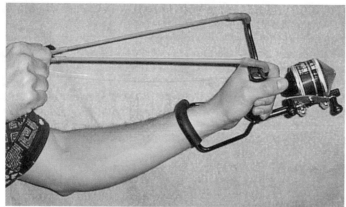

Photo Courtesy of EZ Hang, Inc.
Sling Shot and Fishing Reel Device for Getting Antenna Wires Over Trees.

RF SAFETY FUNDAMENTALS, TERMS AND DEFINITIONS

Author's Note: In 1997, the FCC mandated the addition of questions on Radiofrequency (RF) Safety to the Technician and General class question pools. The addition of these questions reflects the FCC's efforts to make amateurs more aware of the potential danger to themselves and their neighbors from RF radiated energy. Remember, your antenna only emits RF radiation when you are transmitting, not when you are receiving.

The FCC's *OET Bulletin 65* and *Supplement B* contain useful equations and calculation methods for predicting the strength of RF fields when you are transmitting. You can download a copy of this information by visiting the FCC's website: **www.fcc.gov** and searching for OET Bulletin 65. **The W5YI RF Safety Tables** appear on page 209 in the Appendix of this book. These tables also will help you determine the safe distance(s) from your antenna(s) for controlled and uncontrolled environments based on transmitting frequency and transmitter power.

Here are some terms and definitions that you need to know for the exam, and as an amateur operator in order to make sure your run your station in a safe manner in compliance with FCC RF safety regulations:

Near Field — the electromagnetic field located in the immediate vicinity of the antenna. The extent (size) of the near field depends on the size of the antenna, its wavelength, and transmission power.

Far Field — the electromagnetic field located at a great distance from a transmitting antenna. The far field begins at a distance that depends on many factors, including the wavelength and size of the antenna.

Transition Region — the area between the near and far field where power density decreases inversely with distance from the antenna.

Controlled Environment — involves people who are aware of and who can exercise control over RF exposure. Controlled exposure limits apply to both occupational workers and Amateur Radio operators and their immediate households.

Uncontrolled Environment — a location where individuals, such as your neighbors, may have no knowledge of (and therefore no control over) their exposure to RF radiation while you are operating your transmitter.

Maximum Permissible Exposure (MPE) — the maximum amount of electric and magnetic RF energy to which a person may be safely exposed.

Specific Absorption Rate (SAR) — the time rate at which RF energy is absorbed into the human body.

Thermal Effects — as applies to RF radiation, biological tissue damage resulting from the body's inability to cope with or dissipate excessive heat.

Duty Cycle — the percentage of time that a transmitter is "on" versus "off" in a 6- or 30-minute time period.

Can RF energy hurt me, my family, or neighbors?

Staying safe around transmitting antennas will keep you around a long time as a licensed Amateur Radio operator.

T0C01 What is radio frequency radiation?
A. Waves of electric and magnetic energy between 3 kHz and 300 GHz
B. Ultra-violet rays emitted by the sun between 20 Hz and 300 GHz
C. Sound energy given off by a radio receiver
D. Beams of X-Rays and Gamma rays emitted by a radio transmitter

ANSWER A: A radiofrequency signal is considered *radiofrequency radiation* on our popular amateur frequencies *between 3 kHz* at the bottom of the dial *and 300 GHz (300,000 MHz),* which is well into the microwave region.

T0E05 Why are Amateur Radio operators required to meet the FCC RF radiation exposure limits?
A. The standards are applied equally to all radio services
B. To ensure that RF radiation occurs only in a desired direction
C. Because amateur station operations are more easily adjusted than those of commercial radio services
D. To ensure a safe operating environment for amateurs, their families and neighbors

ANSWER D: By observing the FCC *RF radiation exposure limit rules* you will *ensure a safe operating environment* for you to enjoy Amateur Radio, and your families and neighbors to live safely near you when you are on the air.

T0C02 Why is it a good idea to adhere to the FCC's Rules for using the minimum power needed when you are transmitting with your hand-held radio?
A. Large fines are always imposed on operators violating this rule
B. To reduce the level of RF radiation exposure to the operator's head
C. To reduce calcification of the NiCd battery pack
D. To eliminate self-oscillation in the receiver RF amplifier

ANSWER B: The FCC adopted new rules and regulations about radiofrequency safety on August 1, 1996. These Part 97 rules send a clear signal that all amateur operators should be aware of the hazards associated with RF emissions. Always *reduce power to the minimum level* needed when transmitting *with a handheld* radio through a repeater or to another nearby ham on simplex *to protect your head from RF radiation.*

T0C05 Which of the following categories describes most common amateur use of a hand-held transceiver?
A. Mobile devices   C. Fixed devices
B. Portable devices   D. None of these choices is correct

ANSWER B: Your *handheld* transceiver is considered a *portable device.*

T0F13 Why does the FCC consider a hand-held transceiver to be a portable device when evaluating for RF radiation exposure?
A. Because it is generally a low-power device
B. Because it is designed to be carried close to your body
C. Because it's transmitting antenna is generally within 20 centimeters of the human body
D. All of these choices are correct

ANSWER C: The FCC takes a slightly different look at *handheld* radios as a portable device when conducting its exposure limit test because your little handheld transmitting *antenna is generally as close as 20 centimeters* or less from your eyes and face. When operating a single- or dual-band amateur transceiver, always try to position that little rubber antenna as far away from your eyes as possible.
➡ http://n5xu.ae.utexas.edu/rfsafety

The FCC considers handheld transceivers "portable devices."

T0D03 Why might mobile transceivers produce less RF radiation exposure than hand-held transceivers in mobile operations?
 A. They do not produce less exposure because they usually have higher power levels.
 B. They have a higher duty cycle
 C. When mounted on a metal vehicle roof, mobile antennas are generally well shielded from vehicle occupants
 D. Larger transmitters dissipate heat and energy more readily

ANSWER C: Never transmit with your handheld using the little rubber antenna inside the vehicle. You could actually generate more damaging RF exposure that way than you could with a more powerful output using an antenna on the metal roof. You can buy adapters that will let a *roof mounted antenna* work quite nicely on your mobile handheld. This *is the safe way to go!* ➡ www.antennex.com

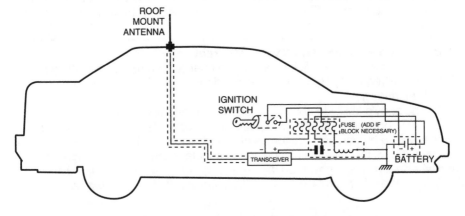

The safest place to mount the mobile antenna for minimum RF exposure is on the metal roof, as indicated.

T0E06 At what frequencies do the FCC's RF radiation exposure guidelines incorporate limits for Maximum Permissible Exposure (MPE)?

A. All frequencies below 30 MHz
B. All frequencies between 20,000 Hz and 10 MHz
C. All frequencies between 300 kHz and 100 GHz
D. All frequencies above 300 GHz

ANSWER C: All frequencies *from 300 kHz through 100 GHz* are covered as part of the Federal Communication Commission's *radiofrequency radiation guidelines.*

T0C04 Over what frequency range are the FCC Regulations most stringent for RF radiation exposure?

A. Frequencies below 300 kHz
B. Frequencies between 300 kHz and 3 MHz
C. Frequencies between 3 MHz and 30 MHz
D. Frequencies between 30 MHz and 300 MHz

ANSWER D: The *RF exposure regulations* specifically target no-code Technician class bands from *30 MHz to 300 MHz* because these frequencies have rather short wavelengths, and the shorter the wavelength, the more susceptible our body is to RF exposure problems. Microwave ovens cook at frequencies near our popular VHF and UHF radio bands. Watch out for high power levels from 30-MHz to 300-MHz, and keep that handheld antenna away from your head and eyes!

T0F01 Is it necessary for you to perform mathematical calculations of the RF radiation exposure if your VHF station delivers more than 50 watts peak envelope power (PEP) to the antenna?

A. Yes, calculations are always required to ensure greatest accuracy
B. Calculations are required if your station is located in a densely populated neighborhood
C. No, calculations may not give accurate results, so measurements are always required
D. No, there are alternate means to determine if your station meets the RF radiation exposure limits

ANSWER D: *Use the Tables and Figures* on pages 209 to 211 to determine RF radiation exposure limits. *This will save you hours* on your calculator trying to work out the complicated math calculations!

T0D02 Why do exposure limits vary with frequency?

A. Lower-frequency RF fields have more energy than higher-frequency fields
B. Lower-frequency RF fields penetrate deeper into the body than higher-frequency fields
C. The body's ability to absorb RF energy varies with frequency
D. It is impossible to measure specific absorption rates at some frequencies

ANSWER C: The human body becomes nice and resonant for roasting between 30 MHz and 300 MHz. This puts us right in the middle of the dangerous portion of the band when we run high power on the 2-meter band at 144 MHz. *The exposure limits are based on our body's ability to absorb the RF energy.*

T0C06 From an RF safety standpoint, what impact does the duty cycle have on the minimum safe distance separating an antenna and people in the neighboring environment?

    A. The lower the duty cycle, the shorter the compliance distance
    B. The compliance distance is increased with an increase in the duty cycle
    C. Lower duty cycles subject people in the environment to lower radio-frequency radiation
    D. All of these answers are correct

ANSWER D: *The less you transmit, the lower the duty cycle,* and the shorter the distance separation required between you and your neighbors. The more you talk, the further away your antenna must be from your neighbor to be within compliance. Lower duty cycle subjects the environment to *lower radiofrequency radiation cycles* – and this is good.

T0C07 Why is the concept of "duty cycle" one factor used to determine safe RF radiation exposure levels?

    A. It takes into account the amount of time the transmitter is operating at full power during a single transmission
    B. It takes into account the transmitter power supply rating
    C. It takes into account the antenna feed line loss
    D. It takes into account the thermal effects of the final amplifier

ANSWER A: *Radiofrequency emissions* from your new ham radio station will *vary* in "duty cycle" *depending on what type of emission you are using.* On FM, every time you key your microphone, your transmitter is working at full tilt. On single sideband, every time you pause between words and syllables, transmitter output drops to almost zero, decreasing the overall duty cycle. When sending CW, your dots and dashes will be active energy, with spaces in between as no energy. This will also affect the duty cycle.

The averaging time period for controlled exposure is six minutes. The averaging time for uncontrolled exposure is 30 minutes. Here are examples of equivalent exposure:

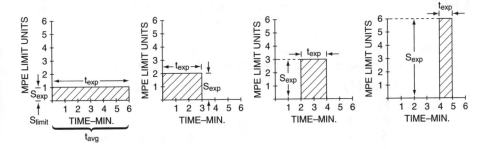

The general equation for time averaging exposure equivalence is:

$$S_{exp}\, t_{exp} = S_{limit}\, t_{avg}$$

The duty cycle is:
$$DC\ (in\ \%) = \frac{t_{exp}}{t_{avg}} \times 100$$

T0D07 What factors determine the location of the boundary between the near and far fields of an antenna?
A. Wavelength and the physical size of the antenna
B. Antenna height and element length
C. Boom length and element diameter
D. Transmitter power and antenna gain

ANSWER A: When predicting the amount of RF radiation that someone may be exposed to from an amateur antenna, we first consider the most dangerous area, the near-field, or Fresnel region. Here is where power density can be at a maximum before it begins to decrease with distance. The distance (in meters) that the near field extends is given by the formula:

$$R_{nf} = \frac{D^2}{4\lambda}$$

Where:
D = Antenna diameter in **meters**
λ = Wavelength in **meters**

The power density in the far-field, called the Fraunhoffer region, decreases inversely as the square of the distance. Power density in the far-field of the radiation pattern can be estimated by the general equation:

$$S_{ff} = \frac{PG}{4\pi R^2}$$

Where:
S_{ff} = Power density in **milliwatts per square centimeter (mW/cm^2)**
P = Power fed to the antenna in **watts**
G = Gain of the antenna relative to an isotropic radiator **(a ratio)**
R = Distance to the point of interest in **centimeters**

It is the *wavelength of the frequency* that you are transmitting *and the physical size of the antenna* that will *determine the boundaries between near-fields and far-fields.*

T0C03 Which of the following units of measurement are used to specify the power density of a radiated RF signal?
A. Milliwatts per square centimeter   C. Amperes per meter
B. Volts per meter   D. All of these choices are correct

ANSWER A: The measurement of *"power density"* of a radiated RF signal at a distance from the antenna, the "far-field," has been pre-calculated for amateur operators. Power density of a radiated radiofrequency signal is measured in *milliwatts per square centimeter (mW/cm^2).* Keep in mind that a radio system used just for receive does not put out a radiated RF signal. Only on transmit.

Quantity	Unit of Measurement
RF Electrical Field Strength	Volts per meter–V/m
RF Magnetic Field Strength	Amperes per meter–A/m
RF Radiated Signal Power Density	Milliwatts per square centimeter–mW/cm^2

Units of RF Radiation

T0F15 In which of the following areas is it most difficult to accurately evaluate the effects of RF radiation exposure?
A. In the far field   C. In the near field
B. In the cybersphere   D. In the low-power field

ANSWER C: An antenna energized by a radio set on transmit produces strong near-field energy where power density is at a maximum. RF radiation decreases with distance. The "near field" is so close to the antenna that a person could easily touch it, or within a few steps, walk over and touch it. Because there is so much power density in close proximity to the antenna when the radio is transmitting, and there are so many other variables to consider, *it is most difficult to accurately evaluate the effects of RF radiation exposure in the near field.*

T0D05 In the near field, how does the field strength vary with distance from the source?
- A. It always increases with the cube of the distance
- B. It always decreases with the cube of the distance
- C. It varies as a sine wave with distance
- D. It depends on the type of antenna being used

ANSWER D: Every antenna has its own radiation pattern. On Yagi antennas, the greatest radiation is from the front director. On a dipole, there may be minimum amounts of radiation off each end, but maximum when standing broadside to the dipole. Remember that the *near field strength of the signal will depend on the type of antenna* that is radiating the power from the transceiver on transmit.

T0D04 In the far field, as the distance from the source increases, how does power density vary?
- A. The power density is proportional to the square of the distance
- B. The power density is proportional to the square root of the distance
- C. The power density is proportional to the inverse square of the distance
- D. The power density is proportional to the inverse cube of the distance

ANSWER C: During our ham radio weekend classes that I teach throughout the country, I use a fluorescent tube to illustrate the power density around a mobile 1/4-wavelength, 10-meter antenna at 100 watts output. We use a nonconducting extension pole to hold the tube next to the antenna. When I speak in the mike, the fluorescent tube glows. But as soon as that tube is more than a foot or so away from the antenna, it no longer glows. This is a graphic example of how the power density radiating off an antenna is proportional to the inverse square of the distance away from the antenna.

We see that the *far-field power density varies with the inverse square of the distance R from the antenna.*

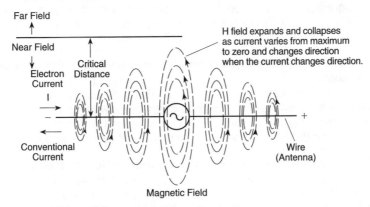

Electromagnetic Antenna Fields

Source: *Antennas,* A.J. Evans, K.E. Britain, ©1998, Master Publishing, Lincolnwood, Illinois

T0D01 What factors must you consider if your repeater station antenna will be located at a site that is occupied by antennas for transmitters in other services?

- A. Your radiated signal must be considered as part of the total RF radiation from the site when determining RF radiation exposure levels
- B. Each individual transmitting station at a multiple transmitter site must meet the RF radiation exposure levels
- C. Each station at a multiple-transmitter site may add no more than 1% of the maximum permissible exposure (MPE) for that site
- D. Amateur stations are categorically excluded from RF radiation exposure evaluation at multiple-transmitter sites

ANSWER A: Now here is an interesting situation – you will be putting up a *repeater station* and antenna system on top of a building where the maximum permissible exposure (MPE) is just barely within the legal limit. You now turn on your system, and when your station is transmitting the collective signals may exceed MPE limits. Do they *judge your system* all by itself, or collectively? That's right, *collectively as part of the total RF radiation from the transmitter site.*
➡ www.ustower.com

All of the RF emissions from a repeater site like this one must be considered collectively when performing an RF safety evaluation.

T0C09 What unit of measurement specifies RF electric field strength?

- A. Coulombs (C) at one wavelength from the antenna
- B. Volts per meter (V/m)
- C. Microfarads (uF) at the transmitter output
- D. Microhenrys (uH) per square centimeter

ANSWER B: The measurement of RF electrical field strength is a complicated process requiring a major amount of expensive equipment. The measurements will specify *RF electrical field strengths in volts per meter, abbreviated V/m.* The electric field is always measured in volts per meter.

T0C10 Which of the following is considered to be non-ionizing radiation?

- A. X-radiation
- B. Gamma radiation
- C. Ultraviolet radiation
- D. Radiofrequency radiation

ANSWER D: The transmission of *radiofrequency energy* from your antenna *is* considered *"nonionizing" radiation.* This is altogether different than x-ray, gamma ray, and ultraviolet radiation, which are far more dangerous.

T0E11 What is one effect of RF non-ionizing radiation on the human body?

- A. Cooling of body tissues
- B. Heating of body tissues
- C. Rapid dehydration
- D. Sudden hair loss

ANSWER B: *"Nonionizing radiation"* is the radio signal coming off of a transmitting Amateur Radio (for that matter, any type of radio or television) antenna system, and it is the *heating of body tissue* that we are most concerned with. Stay away from transmitting antennas.

T0C11 What do the FCC RF radiation exposure regulations establish?

A. Maximum radiated field strength
B. Minimum permissible HF antenna height
C. Maximum permissible exposure limits
D. All of these choices are correct

ANSWER C: The FCC *RF radiation exposure rules and regulations establish maximum permissible exposure (MPE) limits.* It's up to YOU to adjust radiated field strength by the amount of power you are transmitting, and it's up to YOU as to how high up your antenna will be mounted.

T0C08 What factors affect the resulting RF fields emitted by an amateur transceiver that expose people in the environment?

A. Frequency and power level of the RF field
B. Antenna height and distance from the antenna to a person
C. Radiation pattern of the antenna
D. All of these answers are correct

ANSWER D: The term "RF" refers to "radiofrequency" energy that comes off of your ham radio antenna system on transmit. The radiofrequency energy can be analyzed as a radiofrequency "field," and these "RF fields" must be evaluated to determine the environmental effects that this radio energy may have on our well-being. The *important factors in evaluating the environmental effects of RF emissions are: frequencies and power levels* of your transmitter; *how high up your antenna is* and *how far it is away from people*; the radiation pattern of your antenna; and, to some extent, ground reflections of the radiated energy. *"All of these answers" are important to consider.*

T0C12 Which of the following steps would help you to comply with RF-radiation exposure guidelines for uncontrolled RF environments?

A. Reduce transmitting times within a 6-minute period to reduce the station duty cycle
B. Operate only during periods of high solar absorption
C. Reduce transmitting times within a 30-minute period to reduce the station duty cycle
D. Operate only on high duty cycle modes

ANSWER C: One way to *reduce your RF radiation* exposure would be to *reduce transmitting times* within a 30-minute period *to reduce the station duty cycle.* The averaging time for an uncontrolled RF environment is 30 minutes.
➡www.cq73.com

T0E03 To determine compliance with the maximum permitted exposure (MPE) levels, safe exposure levels for RF energy are averaged for an "uncontrolled" RF environment over what time period?

A. 6 minutes   C. 15 minutes
B. 10 minutes   D. 30 minutes

ANSWER D: In an *uncontrolled RF environment,* exposure is based on the averaged transmission made over *30 minutes. Remember "U-30."*
➡ www.universaltower.com

T0C13 Which of the following steps would help you to comply with RF-exposure guidelines for controlled RF environments?
A. Reduce transmitting times within a 30-minute period to reduce the station duty cycle
B. Operate only during periods of high solar absorption
C. Reduce transmitting times within a 6-minute period to reduce the station duty cycle
D. Operate only on high duty cycle modes

ANSWER C: For a *controlled RF environment,* reducing transmitting time within a *6-minute period* will reduce the station duty cycle and lower RF exposure.

T0E04 To determine compliance with the maximum permitted exposure (MPE) levels, safe exposure levels for RF energy are averaged for a "controlled" RF environment over what time period?
A. 6 minutes
B. 10 minutes
C. 15 minutes
D. 30 minutes

ANSWER A: In a *controlled RF environment*, exposure is based on the averaged transmission made over *6 minutes. Remember "C-6."*

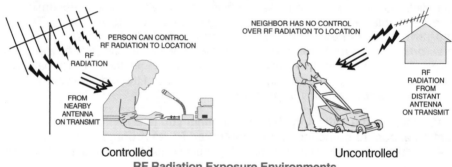

Controlled   Uncontrolled
RF Radiation Exposure Environments

T0C14 To avoid excessively high human exposure to RF fields, how should amateur antennas generally be mounted?
A. With a high current point near ground
B. As far away from accessible areas as possible
C. On a nonmetallic mast
D. With the elements in a horizontal polarization

ANSWER B: Put your *antennas as far away as possible from accessible areas* so no one can come near them on transmit. ➡**www.radioworks.com**

T0E10 Why should you not stand within reach of any transmitting antenna when it is being fed with 1500 watts of RF energy?
A. It could result in the loss of the ability to move muscles
B. Your body would reflect the RF energy back to its source
C. It could cause cooling of body tissue
D. You could accidentally touch the antenna and be injured

ANSWER D: When you pass your Technician class license, you are allowed to operate up to 1500 watts output of RF energy. You might run this amount of power while conducting moon-bounce operations on the 2-meter or 430-MHz band. Make sure that no one can touch the transmitting antenna with this major amount of power on it, because *accidentally touching the antenna will cause someone to be burned and injured.* ➡**www.ameritron.com**

T0D06 Why should you never look into the open end of a microwave feed horn antenna while the transmitter is operating?

A. You may be exposing your eyes to more than the maximum permissible exposure of RF radiation

B. You may be exposing your eyes to more than the maximum permissible exposure level of infrared radiation

C. You may be exposing your eyes to more than the maximum permissible exposure level of ultraviolet radiation

D. All of these choices are correct

ANSWER A: *Microwave* systems may use *feed horns,* parabolic reflectors, or slotted wave guides to radiate the signal in a concentrated beam. Consider any microwave antenna as dangerous, regardless of the low power output that the operator may be transmitting. Never assume that a microwave system is simply receiving signals and is harmless. Always assume that the microwave antenna is transmitting a signal, and always walk behind a microwave transmitting antenna, never in front of it. *Exposing your eyes to more that the maximum permissible exposure of RF radiation is very dangerous.*

Never stand in front of a microwave feedhorn antenna. On transmit, it radiates a concentrated beam of RF energy.

T0C15 What action can amateur operators take to prevent exposure to RF radiation in excess of the FCC-specified limits?

A. Alter antenna patterns

B. Relocate antennas

C. Revise station technical parameters, such as frequency, power, or emission type

D. All of these choices are correct

ANSWER D: In order *to prevent exposure to RF radiation* in excess of the FCC-specified limits, you may need to *relocate your antenna, lower your power, change frequency bands, alter antenna patterns,* and maybe *do all of these,* if necessary. ➡**www.csvhfs.org**

T0C16 Which of the following radio frequency emissions will result in the least RF radiation exposure if they all have the same peak envelope power (PEP)?

A. Two-way exchanges of phase-modulated (PM) telephony

B. Two-way exchanges of frequency-modulated (FM) telephony

C. Two-way exchanges of single-sideband (SSB) telephony

D. Two-way exchanges of Morse code (CW) communication

ANSWER C: *Single-sideband voice* transmissions (telephony) *have less RF radiation than all other types of transmissions* at the same peak envelope power. This is because there is little power output in between syllables, sentences, and when you have stopped talking and are listening and thinking of what you are going to say next. ➡**www.ntms.org**

T0C17 Why is the concept of "specific absorption rate (SAR)" one factor used to determine safe RF radiation exposure levels?
A. It takes into account the overall efficiency of the final amplifier
B. It takes into account the transmit/receive time ratio during normal amateur communication
C. It takes into account the rate at which the human body absorbs RF energy at a particular frequency
D. It takes into account the antenna feed line loss
ANSWER C: The "Soon About to Roast" *(SAR) concept is based on a calculated rate at which the human body absorbs RF energy* at a specific frequency.

T0C18 Why must the frequency of an RF source be considered when evaluating RF radiation exposure?
A. Lower-frequency RF fields have more energy than higher-frequency fields
B. Lower-frequency RF fields penetrate deeper into the body than higher-frequency fields
C. Higher-frequency RF fields are transient in nature, and do not affect the human body
D. The human body absorbs more RF energy at some frequencies than at others
ANSWER D: Remember that your operation on many different radio bands changes the frequency of your RF emissions. *At certain wavelengths around 2 meters, the human body absorbs more RF energy.* On lower-frequency worldwide wavelengths, the body absorbs less energy.

T0E07 On what value are the maximum permissible exposure (MPE) limits based?
A. The square of the mass of the exposed body
B. The square root of the mass of the exposed body
C. The whole-body specific gravity (WBSG)
D. The whole-body specific absorption rate (SAR)
ANSWER D: *Maximum permissible exposure limits are based on our whole-body specific absorption rate.* You can remember "SAR" as "Soon About to Roast".

(A) Limits for Occupational / Controlled Exposure				
Frequency Range (MHz)	Electrical Field Strength (V/m)	Magnetic Field Strength (A/m)	Power Density (mW/cm²)	Averaging Time (minutes)
0.3 – 3.0	614	1.63	(100)*	6
3.0 – 30	1842/f	4.89/f	(900/f²)*	6
30 – 300	61.4	0.163	1.0	6
300 – 1500	—	—	f/300	6
1500 – 100,000	—	—	5	6
(B) Limits for General Population / Uncontrolled Exposure				
Frequency Range (MHz)	Electrical Field Strength (V/m)	Magnetic Field Strength (A/m)	Power Density (mW/cm²)	Averaging Time (minutes)
0.3 – 1.34	614	1.63	(100)*	30
1.34 – 30	824/f	2.19/f	(180/f²)*	30
30 – 300	27.5	0.073	0.2	30
300 – 1500	—	—	f/1500	30
1500 – 100,000	—	—	1.0	30
f = frequency in MHz	*= Plane-wave equivalent power density			

Figure T0-1

T0D08 Referring to Figure T0-1, which of the following equations should you use to calculate the maximum permissible exposure (MPE) on the Technician (with code credit) HF bands for a controlled RF radiation exposure environment?

A. Maximum permissible power density in mW per square cm equals 900 divided by the square of the operating frequency, in MHz

B. Maximum permissible power density in mW per square cm equals 180 divided by the square of the operating frequency, in MHz

C. Maximum permissible power density in mW per square cm equals 900 divided by the operating frequency, in MHz

D. Maximum permissible power density in mW per square cm equals 180 divided by the operating frequency, in MHz

ANSWER A: On your upcoming Technician class examination, you will be given a sheet with figures and tables. Don't panic – if you read them carefully, you'll be able to spot the correct answer quickly. This question deals with a Technician class operator, with code credit, operating on high-frequency bands for a controlled RF radiation exposure environment calculation. *Go to Figure T0-1*, and notice that *table (A) is for controlled exposure.* Now *go to frequency range* and look up *3.0-30,* the second set of frequencies down from the top. Now go over 3 boxes for *power density, and see (900/F²)* which agrees with Answer A, "milliwatts per square centimeter equals 900 divided by the square of the operating frequency, in MHz." The only thing the question does not give you are the actual frequencies, but since they say a frequency on HF, you must remember 3 MHz-30 MHz, and then refer to the figure and the (A) box. ➡ **www.swot.org**

T0D09 Referring to Figure T0-1, what is the formula for calculating the maximum permissible exposure (MPE) limit for uncontrolled environments on the 2-meter (146 MHz) band?

A. There is no formula, MPE is a fixed power density of 1.0 milliwatt per square centimeter averaged over any 6 minutes

B. There is no formula, MPE is a fixed power density of 0.2 milliwatt per square centimeter averaged over any 30 minutes

C. The MPE in milliwatts per square centimeter equals the frequency in megahertz divided by 300 averaged over any 6 minutes

D. The MPE in milliwatts per square centimeter equals the frequency in megahertz divided by 1500 averaged over any 30 minutes

ANSWER B: Here's another one to look up on Figure T0-1, but this time go to the bottom of the figure for the *table (B) limits for uncontrolled exposure.* The question indicates we're operating on *146 MHz,* so this would be between *30-300,* and the power density is not a formula but rather *"0.2 milliwatts per square centimeter averaged over any 30 minutes."* This figure T0-1 chart will be part of your examination paperwork. Just remember (A) is for controlled exposure, and the lower portion of the chart (B) is for uncontrolled exposure. Look up the frequency range, and then look for power density to solve the problem and find the correct answer.

The next 5 questions lead you to figures found in the tables in Figure T0-2. Some examiners may give you the extra job of choosing which of the T0-2 tables may apply to this question – there are actually 5 individual tables that make up Figure T0-2. But you can easily spot which of the 5 to choose by zeroing in on the frequency. One is for 7 MHz, one is for 28 MHz, one is for 144 MHz, one is for 146 MHz, and one is for 446 MHz. They will give you the specific frequency in the question.

T0D10 What is the minimum safe distance for a controlled RF radiation environment from a station using a half-wavelength dipole antenna on 7 MHz at 100 watts PEP, as specified in Figure T0-2?

A. 1.4 foot
B. 2 feet
C. 3.1 feet
D. 6.5 feet

ANSWER A: In THIS question, we are at *7 MHz, 100 watts of power, in a controlled RF radiation environment* with a *halfwave dipole.* The CONTROLLED box for 100 watts output lists *1.4 feet,* which Answer A shows as 1.4 foot safety distance. Feet or foot, who cares? Go for *Answer A!*
➡www.thewireman.com

Estimated distances to meet RF power density guidelines with a horizontal *half-wave dipole* antenna (estimated gain, 2 dBi). Calculations include the EPA ground reflection factor of 2.56.

Frequency: *7 MHz*
Estimated antenna gain: 2 dBi
Controlled limit: 18.37 mw/cm²
Uncontrolled limit: 3.67 mw/cm²

Transmitter power (watts)	Distance to controlled limit	Distance to uncontrolled limit
100	1.4′	3.1′
500	3.1′	6.9′
1000	4.3′	9.7′
1500	5.3′	11.9′

Figure T0-2

T0D11 What is the minimum safe distance for an uncontrolled RF radiation environment from a station using a 3-element "triband" Yagi antenna on 28 MHz at 100 watts PEP, as specified in Figure T0-2?

A. 7 feet
B. 11 feet
C. 24.5 feet
D. 34 feet

ANSWER C: Now we are on *28 MHz, 100 watts, UNCONTROLLED.* Go over to the *right-hand box,* and there is the *correct answer, 24.5 feet.* Be careful – if you go for the first box, it shows 11 feet for controlled. This question asks UNCONTROLLED. ➡www.hy-gain.com

Estimated distances to meet RF power density guidelines in the main beam of a typical *3-element "triband" Yagi* for the 14, 21, and 28 MHz amateur radio bands. Calculations include the EPA ground reflection factor of 2.56.

Frequency: *28 MHz*
Estimated antenna gain: 8 dBi
Controlled limit: 1.5 mw/cm²
Uncontrolled limit: 0.23 mw/cm²

Transmitter power (watts)	Distance to controlled limit	Distance to uncontrolled limit
100	11′	24.5′
500	24.5′	54.9′
1000	34.7′	77.6′
1500	42.5′	95.1′

Figure T0-2

T0D12 What is the minimum safe distance for a controlled RF radiation environment from a station using a 146 MHz quarter-wave whip antenna at 10 watts, as specified in Figure T0-2?

    A. 1.7 feet
    B. 2.5 feet
    C. 1.2 feet
    D. 2 feet

ANSWER A: This question takes us to the *146 MHz box, 10 watts, CONTROLLED. Easy one – 1.7 feet.* And this is a good question to better understand – it describes a simple automobile 2-meter antenna attached to the roof of your car maybe with a magnetic mount. At 10 watts, you need to stay at least 1.7 feet away, and for everybody inside the car (uncontrolled) that have no idea you are transmitting RF power output, they need to be at least 3.7 feet away! Luckily, the antenna is on the roof, and the roof shields everybody within the car so you should be safe and sound yakking on your ham set using 10 watts of power or less. ➡**www.rfparts.com**

Estimated distances to meet RF power density guidelines with a VHF *quarter-wave* ground plane or *mobile whip* antenna (estimated gain, 1 dBi). Calculations include the EPA ground reflection factor of 2.56.

Frequency: *146 MHz*
Estimated antenna gain: 1 dBi
Controlled limit: 1 mw/cm^2
Uncontrolled limit: 0.2 mw/cm^2

Transmitter power (watts)	Distance to controlled limit	Distance to uncontrolled limit
10	1.7´	3.7´
50	3.7´	8.3´
100	6.4´	14.4´

Figure T0-2

T0D13 What is the minimum safe distance for a controlled RF radiation environment from a station using a 17-element Yagi on a five-wavelength boom on 144 MHz at 100 watts, as specified in Figure T0-2?

    A. 72.4 feet
    B. 78.5 feet
    C. 101 feet
    D. 32.4 feet

ANSWER D: Now you are going to a big *monster moonbounce station, running 100 watts on 144 MHz* and they ask about the distance to *controlled environment.* At 100 watts, distance to controlled shows *32.4 feet* on the chart. Read these questions carefully to see whether or not they want controlled or uncontrolled. ➡**www.qsl.net/ac6la**

Estimated distances to meet RF power density guidelines in the main beam of a *17-element Yagi* on a five-wavelength boom designed for weak signal communications on the 144 MHz amateur radio band (estimated gain, 16.8 dBi). Calculations include the EPA ground reflection factor of 2.56.

Frequency: *144 MHz*
Estimated antenna gain: 16.8 dBi
Controlled limit: 1 mw/cm^2
Uncontrolled limit: 0.2 mw/cm^2

Transmitter power (watts)	Distance to controlled limit	Distance to uncontrolled limit
10	10.2´	22.9´
100	32.4´	72.4´
500	72.4´	162´
1500	125.5´	280.6´

Figure T0-2

T0D14 What is the minimum safe distance for an uncontrolled RF radiation environment from a station using a 446 MHz 5/8-wave ground plane vertical antenna at 10 watts, as specified in Figure T0-2?

A. 1 foot
B. 4.3 feet
C. 9.6 feet
D. 6 feet

ANSWER B: Now you are up on the *70 cm 446 MHz band, running 10 watts.* The question asks the distance for an *uncontrolled RF radiation environment.* This is the box all the way to the right, showing *4.3 feet.* Easy stuff, huh?

The only variable on your upcoming exam will be whether or not the exam team gives you a single page with all of the charts, or if they make it easy for you and give you the specific chart next to the specific question as we have. Either way, *look at the exact frequency,* and most important, *look for controlled or uncontrolled distances, check the power,* and then go for the answer that is correct. Be careful – controlled or uncontrolled is what they want you to know to answer these questions correctly.

Estimated distances to meet RF power density guidelines in the main beam of a *UHF 5/8 ground plane* or mobile whip antenna (estimated gain, 4 dBi). Calculations include the EPA ground reflection factor of 2.56.

Frequency: *446 MHz*
Estimated antenna gain: 4 dBi
Controlled limit: 1.49 mw/cm^2
Uncontrolled limit: 0.3 mw/cm^2

Transmitter power (watts)	Distance to controlled limit	Distance to uncontrolled limit
10	1.9´	4.3´
50	4.3´	9.6´
100	7.5´	16.7´

Figure T0-2

T0E09 Which of the following effects on the human body are a result of exposure to high levels of RF energy?

A. Very rapid hair growth
B. Very rapid growth of fingernails and toenails
C. Possible heating of body tissue
D. High levels of RF energy have no known effect on the human body

ANSWER C: What happens to a meatloaf sandwich when you put it in your microwave and turn on the microwave energy? It heats up, doesn't it! Possible *heating of body tissue* is a major concern when we study and evaluate the environmental effects of RF emissions from your ham radio antenna system.

NEVER STAND IN FRONT OF OR TOUCH AN AMATEUR ANTENNA. IT IS EXREMELY DANGEROUS.

RF Radiation Exposure

T0E08 What is one biological effect to the eye that can result from RF exposure?

A. The strong magnetic fields can cause blurred vision
B. The strong magnetic fields can cause polarization lens
C. It can cause heating, which can result in the formation of cataracts
D. It can cause heating, which can result in astigmatism

ANSWER C: *Intense exposure to microwaves* causes heating of our ocular fluids, which *could result in the formation of cataracts.* Don't be overly concerned that a small handheld radio or mobile VHF is going to cause you to go blind. What we are saying is don't stand in front of a 1500-watt, 5-wavelength-long moonbounce Yagi on 1296 MHz and stare down the length of the boom when the station is transmitting. As long as you take reasonable safety precautions to get out of the way of 1500 watt super-station antennas, you're going to be just fine.

T0C19 What is the maximum power density that may be emitted from an amateur station under the FCC RF radiation exposure limits?
    A. The FCC Rules specify a maximum emission of 1.0 milliwatt per square centimeter
    B. The FCC Rules specify a maximum emission of 5.0 milliwatts per square centimeter
    C. The FCC Rules specify exposure limits, not emission limits
    D. The FCC Rules specify maximum emission limits that vary with frequency
ANSWER C: *The rules specify exposure limits,* which are based on many factors and are altogether different than the actual power emission from your ham antenna.

T0F02 What is one method that amateur radio licensees may use to conduct a routine station evaluation to determine whether the station is within the Maximum Permissible Exposure guidelines?
    A. Direct measurement of the RF fields
    B. Indirect measurement of the energy density at the limit of the controlled area
    C. Estimation of field strength by S-meter readings in the controlled area
    D. Estimation of field strength by taking measurements using a directional coupler in the transmission line
ANSWER A: If you really get into this great ham radio hobby and your local club appoints you the local electronics antenna guru, buy yourself a $1,000 calibrated field-strength meter that allows you to make direct measurements of the RF fields up at the repeater site. *Direct measurement is a great way to know how much RF is around you.*

T0F10 Which of the following instruments might you use to measure the RF radiation exposure levels in the vicinity of your station?
    A. A calibrated field strength meter with a calibrated field strength sensor
    B. A calibrated in-line wattmeter with a calibrated length of feed line
    C. A calibrated RF impedance bridge
    D. An amateur receiver with an S meter calibrated to National Bureau of Standards and Technology station WWV
ANSWER A: To *measure RF radiation* exposure levels, you could *use a calibrated field-strength meter* with a calibrated field-strength sensor. A regular, everyday field-strength meter won't work – everything must be well-calibrated.

T0F04 Which category of transceiver is NOT excluded from the requirement to perform a routine station evaluation?
    A. Hand-held transceivers
    B. VHF base station transmitters that deliver more than 50 watts peak envelope power (PEP) to an antenna
    C. Vehicle-mounted push-to-talk mobile radios
    D. Portable transceivers with high duty cycles

ANSWER B: Small radio equipment like handheld transceivers, mobile two-way radios, and any other type of portable two-way radio might be excluded from the routine station evaluation for putting out excessive amounts of RF radiation. However, *a VHF base station transmitting with more than 50 watts output would most definitely NOT be excluded from the evaluation!*

T0F05 Which of the following antennas would (generally) create a stronger RF field on the ground beneath the antenna?
- A. A horizontal loop at 30 meters above ground
- B. A 3-element Yagi at 30 meters above ground
- C. A 1/2 wave dipole antenna 5 meters above ground
- D. A 3-element Quad at 30 meters above ground

ANSWER C: An *antenna real close to the ground will give off maximum RF fields* on the ground beneath it. The half-wave dipole is only 5 meters above the ground, where all the other ones are up at least 30 meters. The dipole just 5 meters up will create the strongest RF field on the ground beneath it.

T0F07 Below what power level at the input to the antenna are amateur radio operators categorically excluded from routine evaluation to predict if the RF exposure from their VHF station could be excessive?
- A. 25 watts peak envelope power (PEP)
- B. 50 watts peak envelope power (PEP)
- C. 100 watts peak envelope power (PEP)
- D. 500 watts peak envelope power (PEP)

ANSWER B: All amateur transmitters are subject to the FCC's RF Safety guidelines, but *only those stations running more than 50 watts PEP must complete a formal RF evaluation.*

T0F08 Above what power level is a routine RF radiation evaluation required for a VHF station?
- A. 25 watts peak envelope power (PEP) measured at the antenna input
- B. 50 watts peak envelope power (PEP) measured at the antenna input
- C. 100 watts input power to the final amplifier stage
- D. 250 watts output power from the final amplifier stage

ANSWER B: At *50 watts of power or more*, you are *required to complete a routine RF radiation evaluation.* This includes VHF equipment operated by the Technician class no-code licensee.

T0F11 What effect does the antenna gain have on a routine RF exposure evaluation?
- A. Antenna gain is part of the formulas used to perform calculations
- B. The maximum permissible exposure (MPE) limits are directly proportional to antenna gain
- C. The maximum permissible exposure (MPE) limits are the same in all locations surrounding an antenna.
- D. All of these choices are correct

ANSWER A: Antenna gain has an important bearing on your exposure evaluations. *Antenna gain also is part of the formulas* that have been used to develop The W5YI RF Safety Tables in the Appendix of this book. You can use the tables to determine RF exposure limits.

T0F12 As a general rule, what effect does antenna height above ground have on the RF exposure environment?
  A. Power density is not related to antenna height or distance from the RF exposure environment
  B. Antennas that are farther above ground produce higher maximum permissible exposures (MPE)
  C. The higher the antenna the less the RF radiation exposure at ground level
  D. RF radiation exposure is increased when the antenna is higher above ground

ANSWER C: Here's an interesting thought – you can assure your neighbors that *the higher your antenna* is in the air on that big tower, *the less the RF radiation* exposure at ground level. Give it a try and let me know what they say.

T0F14 Which of the following factors must be taken into account when using a computer program to model RF fields at your station?
  A. Height above sea level at your station
  B. Ionization level in the F2 region of the ionosphere
  C. Ground interactions
  D. The latitude and longitude of your station location

ANSWER C: *Ground reflections* of your transmitted signal *add to the power density* levels because some of the energy is being reradiated back up into the environment around your new antenna system when you are transmitting.

T0E01 If you do not have the equipment to measure the RF power densities present at your station, what might you do to ensure compliance with the FCC RF radiation exposure limits?
  A. Use one or more of the methods included in the amateur supplement to FCC OET Bulletin 65
  B. Call an FCC-Certified Test Technician to perform the measurements for you
  C. Reduce power from 200 watts PEP to 100 watts PEP
  D. Operate only low-duty-cycle modes such as FM

ANSWER A: *Bulletin 65 from the Office of Engineering and Technology (OET)* lists the elaborate formulas used to calculate power densities on specific frequencies, different types of antennas, ground reflections and a host of other variables. These formulas are so complex that the FCC condensed its findings into the *tables and figures* we have been reviewing to answer some of these questions.

T0E02 Where will you find the applicable FCC RF radiation maximum permissible exposure (MPE) limits defined?
  A. FCC Part 97 Amateur Service Rules and Regulations
  B. FCC Part 15 Radiation Exposure Rules and Regulations
  C. FCC Part 1 and Office of Engineering and Technology (OET) Bulletin 65
  D. Environmental Protection Agency Regulation 65

ANSWER C: The FCC defines the maximum permissible exposure *(MPE) in its Part 1 Rules and Regulations.* The limits are *also found in OET Bulletin 65,* a half-inch-thick document that provides a detailed analysis of how close we can safely get to our own antennas on transmit (controlled environment), and how far away we must keep our antennas from our neighbors and others around us (uncontrolled environment).

T0F03 What document establishes mandatory procedures for evaluating compliance with RF exposure limits?
- A. There are no mandatory procedures
- B. OST/OET Bulletin 65
- C. Part 97 of the FCC rules
- D. ANSI/IEEE C95.1--1992

ANSWER A: This question asks about the actual, MANDATORY PROCEDURES you should follow for evaluating compliance with RF exposure limits. While indeed your first step is looking over OET Bulletin 65, plus FCC rules, plus ANSI/IEEE paperwork, none of these actually mandate a specific PROCEDURE for conducting your exposure limits evaluation. So the correct answer is *there are no mandatory procedures.*

T0F06 How may an amateur determine that his or her station complies with FCC RF-exposure regulations?
- A. By calculation, based on FCC OET Bulletin No. 65
- B. By calculation, based on computer modeling
- C. By measurement, measuring the field strength using calibrated equipment
- D. Any of these choices

ANSWER D: You can determine how your station *complies with FCC RF exposure regulations by using The W5YI RF Safety Tables* in the Appendix on page 209 of this book. You can use the tables to estimate safe distances based on *FCC OET Bulletin No. 65,* or by *your own calculations based on computer modeling.* You also can actually go out there and *measure with a field-strength meter* the power density levels making sure to use calibrated equipment. *All of these choices* are a good way to determine whether or not you are going to expose yourself or your neighbors unnecessarily.

T0F09 What must you do with the records of a routine RF radiation exposure evaluation?
- A. They must be sent to the nearest FCC field office
- B. They must be sent to the Environmental Protection Agency
- C. They must be attached to each Form 605 when it is sent to the FCC for processing
- D. Though not required, records may prove useful if the FCC asks for documentation to substantiate that an evaluation has been performed

ANSWER D: When you perform RF radiation exposure evaluations, you should write down your results and keep them in case the FCC asks for documentation to substantiate that an evaluation has been performed. *Keep the records at your station* in a safe place. You don't need to send them anywhere, but they must be available *if the FCC asks for documentation.*

Well, you've made it through the question pool. Now it's time to go back page 31 and begin reviewing your new found knowledge. Work the book!

5

Learning Morse Code

As of April 15, 2000, the Federal Communications Commission dropped the 20- and 13-wpm Morse code requirements, leaving 5-wpm as the only Morse code requirement for ham radio licensing in the U.S. 5-wpm code speed is so slow that your brain has plenty of time to hear the sound of the code, recall what letter or number it is, and transfer that message to your hand where you write it down and then wait patiently for the next sound group.

In this chapter, we provide you with a look at the code, and lots of helpful hints for learning the code. Learning the code *by ear* is by far the best way to go, however adding some visual learning will help.

So begin memorizing the alphabet, and then see how easy it is to get the pattern down of the numerals. On the special signals and punctuation, all your 5-wpm Element 1 code test will have is the period, the comma, the question mark, the slant bar, break or pause and, at the final end of the test, the AR for "end of message," and SK for "end of work," pro signs.

LOOKING AT MORSE CODE

The International Morse code, originally developed as the American Morse code by Samuel Morse, is truly international — all countries use it, and most commercial worldwide services employ operators who can recognize it. It is made up of short and long duration sounds. Long sounds, called "dahs," are three times longer than short sounds, called "dits." *Figure 4-1* shows the time intervals for Morse code sounds and spaces. *Figure 4-2* indicates the sounds for the characters and symbols.

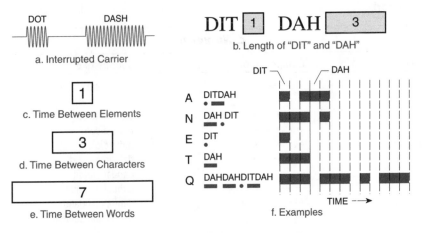

Figure 4-1. Time Intervals for Morse Code

a. Alphabet

LETTER	Composed of:	Sounds like:	LETTER	Composed of:	Sounds like:
A	• —	didah	N	— •	dahdit
B	— • • •	dahdididit	O	— — —	dahdahdah
C	— • — •	dahdidahdit	P	• — — •	didahdahdit
D	— • •	dahdidit	Q	— — • —	dahdahdidah
E	•	dit	R	• — •	didahdit
F	• • — •	dididahdit	S	• • •	dididit
G	— — •	dahdahdit	T	—	dah
H	• • • •	didididit	U	• • —	dididah
I	• •	didit	V	• • • —	didididah
J	• — — —	didahdahdah	W	• — —	ditdahdah
K	— • —	dahdidah	X	— • • —	dahdididah
L	• — • •	didahdidit	Y	— • — —	dahdidahdah
M	— —	dahdah	Z	— — • •	dahdahdidit

b. Special Signals and Punctuation

CHARACTER	Meaning:	Composed of:	Sounds like:
$\overline{AR}$	(end of message)	• — • — •	didahdidahdit
K	invitation to transmit (go ahead)	— • —	dahdidah
$\overline{SK}$	End of work	• • • — • —	didididahdidah
$\overline{SOS}$	International distress call	• • • — — — • • •	didididahdahdahdididit
V	Test letter (V)	• • • —	didididah
R	Received, OK	• — •	didahdit
$\overline{BT}$	Break or Pause	— • • • —	dahdidididah
$\overline{DN}$	Slant Bar	— • • — •	dahdidididahdit
$\overline{KN}$	Back to You Only	— • — — •	dahdidahdahdit
Period		• — • — • —	didahdidahdidah
Comma		— — • • — —	dahdahdididahdah
Question mark		• • — — • •	dididahdahdidit

c. Numerals

NUMBER	Composed of:	Sounds like:
1	• — — — —	didahdahdahdah
2	• • — — —	dididahdahdah
3	• • • — —	didididahdah
4	• • • • —	dididididah
5	• • • • •	dididididit
6	— • • • •	dahdidididit
7	— — • • •	dahdahdididit
8	— — — • •	dahdahdahdidit
9	— — — — •	dahdahdahdahdit
Ø	— — — — —	dahdahdahdahdah

Figure 4-2. Morse Code and Its Sound

CODE KEY

Morse code is usually sent by using a code key. A typical one is shown in *Figure 4-3a*. Normally it is mounted on a thin piece of wood or plexiglass. You can use wood screws, or simply glue the key in place. Make sure that what you mount it on is thin; if the key is raised too high, it will be uncomfortable to the wrist. The correct sending position for the hand is shown in *Figure 4-3b*.

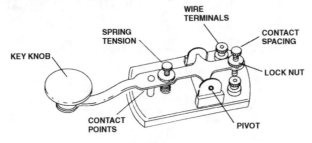

a. Code Key

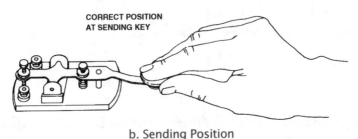

b. Sending Position

Figure 4-3. Code Key for Sending Code

LEARNING MORSE CODE

The reason you are learning the Morse code is to be able to operate on the worldwide bands. Here are five suggestions (four serious ones) on how to learn the code:

1. Memorize the code from the code charts in this book.
2. Use my fun cassette tapes available at all ham radio stores.
3. Go out and spend $1,000 and buy a worldwide radio, and listen to the code live and on the air. You don't need to spend that much, but you can listen to Morse code practice on the air, as shown in *Table 4-1*.
4. Use a code key and oscillator to practice sending the code. Believe it or not, someday you're actually going to do code over the live airwaves, using this same code key hooked up to your new megabuck transceiver.
5. Play with code programs on your computer, and *have fun!*

Table 4-1. Radio Frequencies for Code Reception

Pacific	Mountain	Central	Eastern	Mon.	Tue.	Wed.	Thu.	Fri.
6 a.m.	7 a.m.	8 a.m.	9 a.m.		Fast Code	Slow Code	Fast Code	Slow Code
7 a.m. – 1 p.m.	8 a.m. – 2 p.m.	9 a.m. – 3 p.m.	10 a.m. – 4 p.m.	**VISITING OPERATOR TIME**				
1 p.m.	2 p.m.	3 p.m.	4 p.m.	Fast Code	Slow Code	Fast Code	Slow Code	Fast Code
2 p.m.	3 p.m.	4 p.m.	5 p.m.	Code Bulletin				
3 p.m.	4 p.m.	5 p.m.	6 p.m.	Teleprinter Bulletin				
4 p.m.	5 p.m.	6 p.m.	7 p.m.	Slow Code	Fast Code	Slow Code	Fast Code	Slow Code
5 p.m.	6 p.m.	7 p.m.	8 p.m.	Code Bulletin				
6 p.m.	7 p.m.	8 p.m.	9 p.m.	Teleprinter Bulletin				
6:45 p.m.	7:45 p.m.	8:45 p.m.	9:45 p.m.	Voice Bulletin				
7 p.m.	8 p.m.	9 p.m.	10 p.m.	Fast Code	Slow Code	Fast Code	Slow Code	Fast Code
8 p.m.	9 p.m.	10 p.m.	11 p.m.	Code Bulletin				

CW is broadcast on the following MHz frequencies: 1.818, 3.5815, 7.0475, 14.0475, 18.0975, 21.0675, 28.0675, and 147.555 (local). W1AW schedule courtesy of *QST* magazine.

CODE REQUIREMENTS FOR AMATEUR RADIO LICENSES

Morse code is not required for a Technician class license, but passing the 5-wpm Element 1 code test will give you additional privileges, as explained in Chapter 2. In order to upgrade to General class, and in order to hold the top Extra class ticket, you must pass the Element 1 test. *Table 4-2* summarizes the code requirements for all three amateur radio license classes.

Table 4-2. Amateur Radio Morse Code Requirements

License Class	Code Requirement
Technician	No code test required. Optional 5-wpm code test provides permanent operating privileges on HF worldwide frequencies. Exam credit for upgrade to General class good for 365-days.
General	5-wpm, receiving plain language text
Extra	5-wpm, receiving plain language text

You don't need to take the code test again when you upgrade from General to Extra. If you upgrade from Technician to General, the 5-wpm code test certificate (CSCE) is valid for 365 days. If it expires prior to taking and passing the General class Element 3 written examination, you will be required to re-take and re-pass the Element 1 code test. Once you achieve General or Extra class levels, keeping your license current means never having to repeat the code test or written exams again.

WHY MORSE CODE?

Learning the code to obtain an amateur radio license is an old tradition. Actually, back in the early 1900's, code was the only form of radio transmission, since microphones didn't come into common, commercial radio use until the '20s.

In the '80s, international radio regulations were changed so that a telegraph test was no longer required for those worldwide operators transmitting on frequencies above 30 MHz. And 10 years later, in 1991, the Technician "no-code" class of license was created. For the next nine years, the U.S. code requirements for worldwide frequencies were 5-wpm for Novice CW sub-band operation; 13-wpm for General class voice, data, and code on the worldwide bands; and 20-wpm for Extra class code where the Extra class operator could enjoy any and all worldwide frequencies.

International regulations still require that all amateurs operating on the worldwide frequencies below 30 MHz know the Morse code — but not necessarily at 20- or 13-wpm. Knowing the code at 5-wpm satisfies the international regulations.

In its December 30, 1999, Report & Order restructuring amateur radio licensing requirements, the Federal Communications Commission found that many amateurs believed that the then-current licensing structure over-emphasized the importance of manual telegraphy. So the FCC concluded that the required speed for a single telegraphy examination for all grades of worldwide operation should be 5-wpm.

As a Technician class operator, if all you want are privileges on the VHF and UHF frequency bands, you can skip the code and never learn a dot or dash. But if you want access to all of the worldwide excitement from ionospheric skywave skip communications, knuckle down and learn the code so you can pass that 5-wpm test. When you upgrade to General within 365 days of passing the 5-wpm test during your Tech test, you will be awarded the General class license on successful completion of the Element 3 examination!

Cassette Tapes

Five words per minute is so slow, and so easy, that many ham radio applicants learn it completely in a single week! You can do it, too, by using my code tapes.

Code cassettes personally recorded by me make code learning *fun*. They will train you to send and receive the International Morse code in just a few short weeks. They are narrated and parallel the instructions in this chapter. The tapes have code characters generated at a 13-15-wpm character rate, spaced out to a 5-wpm word rate. This is known as Farnsworth spacing.

Getting Started

The hardest part of learning the code is taking the first cassette out of the case, putting it in your tape player, and pushing the play button! Try it, and you'll be over your biggest hurdle. After that, the tapes will talk you through the code in no time.

The cassette tapes make code learning *fun*. You'll hear how humor has been added to the learning process to keep your interest high. Since ham radio is a hobby, there's no reason we can't poke ourselves in the ribs and have a little fun learning the code as part of this hobby experience. Okay, you're still not convinced — you probably have already made up your mind that trying to learn the code will be the hardest part of getting your ham license. It will not. Give yourself a fair chance.

Don't get discouraged. Have patience and remember these important reminders when practicing to learn the Morse code:

- Learn the code by sound. Don't stare at the tiny dots and dashes that we have here in the book — the dit and dah sounds on the cassette and on the air and with your practice keyer will ultimately create an instant letter at your fingertips and into the pencil.
- *Never* scribble down dots or dashes if you forget a letter. Just put a small dash on your paper for a missed letter. You can go back and figure out what the word is by the letters you did copy!
- Practice only with fast code characters; 15-wpm character speed, spaced down to 5-wpm speed, is ideal. The FCC recommendations are quite clear about the rate that code characters are generated for the code examination. You will find the code speed, character speed, and actual tone (1000 Hz) on my cassette courses identical to cassettes used by most hams who give code tests.
- Practice the code by writing it down whenever possible. This further trains your brain and hand to work together in a subconscious response to the sounds you hear. (Remember Pavlov and his dog "Spot"?)
- Practice only for 15 minutes at a time. The tapes will tell you when to start and when to stop. Your brain and hand will lose that sharp edge once you go beyond 16 minutes of continuous code copy. You will learn much faster with five 15-minute practices per day than a one-hour marathon at night.
- Stay on course with the cassette instructions. Learn the letters, numbers, punctuation marks, and operating signals in the order they are presented here. My code teaching system parallels that of the American Radio Relay League, Boy Scouts of America, the Armed Forces, and has worked for thousands in actual classroom instruction.

It was no accident that Samuel Morse gave the single dit for the letter "E" which occurs most often in the English language. He determined the most used letters in the alphabet by counting letters in a printer's type case. He reasoned a printer would have more of the most commonly-used letters. It worked! With just the first lesson, you will be creating simple words and sentences with no previous background.

Table 4-3 shows the sequence of letters, punctuation marks, operating signals, and numbers covered in six lessons on the cassettes I've recorded.

Table 4-3. Sequence of Lessons on Cassettes

▪ Lesson 1	E T M A N I S O $\overline{SK}$ Period
▪ Lesson 2	R U D C 5 Ø $\overline{AR}$ Question Mark
▪ Lesson 3	K P B G W F H $\overline{BT}$ Comma
▪ Lesson 4	Q L Y J X V Z $\overline{DN}$ 1 2 3 4 6 7 8 9
▪ Lesson 5	Random code with narrated answers
▪ Lesson 6	A typical 5-wpm code test

Code Key and Oscillator — Ham Receiver

All worldwide ham transceivers have provisions for a code key to be plugged in for both CW practice off the air as well as CW operating on the air. If you already own a worldwide set, chances are all you will need is a code key for some additional code-sending practice.

Read over your worldwide radio instruction manual where it talks about hooking up the code key. For code practice, read the notes about operating with a "side tone" but not actually going on the air. This "side tone" capability of most worldwide radios will eliminate your need for a separate code oscillator.

Code Key and Oscillator — Separate Unit

Many students may wish to simply buy a complete code key and oscillator set. They are available from local electronic outlets or through advertisements in the ham magazines.

Look again at the code key in *Figure 4-3a.* Note the terminals for the wires. Connect wires to these terminals and tighten the terminals so the wires won't come loose. The two wires will go either to a code oscillator set or to a plug that connects into your ham transceiver. Hook up the wires to the plug as described in your ham transceiver instruction book or the code oscillator set instruction book.

Mount the key firmly, as previously described, then adjust the gap between the contact points. With most new telegraph keys, you will need a pair of pliers to loosen the contact adjustment knob. It's located on the very end of your keyer. First loosen the lock nut, then screw down the adjustment until you get a gap no wider than the thickness of a business card. You want as little space as possible between the points. The contact points are located close to the sending plastic knob.

Now turn on your set or oscillator and listen. If your hear a constant tone, check that the right-hand movable shorting bar is not closed. If it is, swing it open. Adjust the spring tension adjustment screw so that you get a good "feel" each time you push down on the key knob. Adjust it tight enough to keep the contacts from closing while your fingers are resting on the key knob.

Pick up the key by the knob! This is the exact position your fingers should grasp the knob—one or two on top, and one or two on the side of it. Poking at the knob with one finger is unacceptable. Letting your fingers fly off the knob between dots and dashes (dits and dahs) also is not correct. As you are sending, you should be able to instantly pick up the whole key assembly to verify proper finger position.

Your arm and wrist should barely move as you send CW. All the action is in your hand — and it should be almost effortless. Give it a try, and look at *Figure 4-3b* again to double-check your hand position.

Letting someone else use the key to send CW to you will also help you learn the code.

Morse Code Computer Software

The newest way to learn Morse code is through computer-aided instruction. There are many good PC programs on the market that not only teach you the characters, but build speed and allow you to take actual telegraphy examinations, which the computer constructs.

A big advantage of computer-aided Morse code learning is that you can easily customize the program to fit your own needs! You can select the sending speed, Farnsworth character-spacing speed, duration of transmission, number of characters in a random group, tone frequency — and more!

Some have built-in "weighting." That means the software will determine your weaknesses and automatically adjust future sending to give you more study on your problem characters! All Morse code software programs transmit the tone by keying the PC's internal speaker. Some generate a clearer audio tone through the use of external oscillators or internal computer sound cards.

THE ACTUAL CODE TEST

Now that 5-wpm is the only speed that a code test may be generated at, you need to know a little bit more about what 5-wpm sounds like. The actual character rate is around 13- to 15-wpm. This is called Farnsworth method where you hear the code sounds as a "package," and can much more easily recall what the letter is by their group sound. Code tests are no longer strung-out with extremely slow dits and dahs.

The pitch of the tone will be between 800 Hz to 1,000 Hz. The rate and tone are identical to my code training cassettes. Again, the course should be available at the same place where you purchased this book.

The actual code test will be administered by your accredited test team. They usually generate the code from pre-recorded audio cassettes supplied to them by their Volunteer Examiner Coordinator. These are played over a boom box, and some teams may even offer headsets to decrease the echoes found in a larger room. If you aren't given a headset, sit as close to the audio system speaker as possible.

The code test is preceded with a 1-minute warm-up message sent in Morse code, such as this: THIS IS A TEST. ONE TWO THREE. COPY? Your examiner team will then ask if everyone can hear the code okay and does anyone need to change seats to minimize echoes in the room.

Then the code test begins, usually preceded with a series of 6 Vs. Some examiners will use a typical communication from one ham to another as the 5 to 6 minute test. *Figure 4-4* is an example of what may be sent on your 5-wpm code test:

VVV VVV W2ZE DE K9QY HI CINDY, NAME IS JOE. UR RST 589 BT 589. RIG IS ICOM 746 AND ANTENNA IS BEAM UP 130 FEET. WX VERY COLD / RAIN. I AM A TEACHER. MUST QRT FOR LUNCH, HOW COPY? W2ZE DE K9QY AR SK

Figure 4-4. A Typical Element 1 Code Test

Your examination team will send a plain text message. You won't need to copy random, military-style code groups. The plain text may contain some abbreviations, and you will find some of the more popular ham abbreviations in the Appendix.

By FCC order, the code test must contain every number, every letter of the alphabet, and the procedural signals. At 5-wpm, it is sometimes tough to use up all of the letters and numbers, so many times they may have a statement, "I still have problems copying…," and they stuff in the numbers and letters they couldn't figure out how to use in the text. So you could get some random numbers and characters in the last part of the test.

After the test is over and you hear the final AR SK, your examination team will smile and ask how you did, and then give you instructions for preparing your code copy for their review. If you did really well, look for 1 minute of solid copy, and underline it. This will easily meet the FCC rules. That's 25 letters in a row. And yes, you can go back and correct any errors in your code copy. Watch for spelling errors – your examiners will not intentionally misspell words, so perhaps you copied them down wrong, and this is a good time to correct them for that 1 minute of solid copy.

An alternate way of passing the 5-wpm Element 1 code test is by answering 7 out of 10 questions about the text correctly. Referring to the sample test transmission shown in *Figure 4-4,* here is an example of a "fill in the blank" code test:

1. Call sign of sending station?
   Answer: K9QY
2. Call sign of receiving station?
   Answer: W2ZE
3. Name of sender?
   Answer: Joe
4. RST Report?
   Answer: 589
5. Type of radio?
   Answer: ICOM
6. Type of antenna?
   Answer: Beam
7. Antenna height?
   Answer: 130 feet
8. Weather?
   Answer: Cold/rain
9. Occupation of sender?
   Answer: Teacher
10. Why is sender signing off?
    Answer: Lunch

Trying to squeeze a logical, typical CW exchange into 5 or 6 minutes is tough. It's even more difficult when the Volunteer Exam Coordinators need to come up with 10 questions about the copy. But if you write down every single letter you hear, chances are you'll do just fine.

My audio code course has many tips on how to identify correct answers on the code test. For instance, the call sign of the sender is always preceded by the letters "DE," "FROM." The call sign of the receiver usually comes first, right after the series of Vs. Both call signs are repeated a second time, but just don't get them backwards!

Some code tests may say "handle" instead of "name" for the sending or receiving operator. A "rig" is a type of transceiver. Antenna height might be listed in feet or — be careful — sometimes in meters. On weather reports, they sometimes slip the slant bar in between the 2 weather conditions. The term "QRT" is a name for why the operator is having to sign off. All of this is explained on my code cassette courses.

To take the actual test, your examiners will have a separate station for your code test, different from the written examination.

After the Test

After the test is over, you can go back and work on your copy to fill in where you missed a letter. Since they were using plain language, it's easy to spot letters you accidentally copied wrong, or misspellings because you accidentally wrote an "A" instead of an "N."

When you think you have done the best to correct your material, the examiners will look for one minute of perfect copy, or may ask you ten simple questions about what you copied. These questions will have fill-in-the-blank answers. Seven out of ten is usually a passing score. They might also send another code transmission if you need a second chance — there is no longer a required waiting time between missed examination elements.

At 5-wpm, we have seen some students write down individual dots and dashes for the code received, and then translate them like a cryptogram into letters and numbers after the code test has been completed. This is one way to pass the test, but you'll find it easier just to memorize the characters and recognize them by their sound.

SENDING CODE AS AN ALTERNATIVE

Is your hearing shot from playing your boom box into the headphones too loud a few years ago? If you truly have a hearing disability, your examiners may allow you to take a code test by sending to them a predetermined text. Although the Federal Communications Commission rules mention sending as part of the code test, most examiners will usually do the code test as a receiving test.

Hey, sending is easier than receiving; and if you really do have a hearing disability, opt for the sending test. But I suggest you get a note from your doctor to back up the fact that your ear drums are no longer what they should be. This will allow the examiners to work with you on performing a sending code test, rather than a receiving code test.

ALL YOU NEED IS 5!

There no longer is a 20-wpm code test for Extra. There no longer is a 13-wpm rate for General. Now the only code speed you need for General or Extra — the top ham license — is 5-wpm.

And you don't need to take any code test for Technician class, but you should — because that gets the code test out of the way and gives you permanent operating privileges on 10-meter phone and code excitement on 10-, 15-, 40-, and 80-meters CW. And you'll have 365 days of exam credit to get ready to take your General class Element 3 written exam for your upgrade.

For heaven sake, don't lose that certificate showing you passed the 5-wpm code test. You'll need it when you upgrade to General Class. DON'T LOSE THAT CODE-PASSING CERTIFICATE! This is your proof that you don't have to go through the code test again when you upgrade to General.

NOW WE'RE READY

Obtain the code practice materials that will best suit your listening pleasure and learning needs. If you regularly work with computers, we've mentioned the excellent computer programs for learning code. If you regularly listen to tape cassettes in your automobile, we've mentioned the code learning cassettes developed and recorded by your author. Both of these products are available in the amateur radio marketplace.

You might also consider purchasing your high frequency equipment ahead of time, in preparation for your privileges on 10 meters, 15 meters, 40 meters, and 80 meters. You don't need a license to buy ham equipment; however, don't transmit until your license is granted by the FCC. Listen to the code practice on 80 and 40 meters at night, and at 15 and 10 meters during the day. This is another great way to prepare yourself for the 5-wpm Element 1 code test.

Taking the Exam &
Receiving Your First License

This chapter tells you when and where to test, how the examination will be given, who is qualified to give the Element 2 exam, and what happens after you complete it. There's also some good tips on finding a Volunteer Examiner team near you, and what to look for when asking questions about how they might conduct their Morse code test.

EXAMINATION ADMINISTRATION

All amateur radio service examinations are conducted by licensed amateur operators who volunteer and who are accredited by a Volunteer Examiner Coordinator (VEC). Each exam session is coordinated by a national or regional VEC. Licensed amateurs who hold a General class or higher class license may be accredit by a VEC to administer the Element 2 Technician class examination, and the Element 1 Morse code test. Advanced class VEs may administer Elements 1, 2, and 3 only. Extra class VEs may administer all examinations, including Element 4.

A team of 3 officially-accredited Volunteer Examiners (VEs) are required to form an examination session. No one-on-one or one-on-two. Three examiners must be present for the exam session to be valid.

The VEs who will conduct your exam session are your fellow hams, and as volunteers don't get a penny for their time and skills. However, they are permitted to charge you a fee for certain reimbursable expenses incurred in preparing, administering, and processing the examination. The FCC adjusts the fee annually based on inflation. The current fee is about $12.00.

HOW TO FIND AN EXAM SITE

Exam sessions are held regularly at sites throughout the country to serve their local communities. The exam site could be a public library, a fire house, someone's office, in a warehouse, and maybe even in someone's private home. Each examination team may regularly post their examination locations down at the local ham radio store. They also inform their VEC when and where they regularly hold test sessions. So the easiest way for you to find an exam session that is near you and at a convenient time is to call the VEC.

A complete list of VECs is located on page 208 in the Appendix. The W5YI VEC and the ARRL VEC are the 2 largest examination groups in the country, and they

---

Want to find a test site fast?
Visit the W5YI-VEC website at **www.w5yi.org**, or call 800-669-9594.

---

test in all 50 states. Their 3-member, accredited examination teams are just about *everywhere.* So when you call the W5YI-VEC in Texas, or the ARRL-VEC in Connecticut, be assured they probably have an examination team only a few miles from where you are reading this book right now!

Any of the VECs listed will provide you with the phone number of a local Volunteer Examiner team leader who can tell you the schedule of upcoming exam sessions near you. Go ahead — give them a call now and let them know you are studying my book. Select a session you wish to attend, and make a reservation so the VEs know to expect you. Don't be a "no-show" and don't be a "surprise-show." Make a reservation. And don't hesitate to tell them how much we all appreciate their efforts in supporting ham radio testing.

Ask them ahead of time what you will need to bring to the examination session. And ask them how much the current fee is for your exam session.

Remember, your volunteer examiners don't get paid for their time, so anything that you can do to help out during the exam session will be appreciated. Maybe stick around after the exam session to help the VEs put away the tables and chairs. Someday *you* may be a volunteer examiner, and you will appreciate the help!

WHAT TO BRING TO THE EXAM

Here's what you'll need to bring with you for your Technician Class, Element 2 written examination and/or optional Element 1 Morse code test:
1. Examination fee of approximately $12.00 in cash.
2. Personal identification with a photo.
3. Any Certificates of Successful Completion of Examinations (CSCEs) issued within the last 365 days prior to this test session date. Bring the originals, plus two copies of everything.
4. Some sharp pencils and fine-tip pens. Bring a backup!
5. Calculators may be used, so bring your calculator.
6. Any other item that the VE team asks you to bring. Remember, these volunteer examiners receive no pay for their work.

EXAM CONTENT

Years ago, the FCC staff administered amateur radio exams, and the questions and answers were *secret.* The FCC developed their secret questions, their secret multiple-choice answers, and they had all sorts of secret subjects that you never knew about until after you took the exam for the first time.

In the 80's, things improved when President Ronald Reagan signed legislation providing for volunteer amateur operator examinations, allowing the Federal Communications Commission to transfer testing responsibilities over to the amateur community. This included making up the examination questions and answers, which would then be available in the public domain. It is the role of Volunteer Exam Coordinators — specifically the Question Pool Committee — to review the questions in each of the three pools for the various amateur operator licenses. This procedure has been in effect for years for FAA airplane pilot testing. The amateur radio exam process has been privatized, and has worked out very well.

So, there won't be any surprises on you upcoming Element 2 written examination. Again, every one of the 35 questions on your exam will be taken from the 510 question pool in this book. The wording of the questions, answer, and distracters will be exactly as they appear here. The only change that the VECs are allowed to make is in the order of the A B C D answers.

TAKING THE EXAMINATION

Get a good night's sleep before exam day. Continue to study theory Q&A up to the moment you go into the room. Make a list of questions you have the most difficulty answering. Memorize the answers, and review them as you go to the examination. If someone is going with you to the examination, have them ask you the questions on the way, so that you can practice answering them. Listen to my theory tapes in your car as you drive to the examination session. Speedread *keywords* over and over again before the exam!

Check and Double-Check

When the examiners hand out the examination material, put your name, date, and test number on the answer sheet. *Make no marks on the multiple-choice question sheet.* Only write on the answer sheets.

Read over the examination questions carefully. Take your time in looking for the correct answer. Some answers start out looking correct, but end up wrong. Don't speed read the test.

When you are finished with the examination, go back over every question and double-check your answers. Try a game where you read what you have selected as the correct answer, and see if it agrees with the question.

When you are finished with the exam, turn in all of your paperwork. Tell the examiners how much you appreciate their efforts to help promote ham radio participation. If you are the last one in the room, volunteer to help them take down the testing location. The VE team will appreciate your offer.

And now, wait patiently outside for the examiners to announce that you have passed your examination. Chances are they will greet you with a smile and your Certificate of Successful Completion of Examination. Make sure to immediately sign this certificate when it is handed to you.

COMPLETING NCVEC FORM 605

When you arrive at the examination site, one of the first things you will do is complete the NCVEC Form 605. This form is retained by the Volunteer Exam Coordinator who transfers your printed information to an electronic file and sends it to the FCC for your new license, or upgrade. Your application may be delayed or kicked-back to you if the VEC can't read your writing. Make absolutely sure you print as legibly as you can, and carefully follow the instructions on the form.

Name

This isn't a tough one — your last name, first name, middle initial, and suffix such as junior or senior. You must stay absolutely consistent with your name on any future Form 605s for upgrades or changes of address. If you start out as "Jack" and end up

"John," the computer will throw out your next application. If you don't list a middle initial the first time, but do the second time, the computer will again hiccup. If you decide to use a nickname, this is okay — but down the line when you visit a foreign country, they may ask you for your personal identification that needs to illustrate this same nickname. It is best to stick with the name that is on most of your personal pictured IDs, such as your Driver's License.

NCVEC QUICK-FORM 605 APPLICATION FOR AMATEUR OPERATOR/PRIMARY STATION LICENSE

SECTION 1 - TO BE COMPLETED BY APPLICANT

PRINT LAST NAME	SUFFIX	FIRST NAME	INITIAL	STATION CALL SIGN (IF ANY)
MARCONI		*JOE*	*G*	

MAILING ADDRESS (Number and Street or P.O. Box)		SOCIAL SECURITY NUMBER / TIN (OR LICENSEE ID)
7101 RECTIFIER ROAD		*090-909-090*

CITY	STATE CODE	ZIP CODE (5 or 9 Numbers)	E-MAIL ADDRESS (OPTIONAL)
INDUCTOR	*IL*	*60777*	*SPARKS@MSN.COM*

DAYTIME TELEPHONE NUMBER (Include Area Code) OPTIONAL	FAX NUMBER (Include Area Code) OPTIONAL	ENTITY NAME (IF CLUB, MILITARY RECREATION, RACES)

Type of Applicant: [X] Individual   [ ] Amateur Club   [ ] Military Recreation   [ ] RACES (Renewal Only)

TRUSTEE OR CUSTODIAN CALL SIGN

I HEREBY APPLY FOR (Make an X in the appropriate box(es))

SIGNATURE OF RESPONSIBLE CLUB OFFICIAL

[X] **EXAMINATION** for a **new** license grant

[ ] **EXAMINATION** for **upgrade** of my license class

[ ] **CHANGE** my **name** on my license to my new name

Former Name: _____
(Last name) (Suffix)   (First name)   (MI)

[ ] **CHANGE** my mailing address to **above** address

[ ] **CHANGE** my station **call sign** systematically

Applicant's Initials: _____

[ ] **RENEWAL** of my license grant.

Do you have another license application on file with the FCC which has not been acted upon?	PURPOSE OF OTHER APPLICATION	PENDING FILE NUMBER (FOR VEC USE ONLY)

I certify that:
- I waive any claim to the use of any particular frequency regardless of prior use by license or otherwise;
- All statements and attachments are true, complete and correct to the best of my knowledge and belief and are made in good faith;
- I am not a representative of a foreign government;
- I am not subject to a denial of Federal benefits pursuant to Section 5301 of the Anti-Drug Abuse Act of 1988, 21 U.S.C. § 862;
- The construction of my station will NOT be an action which is likely to have a significant environmental effect (See 47 CFR Sections 1.301-1.319 and Section 97.13(a));
- I have read and WILL COMPLY with Section 97.13(c) of the Commission's Rules regarding RADIOFREQUENCY (RF) RADIATION SAFETY and the amateur service section of OST/OET Bulletin Number 65.

Signature of applicant (Do not print, type, or stamp. Must match applicant's name above.)

X *Jos G Marconi*   Date Signed: *4-15-00*

NCVEC Form 605

Social Security Number

Put in your Social Security Number in the designated box. If you are a citizen of another country, put down the country name in this box. If you are a U.S. citizen and prefer not to disclose your Social Security Number on this application, you will want to check with the VEC ahead of time and follow their detailed instructions on how to secure an FCC "CORES FRN ID" number to use in lieu of your SSN. Take our word for it — just give them your SSN, and you will avoid a lot of grief.

Address

Where do you want your paper license mailed? If you move around frequently, you will need to be contacting the FCC regularly for a change of address. Use a mailing address that you plan to keep as permanent as possible.

E-mail Address

This is optional, but it's a good idea because the amateur radio service is now under the FCC's Universal Licensing System. Once you get your new call sign, you will be able to work with the Federal Communications Commission directly via computer, including change of address, change of name, and license renewals without having to do any paperwork.

Phone Numbers

There are two boxes for phone numbers — one for a daytime contact, and the other for your FAX number. These are optional, but it's a good idea to put these numbers down just in case the VEC or VE team need to re-contact you for some reason.

Signature

When you sign your name, make sure to include all of the letters that you printed as your name at the top of the form. Don't just put down a squiggle or an initial. You need to sign your name all the way out, including all of the letters that were in your printed name.

Final Check

Finally, double-check that your handwriting is legible. If a single letter in your name can't be read clearly and is misinterpreted, subsequent electronic filings may get returned as no action. Make sure your NCVEC Form 605 is as clear as a bell to your Volunteer Examination team, who will then forward it to their VEC. Stay away from red ink, too.

Your Examiners' Portion

The Volunteer Examination Team will carefully review your NCVEC Form 605 to ensure that they can read your handwriting and that everything looks okay. Then VEs will sign and date your form and then send it on to the VEC for processing. The VEC will then electronically file your results with the FCC.

CONGRATULATIONS! YOU PASSED!

After you pass the examination, congratulations and a big welcome to Technician class privileges are in order! The world of microwave and VHF/UHF operating awaits you. And, if you also passed the code test, welcome to the additional HF privileges and the world of long-range, high-frequency operation that you earned.

You can begin operating as soon as you obtain your official FCC call sign. This means you do not have to wait for the hard copy of your license to arrive at the address listed on your NCVEC 605.

Electronic Filing

After you pass your Technician Class examination, your VE team will submit your amateur license application results electronically to their Volunteer Examiner Coordinator (VEC). The VEC will then electronically file for your license grant, and within days of passing your test your call sign is granted and you are permitted to go on the air immediately!

The system of electronic filing has been working so well that most new applicants who pass their exam over the weekend are able to go on the air that following Wednesday or Thursday once they have seen their new call letters appear on the FCC database. Recent rule changes now allow you to instantly go on the air with those call letters, as an FCC grant, even though you don't actually have the official FCC paper license in your possession. It takes about two weeks to receive that official FCC license, which you may wish to frame, or cut off the top portion to keep in your wallet.

Ask your Volunteer Examination team when they will electronically file your test results. They can then give you an approximate date to check the FCC database to find out your new call sign.

YOUR FIRST CALL SIGN

To find your new call sign on the internet, go to: **http://wireless.fcc.gov/**, which will take you to the FCC Wireless Telecommunications Bureau home page. On the right hand side of the screen under Licensing click on "License Search" then search by name entering your last name first, a comma, and then your first name.

Amateur Call Signs

As an aid to enforcement of the radio rules, transmitting stations throughout the world are required to identify themselves at regular intervals when they are in operation. That's the primary purpose of your call sign. A call sign is a very important matter to a ham — sometimes more personal than his or her name!

By international agreement, the prefix letters of a station's call sign indicates the country in which that station is authorized to operate. The national prefixes allocated to the United States are AA through AL, KA through KZ, NA through NZ, and WA through WZ. In addition, U.S. amateur stations with call signs that start with AA-AL, K, N or W are followed by a number indicating their location in a specific U.S. geographic area. *Table 5-1* details these geographical areas. On the DX airwaves, hams can readily identify the national origin of the ham signal they hear by its call sign prefix. The suffix letters indicate a specific amateur station.

The Amateur Operator/Primary Station call sign is issued by the FCC's licensing facility in Gettysburg, Pennsylvania, on a systematic basis after it receives your application information from the VEC. There are four call sign groupings, A, B, C, and D. Tables showing the call sign groups and formats for operator/station licenses within and outside the contiguous U.S. are shown in the Appendix.

- Group A call signs are issued to Extra class licensees, and have a 1-by2, 2-by-1, or 2-by-2 format that begins with the letter A. W9MU is an example.
- Group B call signs are issued to grandfathered Advanced class licensees, and have a 2-by-2 format that begins with K, N, or W. WA6PT is an example.
- Group C call signs are issued to General, grandfathered Technician-Plus, and Technician class licensees, and have a 1-by-3 format. N7LAT is an example. (However, because of the large number of Technician licenses that have been issued since the inception of the "no-code" license in 1991, there are no Group C call signs available. Thus, in accordance with FCC rules, new General and Technician class operators are issued a Group D call sign.)
- Group D call signs are issued to new Technician and General class operators, and to grandfathered Novice class operators. They have a 2-by-3 format. KB9SMG is an example.

Table 5-1. Call Sign Area for U.S. Geographical Areas

Call Sign Area No.	Geographical Area
1	Maine, New Hampshire, Vermont, Massachusetts, Rhode Island, Connecticut
2	New York, New Jersey, Guam and the U.S. Virgin Islands
3	Pennsylvania, Delaware, Maryland, District of Columbia
4	Virginia, North and South Carolina, Georgia, Florida, Alabama, Tennessee, Kentucky, Midway Island, Puerto Rico[1]
5	Mississippi, Louisiana, Arkansas, Oklahoma, Texas, New Mexico
6	California, Hawaii[2]
7	Oregon, Washington, Idaho, Montana, Wyoming, Arizona, Nevada, Utah, Alaska[3]
8	Michigan, Ohio, West Virginia, American Samoa
9	Wisconsin, Illinois, Indiana
0	Colorado, Nebraska, North and South Dakota, Kansas, Minnesota, Iowa, Missouri, Northern Mariana Island

[1] Puerto Rico also issued Area #3.
[2] Hawaii also issued Area #7.
[3] Alaska also issued Areas #1 through #0.

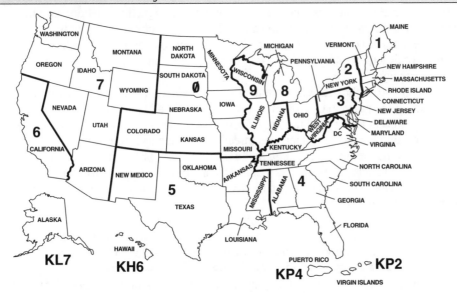

Figure 5-1. U.S. Call Sign Areas

Once assigned, a call sign is never changed unless the licensee specifically requests the change — even if they move out of the continental United States. FCC licensees residing in foreign countries must show a U.S. mailing address on their applications. You may change your call sign to a new group when you upgrade your amateur license.

Of course, if you get a real neat call sign as your first issued call sign, you can elect to hold onto it all the way to the top. My very first call sign was WB6NOA, and I've retained this same call sign all the way up to my current Extra class license.

So what does all this mean? You can no longer easily tell what grade of license someone has by how many letters and single number in their call sign. But you're just a few keystrokes away from finding out on your computer by visiting **www.qrz.com** on the worldwide web. This website contains a data base of call signs that you can scan. You can also look up call signs by the name of the licensee, or by the person's call sign Go to: **http://wireless.fcc.gov**. On the right side of the screen under "Licensing" click on "License Search" and then search either by name or by call sign.

The W5YI VEC also offers several call sign services to amateurs. They can handle address changes and license renewals for you. In addition, they can obtain a "Vanity" call sign for you, request a one-by-one call sign for your special event, or do the research and provide evidence that you were licensed prior to March 21, 1987 and therefore qualify for a General class ticket without further examination. W5YI VEC also can file for your club station call sign. Check their website at **www.w5yi.org** for more information on these and other services it offers, or call 800-669-9594 during regular business hours.

Vanity Call Signs

Once you receive your first "no-choice," computer-assigned call letters, you may be eligible to replace them with a vanity call sign of your choosing. This call sign could be made up of your initials, or represent your love of animals (K9DOG) or could be call letters that your late mom or dad had when they got started in ham radio years ago.

General and Technician class amateur operators may request a vanity call sign from Group D or Group C. However, since Group C call signs beginning with the letter N are completely used up, only Group D call signs are available. These call signs have two letters, a number, and three letters (such as KA5GMO).

You also may request a call sign that was previously assigned to you that may have expired years ago, as well as a call sign of a close relative or former holder who is now deceased. This call sign can be from any group. There is an additional fee for a vanity call sign.

There are two ways to file for a vanity call sign — electronically or in writing.

You can file FCC Form 605 and pay the filing fee using your credit card electronically. Instructions for filing electronically are on the FCC website at **http://wireless.fcc.gov/services/amateur/callsigns/vanity**.

To file in writing, you must complete FCC Form 605 along with Form 159 and include your check or money order and mail it to: FCC, PO Box 358130, Pittsburgh, PA 15251-5130.

To make it easier for you to select a vanity call sign, you may wish to contact the W5YI Group at 800-669-9594 and ask for their vanity call sign application. The W5YI Group can help you to file electronically to get the exact call sign of your choice.

As for me, I'm staying with my original-issue WB6NOA call sign. If I changed it, I would be breaking a 40-year tradition!

THANK YOUR VE TEAM!

Your Volunteer Examination team is made up of men and women who are volunteering their time to provide you with an examination opportunity. Your VE team typically spends three additional hours for every one hour at the actual examination site. Since most exam sessions last for three hours, your three examiners may be spending as much as nine additional hours in electronic processing of your paperwork, handling the paperwork, sending the results to their Volunteer Examiner Coordinators, paying for the examination room, and all of the other chores that go along with conducting a volunteer exam session.

Work closely with your VE team and follow their instructions specifically. They are the absolute boss at the exam session, and you must follow their instructions to the letter.

Keep in mind that the volunteers are not paid. The fee that you are charged to take the exams is used to pay expenses. Your Volunteer Examiners don't keep any part of this fee to pay for their time in volunteering their services. So let them know you are grateful that they have given up their weekend or evening to provide you with an examination opportunity.

When you achieve the General class level, or higher, it's time for you to become a Volunteer Examiner. Ask the Volunteer Examination team how you can sign up when you make General class, and higher.

Finally, please tell your Volunteer Examination Team how much Gordon West Radio School appreciates their testing efforts. Show them these comments in this book. Tell them that Gordon West sincerely appreciates all of the hard work they are putting in to help the amateur service grow.

YOUR NEXT STEP

Did you pass the code test? If not, get my 6-tape audio CW course and learn the code at 5 wpm. Remember, 5-wpm is all that is necessary for General class and Extra class after you have passed the next 2 written exams, Element 3 for General class, and Element 4 for Extra class. Study materials for these two exams are contain in my *General Class* and *Extra Class* books.

SUMMARY

Welcome to the new, improved and simplified Amateur Radio service. One 5-wpm code test for all classes of license. Restructured and simplified Element 2, Technician. Straight-forward Element 3, General class. And for you high-techies, Element 4, the Extra class.

Learn the code. Never in the history of ham radio has 5-wpm given you so many operating privileges on the worldwide bands as the new General class license.

Become an *active* amateur, and help establish new radio clubs and volunteer examination programs near where you live. Introduce ham radio to kids, and let's keep our service growing!

FREE PASSING CERTIFICATE

When you pass your exams, I want to know about it! I have a very nice certificate available to you, suitable for framing plus free operating materials from ham equipment manufacturers. All I need is a large, self-addressed envelope with 10 first-class stamps on the inside to cover postage and handling and I'll send one your way. Write me at:

Gordon West Radio School
2414 College Drive
Costa Mesa, California 92626

Listen for me on the airwaves as WB6NOA. Say "hi" at many of the hamfests that I attend throughout the country every year. And if you ever would just like to speak with me, call me Monday through Friday, 10 am to 4 pm (California time), 714-549-5000.

Welcome to ham radio! It's been **FUN** teaching you the Technician Class.

73

Gordon West, WB6NOA

APPENDIX

U.S. VOLUNTEER EXAMINER COORDINATORS IN THE AMATEUR SERVICE

Anchorage Amateur Radio Club
8023 E. 11th Ct.
Anchorage, AK 99504-2003
907/338-0662
e-mail: jwiley@alaska.net

ARRL/VEC
225 Main Street
Newington, CT 06111-1494
860/594-0300
860/594-0339 (fax)
e-mail: vec@arrl.org
Internet: www.arrl.org

Central America VEC, Inc.
1215 Dale Drive SE
Huntsville, AL 35801-2031
256/536-3904
256/534-5557 (fax)
e-mail: dontunstil@comcast.net

Golden Empire Amateur Radio Society
P.O. Box 508
Chico, CA 95927-0508
530/345-3515
wa6zrt@aol.com

Greater Los Angeles Amateur Radio Group
9737 Noble Avenue
North Hills, CA 91343-2403
818/892-2068
818/892-9855 (fax)
e-mail: gla.arg@gte.net

Jefferson Amateur Radio Club
P.O. Box 24368
New Orleans, LA 70184-4368
e-mail: doug@bellsouth.net

Laurel Amateur Radio Club, Inc.
P.O. Box 1259
Laurel, MD 20725-1259
301/937-0394 (6-9 PM)
e-mail: aa3of@arrl.net

The Milwaukee Radio Amateurs Club, Inc.
P.O. Box 070695
Milwaukee, WI 53207-0695
262/797-6722
e-mail: tfuszard@aero.net

MO-KAN/VEC
228 Tennessee Road
Richmond, KS 66080-9174
785/867-2011
wo0e@pgtv.net

SANDARC-VEC
P.O. Box 2446
La Mesa, CA 91943-2446
619/697-1475
e-mail: n6nyx@arrl.net

Sunnyvale VEC Amateur Radio Club, Inc.
P.O. Box 60307
Sunnyvale, CA 94088-0307
408/255-9000 (exam info 24 hours)
e-mail: vec@amateur-radio.org
Internet: www.amateur-radio.org

W4VEC
3504 Stonehurst Place
High Point, NC 27265-2106
336/841-7576
e-mail: w4vec@aol.com
Internet: www.w4vec.com

Western Carolina Amateur Radio Society/
   VEC, Inc.
6702 Matterhorn Ct.
Knoxville, TN 37918-6314
865/687-5410
e-mail: wcars@korrnet.org
Internet: www.korrnet.org/wcars

W5YI-VEC
P.O. Box 565101
Dallas, TX 75356-5101
817/860-3800
800-669-9495
e-mail: w5yi-vec@w5yi.org
Internet: www.w5yi.org

THE W5YI RF SAFETY TABLES

(Developed by Fred Maia, W5YI, working in cooperation with the ARRL.)

There are two ways to determine whether your station's radio frequency signal radiation is within the MPE (Maximum Permissible Exposure) guidelines established by the FCC for *"controlled"* and *"uncontrolled"* environments. One way is direct *"measurement"* of the RF fields. The second way is through *"prediction"* using various antenna modeling, equations and calculation methods described in the FCC's *OET Bulletin 65* and *Supplement B.*

In general, most amateurs will not have access to the appropriate calibrated equipment to make precise field strength/power density measurements. The field-strength meters in common use by amateur operators are inexpensive, hand-held field strength meters that do not provide the accuracy necessary for reliable measurements, especially when different frequencies may be encountered at a given measurement location. It is more practical for amateurs to determine their PEP output power at the antenna and then look up the required distances to the controlled/uncontrolled environments using the following tables, which were developed using the prediction equations supplied by the FCC.

The FCC has determined that radio operators and their families are in the "controlled" environment and your neighbors and passers-by are in the "uncontrolled" environment. The estimated minimum compliance distances are in meters from the transmitting antenna to either the occupational/controlled exposure environment ("Con") or the general population/uncontrolled exposure environment ("Unc") using typical antenna gains for the amateur service and assuming 100% duty cycle and maximum surface reflection. Therefore, these charts represent the worst case scenario. They do not take into consideration compliance distance reductions that would be caused by:

(1) Feed line losses, which reduce power output at the antenna especially at the VHF and higher frequency levels.

(2) Duty cycle caused by the emission type. The emission type factor accounts for the fact that, for some modulated emission types that have a non-constant envelope, the PEP can be considerably larger than the average power. Multiply the distances by 0.4 if you are using CW Morse telegraphy, and by 0.2 for two-way SSB (single sideband) voice. There is no reduction for FM.

(3) Duty cycle caused by on/off time or "time-averaging." The RF safety guidelines permit RF exposures to be averaged over certain periods of time with the average not to exceed the limit for continuous exposure. The averaging time for occupational/controlled exposures is 6 minutes, while the averaging time for general population/uncontrolled exposures is 30 minutes. For example, if the relevant time interval for time-averaging is 6 minutes, an amateur could be exposed to two times the applicable power density limit for three minutes as long as he or she were not exposed at all for the preceding or following three minutes.

A routine evaluation is not required for vehicular mobile or hand-held transceiver stations. Amateur Radio operators should be aware, however, of the potential for exposure to RF electromagnetic fields from these stations, and take measures (such as reducing transmitting power to the minimum necessary, positioning the radiating antenna as far from humans as practical, and limiting continuous transmitting time) to protect themselves and the occupants of their vehicles.

Amateur Radio operators should also be aware that the FCC radio-frequency safety regulations address exposure to people — and not the strength of the signal. Amateurs may exceed the Maximum Permissible Exposure (MPE) limits as long as no one is exposed to the radiation.

How to read the chart: If you are radiating 500 watts from your 10 meter dipole (about a 3 dB gain), there must be at least 4.5 meters (about 15 feet) between you (and your family) and the antenna — and a distance of 10 meters (about 33 feet) between the antenna and your neighbors.

Medium and High Frequency Amateur Bands
All distances are in meters

Freq. (MF/HF) (MHz/Band)	Antenna Gain (dBi)	Peak Envelope Power (watts) 100 watts		500 watts		1000 watts		1500 watts	
		Con.	Unc.	Con.	Unc.	Con.	Unc.	Con.	Unc.
2.0 (160m)	0	0.1	0.2	0.3	0.5	0.5	0.7	0.6	0.8
2.0 (160m)	3	0.2	0.3	0.5	0.7	0.6	1.06	0.8	1.2
4.0 (75/80m)	0	0.2	0.4	0.4	1.0	0.6	1.3	0.7	1.6
4.0 (75/80m)	3	0.3	0.6	0.6	1.3	0.9	1.9	1.0	2.3
7.3 (40m)	0	0.3	0.8	0.8	1.7	1.1	2.5	1.3	3.0
7.3 (40m)	3	0.5	1.1	1.1	2.5	1.6	3.5	1.9	4.2
7.3 (40m)	6	0.7	1.5	1.5	3.5	2.2	4.9	2.7	6.0
10.15 (30m)	0	0.5	1.1	1.1	2.4	1.5	3.4	1.9	4.2
10.15 (30m)	3	0.7	1.5	1.5	3.4	2.2	4.8	2.6	5.9
10.15 (30m)	6	1.0	2.2	2.2	4.8	3.0	6.8	3.7	8.3
14.35 (20m)	0	0.7	1.5	1.5	3.4	2.2	4.8	2.6	5.9
14.35 (20m)	3	1.0	2.2	2.2	4.8	3.0	6.8	3.7	8.4
14.35 (20m)	6	1.4	3.0	3.0	6.8	4.3	9.6	5.3	11.8
14.35 (20m)	9	1.9	4.3	4.3	9.6	6.1	13.6	7.5	16.7
18.168 (17m)	0	0.9	1.9	1.9	4.3	2.7	6.1	3.3	7.5
18.168 (17m)	3	1.2	2.7	2.7	6.1	3.9	8.6	4.7	10.6
18.168 (17m)	6	1.7	3.9	3.9	8.6	5.5	12.2	6.7	14.9
18.168 (17m)	9	2.4	5.4	5.4	12.2	7.7	17.2	9.4	21.1
21.145 (15m)	0	1.0	2.3	2.3	5.1	3.2	7.2	4.0	8.8
21.145 (15m)	3	1.4	3.2	3.2	7.2	4.6	10.2	5.6	12.5
21.145 (15m)	6	2.0	4.6	4.6	10.2	6.4	14.4	7.9	17.6
21.145 (15m)	9	2.9	6.4	6.4	14.4	9.1	20.3	11.1	24.9
24.99 (12m)	0	1.2	2.7	2.7	5.9	3.8	8.4	4.6	10.3
24.99 (12m)	3	1.7	3.8	3.8	8.4	5.3	11.9	6.5	14.5
24.99 (12m)	6	2.4	5.3	5.3	11.9	7.5	16.8	9.2	20.5
24.99 (12m)	9	3.4	7.5	7.5	16.8	10.6	23.7	13.0	29.0
29.7 (10m)	0	1.4	3.2	3.2	7.1	4.5	10.0	5.5	12.2
29.7 (10m)	3	2.0	4.5	4.5	10.0	6.3	14.1	7.7	17.3
29.7 (10m)	6	2.8	6.3	6.3	14.1	8.9	19.9	10.9	24.4
29.7 (10m)	9	4.0	8.9	8.9	19.9	12.6	28.2	15.4	34.5

VHF/UHF Amateur Bands

All distances are in meters

Freq. (MF/HF) (MHz/Band)	Antenna Gain (dBi)	Peak Envelope Power (watts)							
		50 watts		100 watts		500 watts		1000 watts	
		Con.	Unc.	Con.	Unc.	Con.	Unc.	Con.	Unc.
50 (6m)	0	1.0	2.3	1.4	3.2	3.2	7.1	4.5	10.1
50 (6m)	3	1.4	3.2	2.0	4.5	4.5	10.1	6.4	14.3
50 (6m)	6	2.0	4.5	2.8	6.4	6.4	14.2	9.0	20.1
50 (6m)	9	2.8	6.4	4.0	9.0	9.0	20.1	12.7	28.4
50 (6m)	12	4.0	9.0	5.7	12.7	12.7	28.4	18.0	40.2
50 (6m)	15	5.7	12.7	8.0	18.0	18.0	40.2	25.4	56.8
144 (2m)	0	1.0	2.3	1.4	3.2	3.2	7.1	4.5	10.1
144 (2m)	3	1.4	3.2	2.0	4.5	4.5	10.1	6.4	14.3
144 (2m)	6	2.0	4.5	2.8	6.4	6.4	14.2	9.0	20.1
144 (2m)	9	2.8	6.4	4.0	9.0	9.0	20.1	12.7	28.4
144 (2m)	12	4.0	9.0	5.7	12.7	12.7	28.4	18.0	40.2
144 (2m)	15	5.7	12.7	8.0	18.0	18.0	40.2	25.4	56.8
144 (2m)	20	10.1	22.6	14.3	32.0	32.0	71.4	45.1	101.0
222 (1.25m)	0	1.0	2.3	1.4	3.2	3.2	7.1	4.5	10.1
222 (1.25m)	3	1.4	3.2	2.0	4.5	4.5	10.1	6.4	14.3
222 (1.25m)	6	2.0	4.5	2.8	6.4	6.4	14.2	9.0	20.1
222 (1.25m)	9	2.8	6.4	4.0	9.0	9.0	20.1	12.7	28.4
222 (1.25m)	12	4.0	9.0	5.7	12.7	12.7	28.4	18.0	40.2
222 (1.25m)	15	5.7	12.7	8.0	18.0	18.0	40.2	25.4	56.8
450 (70cm)	0	0.8	1.8	1.2	2.6	2.6	5.8	3.7	8.2
450 (70cm)	3	1.2	2.6	1.6	3.7	3.7	8.2	5.2	11.6
450 (70cm)	6	1.6	3.7	2.3	5.2	5.2	11.6	7.4	16.4
450 (70cm)	9	2.3	5.2	3.3	7.3	7.3	16.4	10.4	23.2
450 (70cm)	12	3.3	7.3	4.6	10.4	10.4	23.2	14.7	32.8
902 (33cm)	0	0.6	1.3	0.8	1.8	1.8	4.1	2.6	5.8
902 (33cm)	3	0.8	1.8	1.2	2.6	2.6	5.8	3.7	8.2
902 (33cm)	6	1.2	2.6	1.6	3.7	3.7	8.2	5.2	11.6
902 (33cm)	9	1.6	3.7	2.3	5.2	5.2	11.6	7.3	16.4
902 (33cm)	12	2.3	5.2	3.3	7.3	7.3	16.4	10.4	23.2
1240 (23cm)	0	0.5	1.1	0.7	1.6	1.6	3.5	2.2	5.0
1240 (23cm)	3	0.7	1.6	1.0	2.2	2.2	5.0	3.1	7.0
1240 (23cm)	6	1.0	2.2	1.4	3.1	3.1	7.0	4.4	9.9
1240 (23cm)	9	1.4	3.1	2.0	4.4	4.4	9.9	6.3	14.0
1240 (23cm)	12	2.0	4.4	2.8	6.2	6.2	14.0	8.8	19.8

All distances are in meters. To convert from meters to feet multiply meters by 3.28. Distance indicated is shortest line-of-sight distance to point where MPE limit for appropriate exposure tier is predicted to occur.

AUTHORIZED FREQUENCY BANDS – AMATEUR SERVICE (for U.S. Amateur Stations operating from ITU-Region 2–North and South America)

Current License Class[1]	Grandfathered[2]	Technician	Tech. w/Code	General	Advanced	Extra Class
METERS	Novice	Technician	Technician Plus	General	Advanced	Extra Class
160				1800-2000 kHz/All	1800-2000 kHz/All	1800-2000 kHz/All
80	3675-3725 kHz/CW		3675-3725 kHz/CW	3525-3750 kHz/CW 3850-4000 kHz/Ph	3525-3750 kHz/CW 3775-4000 kHz/Ph	3500-4000 kHz/CW 3750-4000 kHz/Ph
40	7100-7150 kHz/CW		7100-7150 kHz/CW	7025-7150 kHz/CW 7225-7300 kHz/Ph	7025-7300 kHz/CW 7150-7300 kHz/Ph	7000-7300 kHz/CW 7150-7300 kHz/Ph
30				10.1-10.15 MHz/CW	10.1-10.15 MHz/CW	10.1-10.15 MHz/CW
20				14.025-14.15 MHz/CW 14.225-14.35 MHz/Ph	14.025-14.15 MHz/CW 14.175-14.35 MHz/Ph	14.0-14.35 MHz/CW 14.15-14.35 MHz/Ph
17				18.068-18.11 MHz/CW 18.11-18.168 MHz/Ph	18.068-18.11 MHz/CW 18.11-18.168 MHz/Ph	18.068-18.11 MHz/CW 18.11-18.168 MHz/Ph
15	21.1-21.2 MHz/CW		21.1-21.2 MHz/CW	21.025-21.2 MHz/CW 21.3-21.45 MHz/Ph	21.025-21.2 MHz/CW 21.225-21.45 MHz/Ph	21.0-21.45 MHz/CW 21.2-21.45 MHz/Ph
12				24.89-24.99 MHz/CW 24.93-24.99 MHz/Ph	24.89-24.99 MHz/CW 24.93-24.99 MHz/Ph	24.89-24.99 MHz/CW 24.93-24.99 MHz/Ph
10	28.1-28.5 MHz/CW 28.3-28.5 MHz/Ph		28.1-28.5 MHz/CW 28.3-28.5 MHz/Ph	28.0-29.7 MHz/CW 28.3-29.7 MHz/Ph	28.0-29.7 MHz/CW 28.3-29.7 MHz/Ph	28.0-29.7 MHz/CW 28.3-29.7 MHz/Ph
6		50-54 MHz/CW 50.1-54 MHz/Ph	50-54 MHz/CW 50.1-54 MHz/Ph	50-54 MHz/CW 50.1-54 MHz/Ph	50-54 MHz/CW 50.1-54 MHz/Ph	50-54 MHz/CW 50.1-54 MHz/Ph
2		144-148 MHz/CW 144.1-148 MHz/All	144-148 MHz/CW 144.1-148 MHz/All	144-148 MHz/CW 144.1-148 MHz/All	144-148 MHz/CW 144.1-148 MHz/All	144-148 MHz/CW 144.1-148 MHz/All
1.25	222-225 MHz/All	[3] 222-225 MHz/All	222-225 MHz/All	222-225 MHz/All	222-225 MHz/All	222-225 MHz/All
0.70		420-450 MHz/All	420-450 MHz/All	420-450 MHz/All	420-450 MHz/All	420-450 MHz/All
0.33		902-928 MHz/All	902-928 MHz/All	902-928 MHz/All	902-928 MHz/All	902-928 MHz/All
0.23	1270-1295 MHz/All	1240-1300 MHz/All	1240-1300 MHz/All	1240-1300 MHz/All	1240-1300 MHz/All	1240-1300 MHz/All

[1] Effective 4-15-00 [2] Prior to 4-15-00 [3] Effective 2/1/944 219-220 MHz is authorized for point-to-point fixed digital message forwarding systems.

Note: Morse code (CW, A1A) may be used on any frequency allocated to the amateur service. Telephony emission (abbreviated Ph above) authorized on certain bands as indicated. Higher class licensees may use slow-scan television and facsimile emissions on the Phone bands; radio teletype/digital on the CW bands. All amateur modes and emissions are authorized above 144.1 MHz. In actual practice, the modes/emissions used are somewhat more complicated than shown above due to the existence of various band plans and "gentlemen's agreements" concerning where certain operations should take place.

Appendix

The following CEPT countries allow U.S. Amateurs to operate in their countries without a reciprocal license. Be sure to carry a copy of your FCC license and FCC Public Notice DA99-1098.

Austria	Finland	Liechtenstein	Slovenia
Belgium	France & its	Lithuania	Spain
Bosnia & Herzegovina	possessions	Luxembourg	Sweden
Bulgaria	Germany	Monaco	Switzerland
Croatia	Greenland	Netherlands	Turkey
Cyprus	Hungary	Netherlands Antilles	United Kingdom & its
Czech Republic	Iceland	Norway	possessions
Denmark	Ireland	Portugal	
Estonia	Italy	Romania	
Faroe Islands	Latvia	Slovak Republic	

List of Countries Permitting Third-Party Traffic

Country — Call Sign Prefix	Country — Call Sign Prefix	Country — Call Sign Prefix
Antigua and Barbuda V2	El Salvador . . . . YS	Paraguay . . . . ZP
Argentina . . . . LU	The Gambia C5	Peru. . . . . OA
Australia. . . . . VK	Ghana 9G	Philippines. . . . . DU
Austria, Vienna. 4U1VIC	Grenada J3	St. Christopher & Nevis . . V4
Belize V3	Guatemala. . . . . TG	St. Lucia J6
Bolivia . . . . CP	Guyana 8R	St. Vincent & Grenadines. . J8
Bosnia-Herzegovina T9	Haiti . . . . HH	Sierra Leone 9L
Brazil . . . . PY	Honduras. . . . . HR	South Africa . . . . ZS
Canada . . . . VE, VO, VY	Israel 4X	Swaziland 3D6
Chile . . . . CE	Jamaica 6Y	Trinidad and Tobago 9Y
Colombia . . . . HK	Jordan . . . . JY	Turkey . . . . TA
Comoros D6	Liberia . . . . EL	United Kingdom . . . . GB*
Costa Rica. . . . . TI	Marshall Is V6	Uruguay. CX
Cuba . . . . CO	Mexico . . . . XE	Venezuela . . . . YV
Dominica. J7	Micronesia V6	ITU-Geneva 4U1ITU
Dominican Republic . . . . . HI	Nicaragua . . . . YN	VIC-Vienna. 4U1VIC
Ecuador. . . . . HC	Panama . . . . HP	

Countries Holding U.S. Reciprocal Agreements

Antigua, Barbuda	Chile	Greece	Liberia	Seychelles
Argentina	Colombia	Greenland	Luxembourg	Sierra Leone
Australia	Costa Rica	Grenada	Macedonia	Solomon Islands
Austria	Croatia	Guatemala	Marshall Is.	South Africa
Bahamas	Cyprus	Guyana	Mexico	Spain
Barbados	Denmark	Haiti	Micronesia	St. Lucia
Belgium	Dominica	Honduras	Monaco	St. Vincent and
Belize	Dominican Rep.	Iceland	Netherlands	Grenadines
Bolivia	Ecuador	India	Netherlands Ant.	Surinam
Bosnia-	El Salvador	Indonesia	New Zealand	Sweden
Herzegovina	Fiji	Ireland	Nicaragua	Switzerland
Botswana	Finland	Israel	Norway	Thailand
Brazil	France[2]	Italy	Panama	Trinidad, Tobago
Canada[1]	Germany	Jamaica	Paraguay	Turkey
		Japan	Papua New Guinea	Tuvalu
		Jordan	Peru	United Kingdom[3]
1. Do not need reciprocal permit		Kiribati	Philippines	Uruguay
2. Includes all French Territories		Kuwait	Portugal	Venezuela
3. Includes all British Territories				

POPULAR Q SIGNALS

Given below are a number of Q signals whose meanings most often need to be expressed with brevity and clarity in amateur work. (Q abbreviations take the form of questions only when each is sent followed by a question mark.)

QRG   Will you tell me my exact frequency (or that of _____)? Your exact frequency (or that of _____) is _____ kHz.

QRH   Does my frequency vary? Your frequency varies.

QRI   How is the tone of my transmission? The tone of your transmission is _____ (1. Good; 2. Variable; 3. Bad).

QRJ   Are you receiving me badly? I cannot receive you. Your signals are too weak.

QRK   What is the intelligibility of my signals (or those of _____)? The intelligibility of your signals (or those of _____) is _____ (1. Bad; 2. Poor; 3. Fair; 4. Good; 5. Excellent).

QRL   Are you busy? I am busy (or I am busy with _____). Please do not interfere.

QRM   Is my transmission being interfered with? Your transmission is being interfered with _____ (1. Nil; 2. Slightly; 3. Moderately; 4. Severely; 5. Extremely).

QRN   Are you troubled by static? I am troubled by static _____ (1-5 as under QRM).

QRO   Shall I increase power? Increase power.

QRP   Shall I decrease power? Decrease power.

QRQ   Shall I send faster? Send faster (_____ WPM).

QRS   Shall I send more slowly? Send more slowly (_____ WPM).

QRT   Shall I stop sending? Stop sending.

QRU   Have you anything for me? I have nothing for you.

QRV   Are you ready? I am ready.

QRW   Shall I inform _____ that you are calling on _____ kHz? Please inform _____ that I am calling on _____ kHz.

QRX   When will you call me again? I will call you again at _____ hours (on _____ kHz).

QRY   What is my turn? Your turn is numbered _____ .

QRZ   Who is calling me? You are being called by _____ (on _____ kHz).

QSA   What is the strength of my signals (or those of _____)? The strength of your signals (or those of _____) is _____ (1. Scarcely perceptible; 2. Weak; 3. Fairly good; 4. Good; 5. Very good).

QSB   Are my signals fading? Your signals are fading.

QSD   Is my keying defective? Your keying is defective.

QSG   Shall I send _____ messages at a time? Send _____ messages at a time.

QSK   Can you hear me between your signals and if so can I break in on your transmission? I can hear you between my signals; break in on my transmission.

QSL   Can you acknowledge receipt? I am acknowledging receipt.

QSM   Shall I repeat the last message which I sent you, or some previous message? Repeat the last message which you sent me [or message(s) number(s) _____].

QSN   Did you hear me (or _____) on _____ kHz? I heard you (or _____) on _____ kHz.

QSO   Can you communicate with _____ direct or by relay? I can communicate with _____ direct (or by relay through _____).

QSP   Will you relay to _____ ? I will relay to _____ .

QST   General call preceding a message addressed to all amateurs and ARRL members. This is in effect "CQ ARRL."

QSU   Shall I send or reply on this frequency (or on _____ kHz)?

QSW   Will you send on this frequency (or on _____ kHz)? I am going to send on this frequency (or on _____ kHz).

QSX   Will you listen to _____ on _____ kHz? I am listening to _____ on _____ kHz.

QSY   Shall I change to transmission on another frequency? Change to transmission on another frequency (or on _____ kHz).

QSZ   Shall I send each word or group more than once? Send each word or group twice (or _____ times).

QTA   Shall I cancel message number _____ ? Cancel message number _____ .

QTB   Do you agree with my counting of words? I do not agree with your counting of words. I will repeat the first letter or digit of each word or group.

QTC   How many messages have you to send? I have messages for you (or for _____).

QTH   What is your location? My location is _____ .

QTR   What is the correct time? The time is _____ .

Source: ARRL

COMMON CW ABBREVIATIONS

AA	All after		NW	Now; I resume transmission
AB	All before		OB	Old boy
ABT	About		OM	Old man
ADR	Address		OP-OPR	Operator
AGN	Again		OT	Old timer; old top
ANT	Antenna		PBL	Preable
BCI	Broadcast interference		PSE-PLS	Please
BK	Break; break me; break in		PWR	Power
BN	All between; been		PX	Press
B4	Before		R	Received as transmitted; are
C	Yes		RCD	Received
CFM	Confirm; I confirm		REF	Refer to; referring to; reference
CK	Check		RPT	Repeat; I repeat
CL	I am closing my station; call		SED	Said
CLD-CLG	Called; calling		SEZ	Says
CUD	Could		SIG	Signature; signal
CUL	See you later		SKED	Schedule
CUM	Come		SRI	Sorry
CW	Continuous Wave		SVC	Service; prefix to service message
DLD-DLVD	Delivered		TFC	Traffic
DX	Distance		TMW	Tomorrow
FB	Fine business; excellent		TNX	Thanks
GA	Go ahead (or resume sending)		TU	Thank you
GB	Good-by		TVI	Television interference
GBA	Give better address		TXT	Text
GE	Good evening		UR-URS	Your; you're; yours
GG	Going		VFO-	Variable-frequency oscillator
GM	Good morning		VY	Very
GN	Good night		WA	Word after
GND	Ground		WB	Word before
GUD	Good		WD-WDS	Word; words
HI	The telegraphic laugh; high		WKD-WKG	Worked; working
HR	Here; hear		WL	Well; will
HV	Have		WUD	Would
HW	How		WX	Weather
LID	A poor operator		XMTR	Transmitter
MILS	Milliamperes		XTAL	Crystal
MSG	Message; prefix to radiogram		XYL	Wife
N	No		YL	Young lady
ND	Nothing doing		73	Best regards
NIL	Nothing; I have nothing for you		88	Love and kisses
NR	Number			

SCHEMATIC SYMBOLS

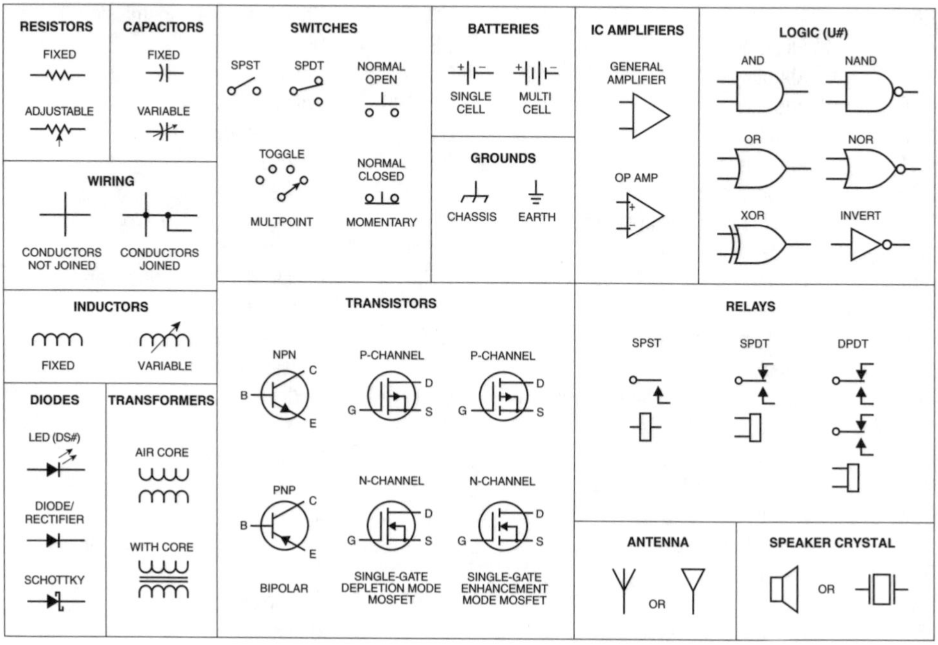

RESISTORS | **CAPACITORS**

FIXED | FIXED

ADJUSTABLE | VARIABLE

WIRING

CONDUCTORS NOT JOINED | CONDUCTORS JOINED

SWITCHES

SPST | SPDT | NORMAL OPEN

TOGGLE | NORMAL CLOSED

MULTPOINT | MOMENTARY

BATTERIES

SINGLE CELL | MULTI CELL

GROUNDS

CHASSIS | EARTH

IC AMPLIFIERS

GENERAL AMPLIFIER

OP AMP

LOGIC (U#)

AND | NAND

OR | NOR

XOR | INVERT

INDUCTORS

FIXED | VARIABLE

DIODES | **TRANSFORMERS**

LED (DS#)

DIODE/ RECTIFIER

SCHOTTKY

AIR CORE

WITH CORE

TRANSISTORS

NPN | P-CHANNEL | P-CHANNEL

PNP | N-CHANNEL | N-CHANNEL

BIPOLAR | SINGLE-GATE DEPLETION MODE MOSFET | SINGLE-GATE ENHANCEMENT MODE MOSFET

RELAYS

SPST | SPDT | DPDT

ANTENNA | **SPEAKER CRYSTAL**

OR | OR

SCIENTIFIC NOTATION

Prefix	Symbol		Multiplication Factor
exa	E	10^{18} =	1,000,000,000,000,000,000
peta	P	10^{15} =	1,000,000,000,000,000
tera	T	10^{12} =	1,000,000,000,000
giga	G	10^{9} =	1,000,000,000
mega	M	10^{6} =	1,000,000
kilo	k	10^{3} =	1,000
hecto	h	10^{2} =	100
deca	da	10^{1} =	10
(unit)		10^{0} =	1

Prefix	Symbol		Multiplication Factor
deci	d	10^{-1} =	0.1
centi	c	10^{-2} =	0.01
milli	m	10^{-3} =	0.001
micro	μ	10^{-6} =	0.000001
nano	n	10^{-9} =	0.000000001
pico	p	10^{-12} =	0.000000000001
femto	f	10^{-15} =	0.000000000000001
atto	a	10^{-18} =	0.000000000000000001

QUESTION POOL SYLLABUS

The syllabus used by the NCVEC Question Pool Committee to develop the question pool is included here as an aid in studying the subelements and topic groups. Reviewing the syllabus will give you an understanding of how the question pool is used to develop the Element 2 written theory examination. Remember, one question will be taken from each topic group within each subelement to create your exam.

Element 2 (Technician Class) Syllabus

T1 - FCC Rules [5 exam questions – 5 groups]
T1A Definition and purpose of Amateur Radio Service, Amateur-Satellite Service in places where the FCC regulates these services and elsewhere; Part 97 and FCC regulation of the amateur services; Penalties for unlicensed operation and for violating FCC rules; Prohibited transmissions.
T1B International aspect of Amateur Radio; International and domestic spectrum allocation; Spectrum sharing; International communications; reciprocal operation; International and domestic spectrum allocation; Spectrum sharing; International communications; reciprocal operation.
T1C All about license grants; Station and operator license grant structure including responsibilities, basic differences; Privileges of the various operator license classes; License grant term; Modifying and renewing license grant; Grace period.
T1D Qualifying for a license; General eligibility; Purpose of examination; Examination elements; Upgrading operator license class; Element credit; Provision for physical disabilities.
T1E Amateur station call sign systems including Sequential, Vanity and Special Event; ITU Regions; Call sign formats.

T2 – Methods of Communication
[2 exam questions – 2 groups]
T2A How Radio Works; Electromagnetic spectrum; Magnetic/Electric Fields; Nature of Radio Waves; Wavelength; Frequency; Velocity; AC Sine wave/Hertz; Audio and Radio frequency.
T2B Frequency privileges granted to Technician class operators; Amateur service bands; Emission types and designators; Modulation principles; AM/FM/Single sideband/upper-lower, international Morse code (CW), RTTY, packet radio and data emission types; Full quieting.

T3 – Radio Phenomena [2 exam questions – 2 groups]
T3A How a radio signal travels; Atmosphere/troposphere/ionosphere and ionized layers; Skip distance; Ground (surface)/sky (space) waves; Single/multihop; Path; Ionospheric absorption; Refraction.
T3B HF vs. VHF vs. UHF characteristics; Types of VHF-UHF propagation; Daylight and seasonal variations; Tropospheric ducting; Line of sight; Maximum usable frequency (MUF); Sunspots and sunspot Cycle, Characteristics of different bands.

T4 – Station Licensee Duties
[3 exam questions -- 3 groups]
T4A Correct name and mailing address on station license grant; Places from where station is authorized to transmit; Selecting station location; Antenna structure location; Stations installed aboard ship or aircraft.
T4B Designation of control operator; FCC presumption of control operator; Physical control of station apparatus; Control point; Immediate station control; Protecting against unauthorized transmissions; Station records; FCC Inspection; Restricted operation.
T4C Providing public service; emergency and disaster communications; Distress calling; Emergency drills and communications; Purpose of RACES.

T5 – Control Operator Duties
[3 exam questions – 3 groups]
T5A Determining operating privileges, Where control operator must be situated while station is locally or remotely controlled; Operating other amateur stations
T5B Transmitter power standards; Interference to stations providing emergency communications; Station identification requirements.
T5C Authorized transmissions, Prohibited practices; Third party communications; Retransmitting radio signals; One way communications.

T6 – Good Operating Practices
[3 exam questions – 3 groups]
T6A Calling another station; Calling CQ; Typical amateur service radio contacts; Courtesy and respect for others; Popular Q-signals; Signal reception reports; Phonetic alphabet for voice operations.
T6B Occupied bandwidth for emission types; Mandated and voluntary band plans; CW operation.
T6C TVI and RFI reduction and elimination, Band/Low/High pass filter, Out of band harmonic Signals, Spurious Emissions, Telephone Interference, Shielding, Receiver Overload.

T7 – Basic Communications Electronics
[3 exam questions – 3 groups]
T7A Fundamentals of electricity; AC/DC power; units and definitions of current, voltage, resistance, inductance, capacitance and impedance; Rectification; Ohm's Law principle (simple math); Decibel; Metric system and prefixes (e.g., pico, nano, micro, milli, deci, centi, kilo, mega, giga).
T7B Basic electric circuits; Analog vs. digital communications; Audio/RF signal; Amplification.
T7C Concepts of Resistance/resistor; Capacitor/capacitance; Inductor/Inductance; Conductor/Insulator; Diode; Transistor; Semiconductor devices; Electrical functions of and schematic symbols of resistors, switches, fuses, batteries, inductors, capacitors, antennas, grounds and polarity; Construction of variable and fixed inductors and capacitors.

T8 – Good Engineering Practice
[6 exam questions - 6 groups]
T8A Basic amateur station apparatus; Choice of apparatus for desired communications; Setting up station; Constructing and modifying amateur station apparatus; Station layout for CW, SSB, FM, Packet and other popular modes.
T8B How transmitters work; Operation and tuning; VFO; Transceiver; Dummy load; Antenna switch; Power supply; Amplifier; Stability; Microphone gain; FM deviation; Block diagrams of typical stations.
T8C How receivers work, operation and tuning, including block diagrams; Super-heterodyne including Intermediate frequency; Reception; Demodulation or Detection; Sensitivity; Selectivity; Frequency standards; Squelch and audio gain (volume) control.
T8D How antennas work; Radiation principles; Basic construction; Half wave dipole length vs. frequency; Polarization; Directivity; ERP; Directional/non-directional antennas; Multiband antennas; Antenna gain; Resonant frequency; Loading coil; Electrical vs. physical length; Radiation pattern; Transmatch.
T8E How transmission lines work; Standing waves/SWR/SWR-meter; Impedance matching; Types of transmission lines; Feed point; Coaxial cable; Balun; Waterproofing Connections.
T8F Voltmeter/ammeter/ohmmeter/multi/S-meter, peak reading and RF watt meter; Building/modifying equipment; Soldering; Making measurements; Test instruments.

T9 – Special Operations [2 exam questions – 2 groups]
T9A How an FM Repeater Works; Repeater operating procedures; Available frequencies; Input/output frequency separation; Repeater ID requirements; Simplex operation; Coordination; Time out; Open/closed repeater; Responsibility for interference.
T9B Beacon, satellite, space, EME communications; Radio control of models; Autopatch; Slow scan television; Telecommand; CTCSS tone access; Duplex/crossband operation.

T0 – Electrical, Antenna Structure and RF Safety Practices [6 exam questions - 6 groups]
T0A Sources of electrical danger in amateur stations: lethal voltages, high current sources, fire; avoiding electrical shock; Station wiring; Wiring a three wire electrical plug; Need for main power switch; Safety interlock switch; Open/short circuit; Fuses; Station grounding.
T0B Lightning protection; Antenna structure installation safety; Tower climbing Safety; Safety belt/hard hat/safety glasses; Antenna structure limitations.
T0C Definition of RF radiation; Procedures for RF environmental safety; Definitions and guidelines.
T0D Radiofrequency exposure standards; Near/far field, Field strength; Compliance distance; Controlled/Uncontrolled environment.
T0E RF Biological effects and potential hazards; Radiation exposure limits; OET Bulletin 65; MPE (Maximum permissible exposure).
T0F Routine station evaluation.

2003-07 ELEMENT 2 Q&A CROSS REFERENCE

The following cross reference presents all 511 question numbers in numerical order included in the 2003-07 Element 2 Question Pool, followed by the page number on which the question begins in the book. This will allow you to locate specific questions by question number. Note: question T1D11 was deleted from the pool by the Question Pool Committee, resulting in an active pool of 510 questions.

Question	Page	Question	Page	Question	Page	Question	Page	Question	Page
T1 – FCC Rules		T1D09	88	**T3 – Radio**		T4B13	96	**T6 – Good Operating**	
Question	Page	T1D10	88	**Phenomena**		T4C01	98	**Practices**	
T1A01	92	T1D11	89	T3A01	110	T4C02	98	T6A01	103
T1A02	31			T3A02	110	T4C03	98	T6A02	103
T1A03	31	T1E01	38	T3A03	111	T4C04	98	T6A03	102
T1A04	92	T1E02	37	T3A04	111	T4C05	97	T6A04	102
T1A05	93	T1E03	38	T3A05	109	T4C06	99	T6A05	103
T1A06	93	T1E04	44	T3A06	113	T4C07	99	T6A06	104
T1A07	92	T1E05	44	T3A07	110	T4C08	99	T6A07	105
T1A08	73	T1E06	38	T3A08	112	T4C09	97	T6A08	107
T1A09	73	T1E07	40	T3A09	111	T4C10	99	T6A09	105
T1A10	93	T1E08	40	T3A10	72	T4C11	100	T6A10	105
T1A11	94	T1E09	41	T3A11	109	T4C12	149	T6A11	103
T1A12	94	T1E10	41	T3A12	109	T4C13	100	T6A12	107
T1A13	94	T1E11	37			T4C14	100	T6A13	107
T1A14	92	T1E12	38	T3B01	70				
T1A15	95			T3B02	70			T6B01	139
T1A16	67	**T2 – Methods of**		T3B03	71	**T5 – Control Operator**		T6B02	140
		Communication		T3B04	71	**Duties**		T6B03	140
T1B01	51	T2A01	85	T3B05	110	T5A01	46	T6B04	140
T1B02	52	T2A02	144	T3B06	70	T5A02	48	T6B05	79
T1B03	53	T2A03	83	T3B07	113	T5A03	46	T6B06	67
T1B04	53	T2A04	84	T3B08	113	T5A04	51	T6B07	106
T1B05	54	T2A05	144	T3B09	111	T5A05	47	T6B08	106
T1B06	54	T2A06	81	T3B10	140	T5A06	47	T6B09	105
T1B07	55	T2A07	86	T3B11	113	T5A07	47	T6B10	106
T1B08	56	T2A08	52	T3B12	112	T5A08	62	T6B11	106
T1B09	62	T2A09	85	T3B13	112	T5A09	49	T6B12	107
T1B10	90	T2A10	83			T5A10	69		
T1B11	53	T2A11	82	**T4 – Station**				T6C01	142
T1B12	43	T2A12	83	**Licenseee Duties**		T5B01	38	T6C02	144
T1B13	57	T2A13	81	Question	Page	T5B02	39	T6C03	142
T1B14	43	T2A14	84	T4A01	43	T5B03	39	T6C04	145
T1B15	54	T2A15	83	T4A02	42	T5B04	106	T6C05	143
		T2A16	83	T4A03	35	T5B05	147	T6C06	145
T1C01	34			T4A04	42	T5B06	87	T6C07	142
T1C02	33	T2B01	89	T4A05	35	T5B07	147	T6C08	146
T1C03	34	T2B02	90	T4A06	36	T5B08	39	T6C09	145
T1C04	36	T2B03	77	T4A07	162	T5B09	97	T6C10	146
T1C05	34	T2B04	79	T4A08	162	T5B10	80	T6C11	146
T1C06	36	T2B05	89	T4A09	162	T5B11	94	T6C12	143
T1C07	32	T2B06	90	T4A10	43	T5B12	56		
T1C08	42	T2B07	53					**T7 – Basic**	
T1C09	101	T2B08	131	T4B01	45	T5C01	39	**Communications**	
T1C10	71	T2B09	59	T4B02	45	T5C02	80	**Electronics**	
T1C11	36	T2B10	131	T4B03	45	T5C03	49	T7A01	119
		T2B11	91	T4B04	45	T5C04	49	T7A02	119
T1D01	32	T2B12	91	T4B05	45	T5C05	50	T7A03	123
T1D02	32	T2B13	58	T4B06	46	T5C06	49	T7A04	123
T1D03	31	T2B14	53	T4B07	47	T5C07	50	T7A05	119
T1D04	33	T2B15	56	T4B08	46	T5C08	94	T7A06	116
T1D05	87	T2B16	102	T4B09	92	T5C09	65	T7A07	121
T1D06	33	T2B17	139	T4B10	48	T5C10	95	T7A08	121
T1D07	33	T2B18	133	T4B11	143	T5C11	95	T7A09	128
T1D08	88	T2B19	136	T4B12	96	T5C12	58	T7A10	125

Glossary

Amateur communication: Noncommercial radio communication by or among amateur stations solely with a personal aim and without personal or business interest.

Amateur operator/primary station license: An instrument of authorization issued by the FCC comprised of a station license, and also incorporating an operator license indicating the class of privileges.

Amateur operator: A person holding a valid license to operate an amateur station issued by the FCC. Amateur operators are frequently referred to as ham operators.

Amateur Radio services: The amateur service, the amateur-satellite service, and the radio amateur civil emergency service.

Amateur-satellite service: A radiocommunication service using stations on Earth satellites for the same purpose as those of the amateur service.

Amateur service: A radiocommunication service for the purpose of self-training, intercommunication and technical investigations carried out by amateurs; that is, duly authorized persons interested in radio technique solely with a personal aim and without pecuniary interest.

Amateur station: A station licensed in the amateur service embracing necessary apparatus at a particular location used for amateur communication.

AMSAT: Radio Amateur Satellite Corporation, a nonprofit scientific organization. (P.O. Box #27, Washington, DC 20044)

ANSI: American National Standards Institute. A non-government organization that develops recommended standards for a variety of applications.

APRS: Automatic Position Radio System, which takes GPS (Global Positioning System) information and translates it into an automatic packet of digital information.

ARES: Amateur Radio Emergency Service — the emergency division of the American Radio Relay League. Also see RACES

ARRL: American Radio Relay League, national organization of U.S. Amateur Radio operators. (225 Main Street, Newington, CT 06111)

Audio Frequency (AF): The range of frequencies that can be heard by the human ear, generally 20 hertz to 20 kilohertz.

Automatic control: The use of devices and procedures for station control without the control operator being present at the control point when the station is transmitting.

Automatic Volume Control (AVC): A circuit that continually maintains a constant audio output volume in spite of deviations in input signal strength.

Beam or Yagi antenna: An antenna array that receives or transmits RF energy in a particular direction. Usually rotatable.

Block diagram: A simplified outline of an electronic system where circuits or components are shown as boxes.

Broadcasting: Information or programming transmitted by radio means intended for the general public.

Bulletin No. 65: The Office of Engineering & Technology bulletin that provides specified safety guidelines for human exposure to radiofrequency (RF) radiation.

Business communications: Any transmission or communication the purpose of which is to facilitate the regular business or commercial affairs of any party. Business communications are prohibited in the amateur service.

Call Book: A published list of all licensed amateur operators available in North American and Foreign editions.

Call sign: The FCC systematically assigns each amateur station its primary call sign.

Certificate of Successful Completion of Examination (CSCE): A certificate providing examination credit for 365 days. Both written and code credit can be authorized.

Coaxial cable, Coax: A concentric, two-conductor cable in which one conductor surrounds the other, separated by an insulator.

Controlled Environment: Involves people who are aware of and who can exercise control over radiofrequency exposure. Controlled exposure limits apply to both occupational workers and Amateur Radio operators and their immediate households.

Control operator: An amateur operator designated by the licensee of an amateur station to be responsible for the station transmissions.

Coordinated repeater station: An amateur repeater station for which the transmitting and receiving frequencies have been recommended by the recognized repeater coordinator.

Coordinated Universal Time (UTC): (Also Greenwich Mean Time, UCT or Zulu time.) The time at the zero-degree (0°) Meridian which passes through Greenwich, England. A universal time among all amateur operators.

Crystal: A quartz or similar material which has been ground to produce natural vibrations of a specific frequency. Quartz crystals produce a high degree of frequency stability in radio transmitters.

CW: See Morse code.

Dipole antenna: The most common wire antenna. Length is equal to one-half of the wavelength. Fed by coaxial cable.

Dummy antenna: A device or resistor which serves as a transmitter's antenna without radiating radio waves. Generally used to tune up a radio transmitter.

Duplexer: A device that allows a single antenna to be simultaneously used for both reception and transmission.

Duty cycle: As applies to RF safety, the percentage of time that a transmitter is "on" versus "off" in a 6- or 30-minute time period.

Effective Radiated Power (ERP): The product of the transmitter (peak envelope) power, expressed in watts, delivered to the antenna, and the relative gain of an antenna over that of a half-wave dipole antenna.

Electromagnetic radiation: The propagation of radiant energy, including infrared, visible light, ultraviolet, radiofrequency, gamma and X-rays, through space and matter.

Emergency communication: Any amateur communication directly relating to the immediate safety of life of individuals or the immediate protection of property.

Examination Element: The written theory exam or CW test required for various classes of FCC Amateur Radio licenses. Technician must pass Element 2 written theory; General must pass Element 3 written theory plus Element 1 CW; Extra must pass Element 4 written theory.

Far Field: The electromagnetic field located at a great distance from a transmitting antenna. The far field begins at a distance that depends on many factors, including the wavelength and the size of the antenna. Radio signals are normally received in the far field.

FCC Form 605: The FCC application form used to apply for a new amateur operator/primary station license or to renew or modify an existing license.

Federal Communications Commission (FCC): A board of five Commissioners, appointed by the President, having the power to regulate wire and radio telecommunications in the U.S.

Feedline: A system of conductors that connects an antenna to a receiver or transmitter.

Field Day: Annual activity sponsored by the ARRL to demonstrate emergency preparedness of amateur operators.

Field strength: A measure of the intensity of an electric or magnetic field. Electric fields are measured in volts per meter; magnetic fields in amperes per meter.

Filter: A device used to block or reduce alternating currents or signals at certain frequencies while allowing others to pass unimpeded.

Frequency: The number of cycles of alternating current in one second.

Frequency coordinator: An individual or organization which recommends frequencies and other operating and/or technical parameters for amateur repeater operation in order to avoid or minimize potential interferences.

Frequency Modulation (FM): A method of varying a radio carrier wave by causing its frequency to vary in accordance with the information to be conveyed.

Frequency privileges: The transmitting frequency bands available to the various classes of amateur operators. The various Class privileges are listed in Part 97.301 of the FCC rules.

Ground: A connection, accidental or intentional, between a device or circuit and the earth or some common body and the earth or some common body serving as the earth.

Ground wave: A radio wave that is propagated near or at the earth's surface.

Handi-Ham system: Amateur organization dedicated to assisting handicapped amateur operators. (3915 Golden Valley Road, Golden Valley, MN 55422)

Harmful interference: Interference which seriously degrades, obstructs or repeatedly interrupts the operation of a radio communication service.

Harmonic: A radio wave that is a multiple of the fundamental frequency. The second harmonic is twice the fundamental frequency, the third harmonic, three times, etc.

Hertz: One complete alternating cycle per second. Named after Heinrich R. Hertz, a German physicist. The number of hertz is the frequency of the audio or radio wave.

High Frequency (HF): The band of frequencies that lie between 3 and 30 Megahertz. It is from these frequencies that radio waves are returned to earth from the ionosphere.

High-Pass filter: A device that allows passage of high frequency signals but attenuates the lower frequencies. When installed on a television set, a high-pass filter allows TV frequencies to pass while blocking lower-frequency amateur signals.

Inverse Square Law: The physical principle by which power density decreases as you get further away from a transmitting antenna. RF power density decreases by the inverse square of the distance.

Ionization: The process of adding or stripping away electrons from atoms or molecules. Ionization occurs when substances are heated at high temperatures or exposed to high voltages. It can lead to significant genetic damage in biological tissue.

Ionosphere: Outer limits of atmosphere from which HF amateur communications signals are returned to earth.

IRC: International Reply Coupon, a method of prepaying postage for a foreign amateur's QSL card.

Jamming: The intentional, malicious interference with another radio signal.

Key clicks, Chirps: Defective keying of a telegraphy signal sounding like tapping or high varying pitches.

Linear amplifier: A device that accurately reproduces a radio wave in magnified form.

Long wire: A horizontal wire antenna that is one wavelength or longer in length.

Low-Pass filter: Device connected to worldwide transmitters that inhibits passage of higher frequencies that cause television interference but does not affect amateur transmissions.

Machine: A ham slang word for an automatic repeater station.

Malicious interference: See jamming.

MARS: The Military Affiliate Radio System. An organization that coordinates the activities of amateur communications with military radio communications.

Maximum authorized transmitting power: Amateur stations must use no more than the maximum transmitter power necessary to carry out the desired communications. The maximum P.E.P. output power levels authorized Novices are 200 watts in the 80-, 40-, 15- and 10-meter bands, 25 watts in the 222-MHz band, and 5 watts in the 1270-MHz bands.

Maximum Permissible Exposure (MPE): The maximum amount of electric and magnetic RF energy to which a person may safely be exposed.

Maximum usable frequency (MFU): The highest frequency that will be returned to earth from the ionosphere.

Medium frequency (MF): The band of frequencies that lies between 300 and 3,000 kHz (3 MHz).

Microwave: Electromagnetic waves with a frequency of 300 MHz to 300 GHz. Microwaves can cause heating of biological tissue.

Mobile operation: Radio communications conducted while in motion or during halts at unspecified locations.

Mode: Type of transmission such as voice, teletype, code, television, facsimile.

Modulate: To vary the amplitude, frequency, or phase of a radiofrequency wave in accordance with the information to be conveyed.

Morse code: The International Morse code, A1A emission. Interrupted continuous wave communications conducted using a dot-dash code for letters, numbers and operating procedure signs.

Near Field: The electromagnetic field located in the immediate vicinity of the antenna. Energy in the near field depends on the size of the antenna, its wavelength and transmission power.

Nonionizing radiation: Electromagnetic waves, or fields, which do not have the capability to alter the molecular structure of substances. RF energy is nonionizing radiation.

Novice operator: An FCC licensed, entry-level amateur operator in the amateur service.

Occupational exposure: See controlled environment.

OET: Office of Engineering & Technology, a branch of the FCC that has developed the guidelines for radiofrequency (RF) safety.

Ohm's law: The basic electrical law explaining the relationship between voltage, current and resistance. The current (I) in a circuit is equal to the voltage (E) divided by the resistance (R), or $I = E/R$.

OSCAR: "Orbiting Satellite Carrying Amateur Radio." A series of satellites designed and built by amateur operators of several nations.

Oscillator: A device for generating oscillations or vibrations of an audio or radiofrequency signal.

Packet radio: A digital method of communicating computer-to-computer. A terminal-node controller makes up the packet of data and directs it to another packet station.

Peak Envelope Power (PEP): 1. The power during one radiofrequency cycle at the crest of the modulation envelope, taken under normal operating conditions. 2. The maximum power that can be obtained from a transmitter.

Phone patch: Interconnection of amateur radio to the public switched telephone network, and operated by the control operator of the station.

Power density: A measure of the strength of an electro-magnetic field at a distance from its source. Usually expressed in milliwatts per square centimeter (mW/cm2). Far-field power density decreases according to the Law of Inverse Squares.

Power supply: A device or circuit that provides the appropriate voltage and current to another device or circuit.

Propagation: The travel of electromagnetic waves or sound waves through a medium.

Public exposure: See "uncontrolled" environment.

Q-signals: International three-letter abbreviations beginning with the letter Q used primarily to convey information using the Morse code.

QSL Bureau: An office that bulk processes QSL (radio confirmation) cards for (or from) foreign amateur operators as a postage-saving mechanism.

RACES (Radio Amateur Civil Emergency Service): A radio service using amateur stations for civil defense communications during periods of local, regional, or national emergencies.

Radiation: Electromagnetic energy, such as radio waves, traveling forth into space from a transmitter.

Radiofrequency (RF): The range of frequencies over 20 kilohertz that can be propagated through space.

Radiofrequency (RF) radiation: Electromagnetic fields or waves having a frequency between 3 kHz and 300 GHz.

Radiofrequency spectrum: The eight electromagnetic bands ranked according to their frequency and wavelength. Specifically, the very-low, low, medium, high, very-high, ultra-high, super-high, and extremely-high frequency bands.

Radio wave: A combination of electric and magnetic fields varying at a radiofrequency and traveling through space at the speed of light.

Repeater operation: Automatic amateur stations that retransmit the signals of other amateur stations.

Routine RF radiation evaluation: The process of determining if the RF energy from a transmitter exceeds the Maximum Permissible Exposure (MPE) limits in a controlled or uncontrolled environment.

RST Report: A telegraphy signal report system of Readability, Strength and Tone.

S-meter: A voltmeter calibrated from 0 to 9 that indicates the relative signal strength of an incoming signal at a radio receiver.

Selectivity: The ability of a circuit (or radio receiver) to separate the desired signal from those not wanted.

Sensitivity: The ability of a circuit (or radio receiver) to detect a specified input signal.

Short circuit: An unintended, low-resistance connection across a voltage source resulting in high current and possible damage.

Shortwave: The high frequencies that lie between 3 and 30 Megahertz that are propagated long distances.

Single-Sideband (SSB): A method of radio transmission in which the RF carrier and one of the sidebands is suppressed and all of the information is carried in the one remaining sideband.

Skip wave, Skip zone: A radio wave reflected back to earth. The distance between the radio transmitter and the site of a radio wave's return to earth.

Sky-wave: A radio wave that is refracted back to earth. Sometimes called an ionospheric wave.

Specific Absorption Rate (SAR): The time rate at which radiofrequency energy is absorbed into the human body.

Spectrum: A series of radiated energies arranged in order of wavelength. The radio spectrum extends from 20 kilohertz upward.

Spurious Emissions: Unwanted radiofrequency signals emitted from a transmitter that sometimes cause interference.

Station license, location: No transmitting station shall be operated in the amateur service without being licensed by the FCC. Each amateur station shall have one land location, the address of which appears in the station license.

Sunspot Cycle: An 11-year cycle of solar disturbances which greatly affects radio wave propagation.

Technician operator: An Amateur Radio operator who has successfully passed Element 2.

Technician-Plus: An amateur operator who has passed a 5-wpm code test in addition to Technician Class requirements.

Telegraphy: Communications transmission and reception using CW, International Morse code.

Telephony: Communications transmission and reception in the voice mode.

Telecommunications: The electrical conversion, switching, transmission and control of audio video and data signals by wire or radio.

Temporary operating authority: Authority to operate your amateur station while awaiting arrival of an upgraded license.

Terrestrial station location: Any location of a radio station on the surface of the earth including the sea.

Thermal effects: As applies to RF radiation, biological tissue damage resulting because of the body's inability to cope with or dissipate excessive heat.

Third-party traffic: Amateur communication by or under the supervision of the control operator at an amateur station to another amateur station on behalf of others.

Time-averaging: As applies to RF safety, the amount of electromagnetic radiation over a given time. The premise of time-averaging is that the human body can tolerate the thermal load caused by high, localized RF exposures for short periods of time.

Transceiver: A combination radio transmitter and receiver.

Transition region: Area where power density decreases inversely with distance from the antenna.

Transmatch: An antenna tuner used to match the impedance of the transmitter output to the transmission line of an antenna.

Transmitter: Equipment used to generate radio waves. Most commonly, this radio carrier signal is amplitude varied or frequency varied (modulated) with information and radiated into space.

Transmitter power: The average peak envelope power (output) present at the antenna terminals of the transmitter. The term "transmitted" includes any external radio-frequency power amplifier which may be used.

Ultra High Frequency (UHF): Ultra high frequency radio waves that are in the range of 300 to 3,000 MHz.

Uncontrolled environment: Applies to those persons who have no control over their exposure to RF energy in the environment. Residences adjacent to ham radio installations are considered to be in an "uncontrolled" environment.

Upper Sideband (USB): The proper operating mode for sideband transmissions made in the new Novice 10-meter voice band. Amateurs generally operate USB at 20 meters and higher frequencies; lower sideband (LSB) at 40 meters and lower frequencies.

Very High Frequency (VHF): Very high frequency radio waves that are in the range of 30 to 300 MHz.

Volunteer Examiner: An amateur operator of at least a General Class level who prepares and administers amateur operator license examinations.

Volunteer Examiner Coordinator (VEC): A member of an organization which has entered into an agreement with the FCC to coordinate the efforts of volunteer examiners in preparing and administering examinations for amateur operator licenses.

Index